BATTLE OF THE
ATLANTIC

BATTLE OF THE
ATLANTIC

Marc Milner

TEMPUS

Vanwell Publishing Limited
St. Catharines, Ontario

First published 2003

Tempus Publishing Limited
The Mill, Brimscombe Port,
Stroud, Gloucestershire, GL5 2QG
www.tempus-publishing.com

Vanwell Publishing Limited
PO Box 2131, 1 Northrup Crescent
St Catharines ON
L2R 7S2
sales@vanwell.com
Phone 905-937-3100
Fax 905-937-1760

British Library Cataloguing in Publication Data.
A catalogue record for this book is available from the British Library.
ISBN 0 7524 2853 5

National Library of Canada Cataloguing in Publication
ISBN 1 55068 125 7

Vanwell Publishing acknowledges the financial support of the Government
of Canada through the Book Publishing Industry Development Programme
for our publishing activities.

Vanwell Publishing acknowledges the Government of Ontario through the
Ontario Media Development Corporation's Book Initiative.

Typesetting and origination by Tempus Publishing Limited
Printed in Great Britain by Midway Colour Print, Wiltshire

Introduction

The Second World War was only a few hours old when a look-out on the conning tower of the German submarine U-30, cruising 600km north-west of Ireland, spotted a large vessel on the horizon. The U-boat's twenty-six-year-old captain, Lieutenant Fritz Julius Lemp, spent the next two-and-a-half hours working around ahead of the contact so that he could make a close inspection from the safety of periscope depth. What Lemp saw through the lens in the gathering twilight was a small liner, running a zigzag course without lights and – apparently – armed. Such a target could only be an Armed Merchant Cruiser (AMC), typically a small passenger ship equipped with guns, manned by a naval crew, commissioned as a warship and used for patrolling. Lemp moved U-30 into firing position and, forty minutes later at 19:40 hours Greenwich Mean Time on 3 September 1939, he fired two torpedoes. Thus began the Battle of the Atlantic, the longest campaign of the Second World War and the longest and most complex submarine war in history.

The idea that German submarines might attack shipping in the North Atlantic was, of course, hardly unexpected in 1939. After all, they had done so with remarkable success during the First World War and in 1917 had brought Britain perilously close to ruin. That crisis was precipitated by a combination of wishful thinking, poor organisation and planning, and a lack of proper anti-submarine equipment – primarily a good underwater locating device. In the early years of the First World War, no one really believed that the Germans would launch a submarine campaign against unarmed merchant vessels. Submarines were ill-suited to capturing enemy vessels, or to the obligations under international law to inspect cargoes and ensure crew safety prior to sinking a ship. Simply sinking ships on sight and sending cargoes and crews alike to a watery grave not only contravened international law, but such wanton destruction of property and the lives of civilians had never occurred in maritime war before. Indeed, even the Germans were loath to undertake a submarine campaign against merchant shipping, though it was the only way to strike a blow at the Allies through their largely impenetrable surface blockade. Every time there was a mistake, like the sinking of the liner *Lusitania* in May 1915 or the *Sussex* a year later, howls of international condemnation followed – especially from the world's most powerful neutral country, the United States.

So between 1914 and 1917, the expectation that the Germans would not slip outside the bounds of acceptable behaviour – albeit stretched and modified by the new horrors of total war – governed British attitudes towards trade defence and anti-submarine warfare. Losses to shipping were sustainable, while defence rested on 'protected lanes' swarming with patrol vessels and aircraft, dispersion of ships along individual routes on the high seas and, ultimately, on keeping ships in port. German U-boats wisely stayed out of the heavily patrolled zones, operating offshore in individual patrol areas through which a solitary vessel sooner or later – because of the

Allied practice of dispersion – was bound to pass. In the early years, it was this that gave the submarine the advantage, since it was heavily armed and faster than the average merchant vessel. Confronted by this lethal spectre from the deep, merchant seamen usually took to their boats, leaving the U-boat crew to the leisurely business of sinking the ship by gunfire or scuttling charges. As merchant ships began to fit guns, however, running gun battles developed and wary submariners grew more and more inclined to fire torpedoes first and ask questions later. This became increasingly so when the British sent disguised and heavily armed 'Q' ships to sea with the express purpose of ambushing submarines on the surface as they approached. In fact, until 1917 the principal weapons in both submarine and anti-submarine warfare were guns, which says a great deal about the power of international opinion and the nature of the fighting at sea.

All that changed in February 1917, when the Germans, out of sheer frustration at their failure on all fronts and an earnest desire to win the war, declared unrestricted submarine warfare against Allied merchant shipping. With U-boats now free to simply torpedo without warning any ship in the war zone around the British Isles, losses to Allied shipping skyrocketed and through the spring of 1917 the new practice looked like being a success. By April, Britain was on the brink of crisis. Ships and cargoes were going down much faster than they could be replaced, and the existing defensive system of high seas dispersion and safe lanes inshore no longer worked. It appeared that the only way to preserve shipping was to keep it in port. What saved the situation in 1917 was the decision taken at the end of April to put all ocean-going shipping into escorted convoys.

Convoys were an ancient idea. They had been used successfully throughout the great age of sail, and were used extensively during the First World War for troopships and other vital traffic. Indeed, by early 1917 heavy losses in routine merchant traffic to Norway and Holland had been virtually eliminated by the adoption of convoys. Even the crucial coal traffic to France was convoyed without loss.

Extending this system to ocean shipping brought immediate results: losses went down steadily and shipping moved. It was the new convoy system, rather than anything technological or tactical, which defeated the 1917 U-boat campaign. Gathering shipping into compact, escorted groups cleared the ocean of easy, individual targets. This made target location for lone U-boats operating off-shore extremely difficult. And then when they did find a target, it was now a mass of ships heavily escorted by destroyers and, increasingly, long-range patrol aircraft: a daunting task for submariners used to handling a single lumbering merchant vessel.

The oppressive nature of constant naval and air escort around convoys forced significant changes in German submarine tactics. To find and attack shipping they had now to move inshore, where the convoy routes converged in channels and the approaches to ports, or where they were canalised by shorelines. Since this brought U-boats well within range of powerful land-based air patrols, including those by airships, it was necessary for the submarines to operate submerged most of the time, and attack shipping from submerged positions. Thus, the adoption of mercantile convoys in 1917 drove U-boats inshore to find targets and forced them to operate primarily as submarines. In the process, losses to Allied merchant shipping returned to a sustainable rate for the balance of the war. The problem of dealing with the sub became one of finding it in the water.

The Allies worked continuously throughout the war to solve the riddle of the submerged submarine. The depth charge, a form of underwater bomb detonated by water pressure, had been invented before the war and became increasingly more effective as the war progressed. It 'killed' submarines not by direct strikes, but by the concussive effect of its detonation nearby, splitting hull seams, popping rivets, wrecking machinery and forcing the submarine to either fill with water or surface. With U-boats increasingly operating submerged, the depth charge supplanted the gun as the most important anti-submarine weapon. Only two U-boats were sunk with depth charges prior to 1917. In that year, depth charges sank six and in 1918 twenty-two. The only major problem with depth charges was that their lethal radius, which depended on depth and therefore water pressure, was normally no more than about twenty-five feet. Placing them with precision on a target moving in three dimensions was a difficult task, especially if you only had a vague idea where the target was.

Finding the submarine once it submerged was the problem and there was no easy solution. Most hunters had to rely on a visual fix on a submerging submarine or its periscope, random depth charging at the end of the bubble trace left by the compressed air of the U-boat's torpedoes, or – for flyers – catching a glimpse of the sub through clear water, as happened on occasion in the Mediterranean. Precise location of a fully submerged submarine might be accomplished by primitive hydrophones: underwater microphones that picked up the sound of the sub's engines. Both warships and aircraft began to use such listening devices early in the war. But all First World War hydrophones were passive and non-directional. Using a series of passive hydrophones to localise a sound was possible, but very time consuming; it was all weather dependent, and submarines got quieter as the war went on.

The ultimate solution was an active sound-locating device, some way to send out a signal in the water and receive an echo from whatever was out there. British scientists, building on a French breakthrough in quartz and steel transducers, conducted the first successful trials of an active underwater location system in March 1918, when echoes were received from a sub at a range of 500 yards. The technical problems of making a combined transmitter-receiver were quickly solved and the first sets of echo-location devices were ordered for the Royal Navy in June. The whole affair – a few primitive sets, trained maintainers and operators – was nearly ready when the war ended in November. Further and extensive technical improvements were made in what the British dubbed 'asdic' (for the Anti-Submarine Divisionics, that is the technical side of the AS Division of the Admiralty) during the immediate post-war period, but the nub of the submarine location problem had been solved – or so it was thought. The interval between transmitting and the return of the echo was measured in time, which was then easily converted to distance. Range and the fixed angle of the transducer (about ten degrees from the horizontal) allowed the depth of the submarine to be calculated as well, and therefore enabled an accurate attack using depth charges. Asdic – or sonar, as it's now known – was one of the most important technological developments in naval warfare during the inter-war years. In theory, at least, it stripped submarines of their uniqueness – the cloak of invisibility which masked an otherwise frail warship – and it led many to even question the long-term viability of the submarine itself.

If the technical and tactical problem of the submarine seemed solved by 1918, it was also true that the larger issue of its indiscriminate use against merchant vessels had also been resolved. Within weeks of the commencement of Germany's unrestricted U-boat campaign in February 1917, the United States of America entered the war as an 'Associated Power' of the Allies. Their choice of designation was deliberate. Americans had been deeply embittered by the Allied economic and military blockade of Europe, which contravened international law just as the German use of U-boats did. But the Anglo-French blockade was sparing of life and it compensated for some economic losses as well; the German blockade was of necessity unsparing of life or property. Thus the bitterness the Americans felt towards the Allies for their heavy-handed blockade was swept aside by the moral outrage that arose from the 1917 unrestricted submarine campaign. America subsequently entered the war, offsetting the collapse of Russia into revolution, and making Allied victory a certainty.

The lesson here was simple: in future, no nation would risk such an international sanction as a global coalition by resorting to indiscriminate use of submarines against merchant shipping.Nonetheless, during the inter-war years the international community moved to draw submarine operations back under the conventions of international law, especially the Prize Laws governing capture at sea. These obliged an attacking ship to visit and search enemy merchant vessels to determine if the ship was carrying contraband or war cargo. Then, in the event the ship was to be sunk, it was necessary to provide for the safety of the civilian crew. Troopships, ships in convoy or under escort, or those engaged in hostile actions, could be sunk on sight. These regulations were embodied in the 1930 Submarine Protocol, which was signed by most major states, including Nazi Germany in 1936. It was this agreement which prompted Commodore Percy Walker Nelles, Chief of Naval Staff of the tiny Royal Canadian Navy, to observe in 1937 that, 'If international law is complied with, submarine attack should not prove serious.' In this Nelles reflected the general senti- ment of the whole British Empire and Commonwealth.

But the 'if' was the big part, and Nelles and senior British offcers were not so naive as to believe that international law would hold the U-boats at bay. They were also fully confident in the organisational and technical measures now available to deal with subs. By the late 1930s asdic had improved steadily and it was fitted in 220 Royal Navy destroyers, sloops and trawlers. Although later experience – and many historians – suggested that this was not enough, it is probably true that the RN had more asdic sets at sea in 1939 than the rest of the world's navies combined. And the British had faith in them. In 1936 the First Lord of the Admiralty, Admiral E.M. Chatfield, claimed that the RN's anti-submarine measures were eighty per cent effec- tive: subs could easily be found using asdic and depth charges could follow with great precision. In theory, no U-boat was safe.

In truth, however, there were some serious flaws in Chatfield's assumptions, not least of which was the toughness of modern sub- marines. This remained a mystery to the British because no proper trials of depth charges against submarine hulls were conducted during the 1920s and 1930s. Moreover, asdic training and trials were invariably conducted against submarines confined to small training areas in water that produced good results. The RN had no real experience of asdic in deep water, or in conditions that produced confused returns (like that from rough bottoms returning echoes in a random fashion). Nor did they understand that the sound beam from the asdic was distorted by temperature layers in the water (although submariners evidently knew this well enough). Finally, in most British warships asdic training was limited to once a year at best, and on foreign stations seldom that. In short, the potential of asdic was assumed, its real limitations were poorly understood, and enormous faith was placed upon it to solve the submarine problem in war.

In fairness, the British had not forgotten the two other essential lessons of battling U-boats and trade defence from the First World War: the importance of air power and the role of convoys. It was generally understood that it was air power that forced U-boats to operate fully submerged, which reduced their effectiveness and drove them inshore where, presumably, they could be found and attacked by warships. Unfortunately, the founding of the Royal Air Force in 1918 and its subsequent struggle to remain an independent service during the inter-war years resulted in a very low priority for anti-submarine aircraft prior to 1939. It took virtually the entire inter-war period to devise and develop an aerial anti-submarine bomb, which in the end was so badly fused, so light and so lacking in proper bombsights, that it was almost entirely ineffective. Most of the aircraft of Coastal Command by the late 1930s were obsolete and even the range and bomb load of the newest, the American Hudson bomber, was no improvement over the Blackburn Kangaroo of 1918 – the workhorse of the inshore maritime patrol squadrons of an earlier war. Only two squadrons of Sunderland flying boats were up to date, albeit with a poor bomb and almost useless bombsights. The ability of aircraft to kill submarines was, in fact, not a serious problem from the viewpoint of trade defence. The real value of aircraft was in aggressive patrolling and in forcing the submarines down, to render them largely immobile and short-sighted. This was true especially when they were used in conjunction with a system of convoy.

Whatever shortcomings the British may have suffered on the technical side before 1939, they were compensated for them in considerable measure by their efforts in organising and maintaining the infrastructure needed to carry out convoy and escort shipping. During the First World War the British, in conjunction with their allies and empire, erected a global naval control of shipping and naval intelligence systems. This was expanded and enhanced enormously in 1917, when oceanic convoys were adopted and the US entered the war. This organisation remained largely in place after 1918, and it was upgraded systematically and thoroughly in the late 1930s by Rear Admiral Eldon Manisty, RN, the officer responsible for perfecting it in 1917-18. It was enhanced by the establishment of an Operational Intelligence Centre (OIC) at the Admiralty in 1937, an office which would play a key role in years to come. By 1939 the British and the Empire and Commonwealth had everything in place to immediately establish a system of oceanic convoys if required.

As a result of all these measures, Commodore Nelles of the RCN was able to report confidently in 1937, when the subject of submarine attack on merchant shipping was reviewed in Canada and the Empire, that the menace was a manageable one:

> If unrestricted [submarine] warfare is again resorted to, the means of combating submarines are considered to have advanced so far that by employing a system of convoy and utilising Air Forces, losses to submarines would be very heavy and might compel the enemy to give up this form of attack.

In this Nelles accurately reflected British sentiment as well. Admiral Sir Reginald Bacon, in one of his final publications, *Modern Naval Strategy* (1940), could only conceive of a U-boat attack on escorted convoys in daylight from periscope depth: a rash act which Bacon and his co-author were sure would lead to the hasty destruction of the U-boat.

Apart from international law and technological and organisational improvements, what confirmed British belief in the remoteness and manageability of the submarine menace was simply the relatively small size of Nazi Germany's submarine fleet. The 1935 Anglo-German Naval Agreement allowed Germany to build a submarine fleet comparable in tonnage to that of the Royal Navy.

But that still meant that the Nazi's U-boat fleet was small. By 1939 it numbered only some thirty-nine operational subs, of which barely twenty-five were ocean-going; enough to keep perhaps seven or eight on station at a time. After the war, Grand Admiral Karl Dönitz opined that with 300 U-boats in 1939 he could easily have beaten Britain. Perhaps. But if Germany had possessed 300 U-boats in 1939 the British would have been much better prepared to meet them. As it was, the RN had seventy-eight small escorts on order by the summer of 1939, with plans ready for a crash programme of auxiliary 'whale catchers' should the need arise. The fact is, given the submarine threat as it existed in 1939, the precautions taken to meet it were sensible. The bedrock of trade defence was largely in place. The small ships needed to make that work, and to supplement anti-submarine forces, could be improvised in the event of war, as they had been in 1914-1918.

Naturally, then, the primary focus of British naval planners during the inter-war years was on the large cruisers and battleships of their real and potential enemies. That kind of threat could only be met by investing in comparable ships (with all their attendant specialists and trades), the new aircraft carriers that profoundly influenced modern fleet actions, dockyards and bases – little of which could be improvised in time of crisis. Indeed, the Royal Navy's main battlefleet was stretched around the globe, from the North Atlantic and North Sea, where it faced a rapidly rearming Germany, through the Mediterranean, which was patrolled by a small but modern Italian battlefleet, to the Far East where Imperial Japan, a powerful regional superpower, operated one of the great fleets of the world. Only the western hemisphere, left to the tender mercies of the USN, lay beyond British care. It is true that by 1939 the German surface fleet was small and principally a threat to merchant shipping. But the famous 'Z' plan of 1938 called for a major expansion of the German battlefleet, with massive new battlecruisers and battleships to challenge the RN directly for dominance of the eastern Atlantic. Under these circumstances, it was no wonder that the potential for the submarine problem to spiral out of control was seen to be – or was hoped to be – remote. In 1939 it could threaten, but it could not deal a mortal blow; however, enemy battlefleets could, and that threat had to be met head on.

While pre-1939 planning to deal with the U-boat threat was then based largely on common sense, no one really believed that Nazi Germany would abide by the Submarine Protocol. Moreover, submarines presented a very credible threat to warships, and so the basic technology and methods for handling submarines had – it seemed – been worked out. Senior British naval officers believed that they could deal effectively with the U-boats regardless of the strategy they adopted. In this they were proven sadly mistaken. Submerged submarines were tremendously hard to locate, even with asdic, under operational conditions, and very hard to kill once they were found. Moreover, the commander of the German submarine fleet in 1939, then Commodore Karl Dönitz, himself an experienced First World War submariner, was not convinced that submerged operations were the best way to employ submarines. During his last wartime operation, Dönitz had attacked a Mediterranean convoy at night while travelling on the surface, using his submarine as a form of torpedo boat. His U-boat was seen, driven down by gunfire and subsequently brought to the surface in a damaged state and abandoned. Dönitz was captured, but he remained convinced that the idea was sound. So much so that he published his ideas for night surface attacks in a small book in January 1939, *Die U-Bootwaffe*, which evidently went unnoticed in Britain.

The irony in all this is that when Lemp approached his target on 3 September 1939, he was operating strictly in accordance with the Submarine Protocol on direct orders from Adolph Hitler himself, and he made his final approach and attack submerged against a fast, zigzagging, darkened lone target on the high seas. This was not quite what the British imagined the submarine war to be, and not at all what the German's wanted at the time. Mindful of the court of international opinion, anxious not to inflame relations with Britain beyond salvage and not to antagonise the French, German forces had been deployed into the eastern Atlantic in late August

1939 with absolutely strict orders to abide by international law and not to attack French shipping at all. By identifying his target as an Armed Merchant Cruiser, Lemp believed he was within his orders.

U-30's two torpedoes had only a short distance to travel, about a thousand yards, but things immediately went wrong. One of the torpedoes turned once it left the tube and began to circle, posing a direct threat to the submarine. Lemp ordered a crash drive and evasive manoeuvres. While U-30 plunged and twisted away, the other torpedo completed the short sprint to the target, detonating against the port side engine room and opening a fatal wound. The ship soon stopped and began to settle in the water, with the sea pouring in and bulkheads collapsing. Emboldened by the ship's distress, Lemp brought U-30 to the surface only 800 yards away only to realise to his sudden horror that he had hit the 13,581-ton passenger ship *Athenia*, outbound from the Clyde for Canada with 1,418 people aboard. Lemp then compounded his error by trying to shoot away the ship's antenna, before submerging and making off. Germany naturally denied any involvement and U-30's log for that day was deliberately falsified on order to mask the disaster: the only known instance of a falsified U-boat log during the war.

Aboard *Athenia,* the scene was one of chaos and carnage. Passengers perished in their compartments below deck as the water rose, and they died as their lifeboats plunged awkwardly into the sea, or capsized. One boat filled with fifty-two women was ripped open by the propeller of a rescuing ship, drowning all but eight or nine of its occupants. In the end 118 passengers died, including sixty-nine women and sixteen children, of whom twenty-two were Americans.

No protest of error by the German government found a willing ear. Clearly, the Nazis intended to pick up where Imperial Germany had left off in 1918. The British Admiralty ordered all ships into convoy, and the whole apparatus of trade defence against submarine attack was stood up. The longest campaign of the Second World War had begun.

1
Opening Skirmishes
September 1939-March 1940

Within hours of the sinking of *Athenia,* the Royal Navy began its system of convoys, and deployed forces to stop German trade, intercept raiders and sink U-boats. German merchant vessels were harried at sea, some were sunk or captured, but the German surface raider fleet proved to be remarkably resilient. *Kriegsmarine* battlecruisers and pocket battleships struck into the broad ocean with comparative impunity. Although their success against Allied merchant vessels was slight, only one German raider was hunted down and destroyed in these early months. The others seemed to come and go as they pleased, and the lingering threat from a powerful and growing German battlefleet remained the primary concern of the British Admiralty. None of this was helped by the fact that the initial British anti-submarine offensive was a catastrophic failure.

In fact, the first month of war indicated that the submarine remained a very effective weapon. Of the fifty-three Allied vessels sunk by the end of September, forty-one were claimed by U-boats, and of the remainder most fell to mines, many of which were sub-marine-laid. In exchange, two U-boats were lost. British attempts to find and sink U-boats with hunting groups and aircraft were tragi-cally futile. The first RAF Coastal Command aircraft to attack a sub in September 1939 crashed when its own anti-submarine bombs skipped on the water and exploded under the aircraft. The sub, which happened to be British in any event, escaped unharmed. Meanwhile, the Royal Navy began deploying its aircraft carriers into the Atlantic to hunt and sink U-boats. It proved a poor idea. On 14 September, U-39 fired a spread of three torpedoes at the aircraft carrier *Ark Royal*, which was on anti-submarine patrol west of Ireland. The torpedoes narrowly missed. U-39 was promptly sunk by the car-rier's escorting destroyers, which also rescued the submarine's crew. It was the first U-boat kill of the war. But U-39 was an exception, one of only two U-boats found and destroyed by British hunting forces in the first six months of the war. The kill was also a stroke of luck. Shortly after U-39 was despatched, two Skua dive-bombers from *Ark Royal* located U-30 and attacked it with anti-submarine bombs. These bombs – like those dropped by RAF aircraft earlier in the month – also skipped on the surface, detonated in the air and brought both attacking aircraft down. The Skua's crews were rescued by the U-boat; surely one of the most bizarre episodes of the war.

The British were not so lucky with the second aircraft carrier sent to hunt U-boats west of Ireland in September. When HMS *Courageous* suddenly altered course to retrieve her aircraft late in the afternoon of 17 September, she turned right in front of U-29 at a range of only 3,000 yards. Two of three torpedoes hit, sending the carrier to the bottom in fifteen minutes with heavy loss of life. *Courageous'* escort hunted the U-boat without success and Kapitänleutnant Otto Schuhart arrived home to a hero's welcome. No more fleet class carriers were sent to hunt submarines. The British had the right idea, but the best carrier for anti-submarine operations proved to be small – and expendable – and aircraft needed much better weaponry. Not surprisingly, the Flag Officer

Contents

To Dominick S. 'Toby' Graham – soldier, scholar, mentor, friend.

for U-boats, Commodore Karl Dönitz, reported optimistically on 28 September that, 'It is not true that Britain possesses the means to eliminate the U-boat menace . . . Enemy technique has doubtless improved, but so has the U-boat, which now moves more silently.'

To prove his case, Dönitz ordered U-47, commanded by Günther Prien, to raid the main British fleet anchorage at Scapa Flow. In one of the most memorable feats of wartime navigation and skill, Prien slipped silently into the anchorage on the night of 13 October and attacked the battleship *Royal Oak* as she rode quietly at her mooring. Approaching on the surface, Prien fired all four torpedoes from his bow tubes at a range of only 4,000 yards. One failed to leave the tube, two missed the target, and one struck either the bow of the battleship or its mooring cable. The detonation occasioned surprisingly little alarm. *Royal Oak's* officers concluded that the detonation was some kind of internal explosion. Meanwhile, Prien swung U-47 around and fired his stern tube: that torpedo failed to hit. Stunned by his inability to hit a huge stationary target at point blank range, Prien waited patiently for the next twenty minutes while his crew frantically reloaded the forward tubes. Then, at 01:16 hours, he fired another spread of three torpedoes: all of them hit. 'Over there a curtain of water rises,' Prien wrote afterwards. 'It is as if the sea is suddenly standing up. Dull thumps sound rapidly in succession, like an artillery barrage in a battle, and grow together into a single ear-splitting crash – bursts of flame spring up, blue, yellow, red. . . . Black shadows fly like giant birds through the flames . . . Fountains metres high spring up where they fall. They are huge fragments from the masts, the bridge, the funnels. We must have made a direct hit on the magazine. . .' And so he had. Nearly 900 men perished aboard *Royal Oak*, and the vulnerability of the fleet was exposed. Prien received a hero's welcome, and even the British had to admit his penetration of the Home Fleet anchorage and the attack on *Royal Oak* was a remarkable accomplishment.

But the Atlantic war was not about sinking carriers and battleships, it was about sinking the humble merchant vessels that carried the sinews of war. In that respect, German prospects were not entirely rosy in the late summer of 1939, and the foundations of the solid organisation that would ultimately defeat the German war at sea were being laid. In fact, the war began about five years too early for the German navy, which hoped to be in a position to challenge British sea power directly by 1944 or 1945. With the limited resources available in 1939, Grand Admiral Erich Raeder, head of the *Kriegsmarine*, chose a strategy of disruption against the Allies. Operations were aimed primarily at Allied merchant shipping in the hopes that they might occasion delay and embarrassment to Allied plans, and perhaps even stop some operations. Raeder was under no illusions that against the combined might of the French and the British, the Germans could achieve much. Indeed, as he confessed in his memoirs, the best that the German navy could do in 1939 was to 'show that they knew how to die gallantly'.

Many did. In the early stages of the war, Anglo-French sea power dominated the surface of the world's oceans and made fugitives of German raiders or confined them to more remote seas. Of the two major warships deployed in August 1939, the pocket battleship *Graf Spee* was tracked down and forced into an ignominious scuttling on a sand bar in the River Plate off Uruguay in December following a classic gunnery battle with three British cruisers. She might well have escaped but for an ill-conceived decision by her captain to fight when cornered. *Graf Spee's* supporting tanker, the *Altmark*, was tracked and finally trapped in a Norwegian fjord in February, where by international law the ship ought to have been immune from attack. But the British government ordered the destroyer *Cossack* to take off the 299 British seamen prisoners she carried. The scuttling of the *Graf Spee* and the boarding of the *Altmark* 'caught the imagination of the British people,' the Royal Navy's official historian wrote later, and 'showed that once again the Germans could not challenge us on the seas with impunity…'.

The other pocket battleship, *Deutschland*, made it home safely with little to show for her efforts. In the last four months of 1939, cruises by major warships – including the first by the new battle-cruisers *Scharnhorst* and *Gneisenau,* and a sortie by the pocket battleship *Scheer* – accounted for only fifteen Allied vessels, and sank only seventeen during the whole of 1940. But the British did not have it all their way. When *Scharnhorst* and *Gneisenau* tried to slip into the North Atlantic in November through the Faeroes-Iceland gap, they stumbled on the 16,700-ton armed merchant cruiser *Rawalpindi*, which was on patrol and supported by heavier vessels nearby. *Rawalpindi* answered the German summons to 'heave to' with gunfire, smoke and a radio transmission calling for help. But no help could arrive during the fifteen minutes it took the two battlecruisers to pound the old liner into a wreck. Then, for the next two hours, the German ships engaged in rescue work, the only time during the war large raiders were afforded that luxury in the North Atlantic. The effort was only given up when, in the light from the burning hulk of *Rawalpindi*, the Germans sighted a shadow cast by the light cruiser *Newcastle*. Her guns were no match for *Scharnhorst* and *Gneisenau* either, but her torpedoes, delivered at close range in the dark, were, and so the powerful German raiders beat a hasty retreat.

The direct impact of major German warships on the war against shipping remained negligible: by 1945 only forty-seven Allied ships had been lost to the guns of battleships and cruisers – about the same number were lost to mines during any three-month period during the war. It is easy to dismiss this raiding effort by capital ships as ineffective and rather pointless, but it tied down huge Allied naval and air forces, and did so until nearly the end of the war. Large units of the German fleet could not be ignored and they proved remarkably difficult to destroy. *Scharnhorst*, *Gneisenau*, *Scheer*, *Lutzow* (the renamed *Deutschland*) and the heavy cruiser *Prinz Eugen* all operated in the Atlantic without fatal interception. Indeed, in early 1941 *Scharnhorst* and *Gneisenau* cruised to the Grand Banks of Newfoundland, raiding shipping where *Scheer* had attacked a convoy weeks earlier and sank the small armed merchant cruiser *Jervis Bay*. Only *Bismarck* – the last to sortie into the Atlantic in May 1941 and unlucky as well – was actually caught in the noose and sunk. It is important to bear in mind this ongoing struggle with powerful German surface ships when the focus of the war at sea shifted to submarines.

Added to the problem of a small but modern and highly efficient German surface navy was that of their equally small – consisting of only some seven vessels – fleet of disguised merchant raiders. These regular trading vessels had been refitted as auxiliary warships, manned by naval crews and prepared with a number of disguises to cruise the distant oceans of the world and attack unwary Allied shipping. In 1940, their first and best year of operations, such raiders accounted for fifty-four Allied vessels, many of these in the southern ocean where *Atlantis*, *Kormoran* and *Penguin* made reputations as particularly effective raiders. For the Allies, the elimination of these marauders, and indeed the interception and destruction of major warships, depended upon the power of the main fleet, good luck of patrols, and, equally importantly, on the progressive expansion of the British Commonwealth's system of naval intelligence and naval control of shipping.

The bedrock of the whole system of trade defence in the North Atlantic was the British Home Fleet. Its superior force of battleships, aircraft carriers, cruisers and destroyers checked the main power of the German navy and made it a fugitive presence at sea. This had been understood clearly by the Admiralty in the inter-war years. Battlefleets could not be improvised in times of crisis, as the smaller escorts of the anti-submarine fleet could. So the limited inter-war budgets had been wisely spent.

Naturally, it would have been best for the British to destroy the *Kriegsmarine* battlefleet outright early in the war, thus freeing men and materiel for other duties. But the Germans understood this perfectly well, and there was little to be gained by being crushed in a gunnery duel with the Royal Navy. With a small but modern force it made sense to maintain a fleet in being, to probe and upset defences, to spread them thin, and force the British to be strong everywhere. It was a logical and effective strategy. By October 1939, the British had four battleships and battlecruisers, thirteen cruisers and five aircraft carriers chasing raiders in the Atlantic, and four battleships and battlecruisers, two cruisers and a carrier assigned to convoy escort in the North Atlantic. All this in response to the two pocket battleships, *Deutschland* and *Graf Spee*. Meanwhile, patrols maintained by the powerful French navy secured convoys operating southward, towards Africa and the Mediterranean.

For the Allies, the second crucial component to securing the North Atlantic was therefore sound naval intelligence. This allowed enemy forces to be tracked, against the backdrop of known Allied warship and merchant vessel movements, and fleet units to be deployed to intercept them or to screen shipping. Gathering intelligence included not only keeping watch on major naval units, like *Scheer* or *Bismarck*, but also trying to track everything that moved. By keeping track of all the pieces of the puzzle, it was easier for patrols to know if the vessel they had in sight was what it claimed to be, or if it was a raider in disguise. In one of the most remarkable incidents of the war, the raider *Kormoran* maintained her disguise long enough to entice the Australian light cruiser *Sydney* to within 900 yards – a fatal error in judgement – when that warship stopped her on 19 November 1941 in the Indian Ocean. While the crew of *Sydney* tried to figure out just whom they were dealing with, *Kormoran* unmasked her guns, shattered *Sydney* with the first salvoes and put at least one torpedo into her. The burning cruiser was last seen drifting away over the horizon while the Germans aboard *Kormoran* fought their own fires and steamed for the Australian coast. Most of the Germans were later rescued; *Sydney* and her crew were never seen again. Naval intelligence was, therefore, crucial, and British Commonwealth naval intelligence began tracking the movements of potential merchant raiders – ships which had strengthened decks to take guns in times of war – as early as 1934, when they began to track Japanese vessels. That attention was extended to potential German raiders in September of 1938, and to similar Italian ships in February 1939. It was essential for operational naval forces to know where the enemy was so he could be attacked, but such intelligence was also crucial for diverting merchant shipping away from danger areas. Basic avoidance of

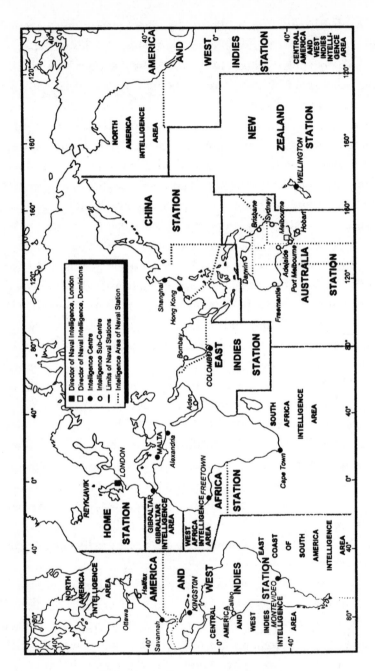

Naval stations, intelligence centres and sub centres.

the enemy remained, in fact, the principal means of defending shipping during the Second World War.

In order to make the most of covering actions by the fleet and information provided by naval intelligence, it was necessary that merchant shipping be brought under some form of effective control, what was known as 'naval control of shipping' (NCS). Eventually the NCS organisation tracked the movements, cargoes and destinations of, eventually, all Allied merchant shipping. Working in conjunction with naval intelligence, NCS organised convoys, controlled the movements of independently routed shipping, co-ordinated departures with operational forces, and worked closely with civilian agencies, shipping firms and economic and transportation ministries to keep the ships moving. This global system had been maintained between the wars and was in good running order in 1939. Information moved around the globe via secure underwater telegraph cables through an information exchange known as the VESCA system. Daily summaries of local movements were passed to the central plots in London, and to and from local naval intelligence and NCS regions around the world. With assigned routes given out to merchant captains and convoys it was, in theory, possible to know exactly where everything was at any given time on any given day. Even safe routes for neutral shipping were promulgated. During the war, the NCS system worked well enough to route most shipping away from most dangers, and to help track down German merchant raiders as well.

It is because of this complex and effective system of trade defence that the German submariners reported in late September 1939 that a large proportion of shipping was already sailing in convoys, well screened by destroyers and in some cases cruisers, and well supported inshore by aircraft. This was not unexpected by the Germans, and Commodore Karl Dönitz had developed an operational and tactical scheme for finding and attacking them. The solution was to operate U-boats in groups, deploying them in a line across the path of the convoys to ensure interception, and then attacking the convoys on the surface at night, using the U-boats like motor-torpedo boats, slipping in on the surface at high speed and using the same high speed or submergence to escape the escort following the attack.

In response to the early introduction of escorted convoys around Great Britain, Dönitz launched the first pack operation in early October 1939. Six U-boats were ordered to concentrate south of Ireland and work as a pack to attack convoys. Kapitänleutnant W. Hartmann in U-37 was designated as tactical comander of the group. As things turned out, three of the group failed to make the rendezvous. U-40 took the shortcut through the English Channel and paid for its audacity when it was sunk by a mine off Dover. U-42 and U-45 fared no better: both were sunk by escort vessels of convoys while en route to the rendezvous. That left Hartmann with only his own submarine, plus U-46 and U-48. Undaunted, on 17 October the tiny group launched an operation against the homeward-bound convoy HG 3 while it was still well out to sea and still unescorted. The attacks were plagued by torpedo failures, but each U-boat claimed one vessel before air support arrived to drive them off. From the German perspective the assault on HG 3, which warrants no notice in British accounts, was a qualified success: proof of the basic concept of pack attacks on convoys. But for the moment, there was little point in trying to attack convoys. After the 'battle' for HG 3, Hartmann went on to sink seven independently routed ships during the rest of his autumn 1939 cruise.

The second pack operation, launched in November, was less successful. It, too, had difficulty getting the designated U-boats to the rendezvous when two of the five were reassigned, leaving only three for operations. More significantly, strong naval and air escorts and torpedo failures hampered attacks on both French and British convoys in the South Western Approaches. And again the U-boats of the pack had their greatest success sinking stragglers and independents. Given the difficulty of organising packs from such a small U-boat fleet and the constant distraction of easy targets, attempts to launch pack operations were temporarily abandoned in November 1939.

The abandonment of pack operations in late autumn 1939 meant that convoys enjoyed something of a false sense of security in the first phase of the war. From the submariner's perspective, there was little point in attacking escorted convoys while the ocean remained full of independently routed shipping. In fact, while all Allied merchant shipping immediately came under effective control of the NCS in 1939, it was not until 1943 that the majority of Allied shipping worldwide moved in escorted convoys. Much of the German U-boat effort in the first years of the war was therefore devoted to finding and attacking the weak and the unescorted.

Given the overall shortage of escort vessels early in the war, convoy systems naturally developed first in the areas of greatest danger, like the eastern Atlantic, and they spread out in response to German pressure and availability of escorts. It was a sensible approach. North Atlantic trade convoys were also restricted initially to vessels in the nine to fifteen knots speed range. Slower vessels and those fast enough to be difficult targets for U-boats were routed independently along courses designed to keep them clear of the enemy. Although fast independents suffered very few losses, independent routing of slow vessels was never very successful. In the first six months of the war, seventy-two per cent of sinkings by U-boats were independents. Only thirteen per cent were lost from convoys (the rest were accounted for primarily by U-boat-laid mines). Furthermore, because of the shortage of escorts, anti-submarine protection to convoys was limited in range, and often confined to the immediate approaches to ports where U-boats were primarily expected to lurk. Oceanic convoys originating in the UK initially received anti-submarine escort only to fifteen degrees west and forty-seven degrees north. Inbound convoys picked up their A/S escort at about the same place. Beyond that point outbound convoys either dispersed or – as with inbound convoys – sailed with an ocean escort comprising of an old battleship, perhaps a cruiser or armed merchant cruiser, and sometimes even a submarine. This weakness was exploited by the German submariners.

Nonetheless, by any measure, the limited U-boat offensive against Allied shipping during the first six months of the war was successful. From September 1939 until the campaign in the Atlantic eased off in March 1940 in preparation for the assault on Norway, U-boats sank roughly 200 Allied vessels. The score ought to have been substantially higher, and would have been but for major problems with the depth control and detonators of German torpedoes, as Günther Prien discovered in his attack on *Royal Oak*. It is estimated that torpedo failures alone prevented the Germans from sinking an additional 300,000 tons – roughly fifty to sixty vessels – up to the spring of 1940, and the problem remained for several years to come.

In addition, the British improved at anti-submarine warfare and began to build the small craft and secure the aircraft need to fight the U-boats. Minefields were laid in the English Channel, around the British coast, in St George's Channel between Cornwall and Ireland, in the Helgoland Bight off German naval bases and across the North Sea towards Norway, to impede U-boat movements and sink them. Much of this effort was negated in the spring of 1940 by the German conquests of Norway and France. The RAF was in the process of developing a proper air-launched depth charge, and had shifted the balance of its flying effort away from largely fruitless searches for escaping surface raiders to reflect the need for increased anti-submarine operations. 'Scarecrow Patrols' of First World War vintage were reintroduced, making inshore waters untenable for U-boats, and driving them further out to sea in search of targets. Moreover, trials were soon underway on airborne radar systems designed to detect ships on the surface, while more modern aircraft, like the American Hudson bomber and Catalina flying boat, were being acquired for Coastal Command.

The British and their allies also launched crash programmes of small warship construction designed to deal with the submarine menace, and permit the expansion of the convoy system. The RN had actually developed a number of escort designs prior to 1939 that it hoped to build in large numbers once the war started. The most prominent of these pre-war designs – Black Swan class sloops and Hunt class destroyers – were built to naval standards and fitted with geared turbine propulsion. As it turned out, these vessels were too complicated for emergency wartime construction, and the short-ranged Hunts proved a disappointment under operational conditions. The Black Swans, however, were superb anti-submarine and escort vessels, and although only forty-two were ever built, they made a contribution to the Atlantic war well beyond what their numbers warranted.

It soon became clear that the future of wartime escort classes lay with a simple design built to mercantile standards propelled by basic steam engines. The most famous of these designs was the whale catcher developed by Smith's Dock that the Admiralty soon dubbed the Flower Class Corvette. Less than 200 feet in length, constructed to mercantile standards and powered by a simple combination of Scotch marine boilers and a four-cylinder triple expansion engine, the corvette could be built by any firm that could cut and bend plate. In mid-1939, as war clouds gathered over Europe, the RN ordered sixty of the vessels, and in July plans were passed to Canada. A further fifty were ordered in Britain before the end of 1939, by which time fifty-four had been ordered in Canada for the Royal Canadian Navy (RCN) and the French had begun a modest programme as well. Other classes of emergency vessels would emerge as the war went on – most some form of 'frigate', a term resuscitated by the Chief of the Canadian Naval Staff for the 'Twin Screw Corvette' – but the corvettes ordered in 1939 carried the burden of the war against the U-boats until the end of 1943. The British had gambled during the inter-war era that they would be able to meet any new submarine menace with a crash programme of escort vessels, and events would prove them right.

While the new escorts tumbled down the slipways of Britain over the winter of 1939-40, naval vessels enjoyed considerable success against U-boats imprudent enough to lurk around convoys. By February 1940, fifteen U-boats had been sunk in the Atlantic, nine of them by escorts operating around convoys in what most believed was essentially a defensive role. In contrast, the dedicated anti-submarine hunting forces were much less successful, accounting for only three submarines and suffering the loss of the fleet carrier *Courageous*. The balance succumbed primarily to mines, one to a British submarine, one to an accidental ramming by a German warship and one – the first – to an aircraft. By April 1940, the number of U-boats lost to all causes had reached twenty-three, a figure that included a number of training submarines. Against this total only thirteen new U-boats had been launched, leaving the overall operational strength of the U-boat fleet largely unchanged from September 1939.

Finally, as impressive as the shipping losses to U-boats were, especially when set against other forms of attack, their total impact on Allied trade between September 1939 and March 1940 was small. The monthly average of Allied shipping losses was less than 200,000 tons, a sustainable rate and indeed one matched by new construction. Moreover, with German raiders forced to make dangerous passages through the North Sea to their patrol areas, the disruption of Allied shipping patterns remained negligible as well. One recent historian of the U-boat war, V.E. Tarrant, describes this opening phase as 'little more than a nuisance...a preliminary skirmish'.

Winston Churchill, who joined Neville Chamberlain's government as First Lord of the Admiralty on the day *Athenia* was sunk, saw it much the same way after the war. Writing in his memoirs, Churchill expressed what at the time was a risky but understandable strategy for dealing with the U-boats over the long term, 'It was obvious that the Germans would build submarines by the hundred...', once the war began. But that would give the British time to react. 'In twelve months, maybe eighteen, we must expect the main U-boat war to begin. But by that time we hoped that our masses of new flotillas and anti-U-boat craft, which was our First [wartime] Priority, would be ready to meet it...'. In fact, the Germans gave the British an even longer lead in which to prepare. It was only in July 1940, with all of western Europe under Nazi domination except for Britain, that U-boat construction was given absolute priority, with a target of twenty-five new boats per month and an operational fleet of 300 submarines. This delay provided Britain with virtually a year's head start on building resources for the U-boat war in the Atlantic, a delay which ultimately proved fatal to the U-boat campaign itself.

2

The Battle of the Atlantic
Begins: April 1940-March 1941

The period from spring 1940 until spring 1941 represents the only time during the war when the Germans could have achieved a decisive strategic result in the Atlantic. Throughout this period, Britain was menaced by a hostile European shore from North Cape to the Biscay and was uniquely vulnerable to blockade. This had happened only once before in all of British history, a century and a half earlier when Napoleon ruled the continent. Nothing in British pre-war planning had anticipated this. The Germans had simply to make Britain's sea-lanes untenable and smash her ports from the air. With the right combination of punches, the British would be either knocked-out or put down on the mat for a count. Either outcome – a clear decision or a technical knock-out – constituted a German victory. Fortunately for the British, however, nothing in German pre-war planning allowed for such an eventuality either, and, although the events of 1940 and early 1941 produced some high drama, the Germans lacked the force needed at the time to deliver the knock-out punch.

The central feature of 1940 was the German victory in the west, starting with Denmark and Norway in April, followed by France and the Low Countries in May and June. These victories not only eliminated Britain's greatest ally, France, but they gave Germany a string of air and naval bases that threatened Britain directly. The occupation of Norway and France also provided direct access to the broad North Atlantic. Britain was still able to maintain an economic blockade of Germany by virtue of her general control over the world's oceans, but it was now proving all but impossible to keep German warships from slipping into the Atlantic and, once there, from being sustained by bases in occupied France. Moreover, the domination of the European coast by German air power virtually prohibited the use of Allied sea power along that hostile shore, while British cities, coastal shipping and major ports were vulnerable to devastating attack by large and powerful enemy air fleets operating from nearby bases. Never before, not even in 1805 when Napoleon's army waited at Boulogne and Nelson searched the vast Atlantic for the French fleet, was Britain's position so perilous. But Britain weathered the storm and by the spring of 1941 the complex and manifold dangers of 1940 had resolved themselves down to the lingering and deadly menace of the U-boat.

The process began in March 1940 as German forces withdrew from the North Atlantic in preparation for the invasion of Denmark and Norway. That operation, which commenced on 9 April, was the most dramatic expression of combined German naval, air and military power in the war. Virtually under the noses of the British, the Germans landed forces along the Norwegian coast as far north as Narvik, dropped them from the sky and then established the air superiority which allowed the operation to move to an eventual success. It was, in the end, an astonishingly bold act. But it was one that cost the small German navy forces it could not quickly or easily replace: one heavy cruiser, two light cruisers, ten modern destroyers and four U-boats sunk, as well as damage to most of the major ships in the fleet – including the new battle-cruisers, *Scharnhorst* and *Gneisenau*. Success in Norway meant that the U-boat fleet was appreciably smaller and the main fleet was largely out of action until late in the year. The significance of this was only apparent after France fell – to everyone's surprise – like a house of cards a few months later.

The other disturbing development for the Germans coming from their strategic success in Norway in April was the comparative failure of their U-boat fleet to inflict serious damage on the British during the campaign. Some twenty-eight U-boats, basically the entire oceanic fleet, were deployed in Norwegian waters and off British ports, and they launched repeated but failed attempts to hit all manner of targets. A subsequent investigation revealed what Günther Prien and many other U-boat captains already knew; their torpedoes were almost totally useless. There were problems with virtually all the key components. The crucial magnetic pistol was a complete failure. It was developed to permit a single torpedo to explode under the keel of a ship and so break its back. This was much more effective than a direct hit, allowed for less precision in targeting (and for movement in the target at the last minute) and offered much more efficient use of the limited numbers of torpedoes carried aboard a submarine. But, as Prien had discovered during his attack on *Royal Oak* and others had since, the magnetic pistol was unreliable, especially in northern waters. The Norwegian campaign also revealed serious faults in the depth control mechanism, which allowed even contact-fused torpedoes to pass harmlessly under unsuspecting targets. And, if that was not enough, even the contact detonator was fickle and would only operate when a target was struck at a right angle. By German reckoning, at least twenty certain hits on battleships, cruisers, destroyers and transports failed to occur during the Norwegian campaign alone because of faulty torpedoes. Prien himself had fired no fewer than ten in quick succession against prime targets at close range in the entrance to Narvik fjord – none hit. 'In all the history of war,' Dönitz opined in

May 1940, 'I doubt whether men have ever had to rely on such a useless weapon.'

As a result, Dönitz ordered the disarming of the magnetic pistols in June, leaving only the contact fuses – and their faulty depth control systems – in service for the time being. The depth control problem was eventually solved, as was the contact pistol problem. The latter was simply replaced by a British design from the submarine *Seal*, which was captured in May 1940. But it was not until December 1942 that a new influence detonator entered service. The impact on the operational potential of the U-boat fleet was, by some measures, enormous. In theory, magnetic pistols used against merchant vessels ought to have guaranteed one kill per torpedo whereas, in practice, it required an average of two contact-fused torpedoes to sink a merchant ship. In these early years of the war, when targets were plentiful, a U-boat's operational cruise was typically determined by the number of torpedoes it carried: once they were gone, the U-boat had to return for more. By some estimates, reliable magnetic pistols would have doubled the effectiveness of the U-boat fleet, with tremendous potential impact on the war itself.

Perhaps. But there were still too few U-boats in 1940. In fact, the number of operational submarines declined during that year as a result of losses and delays in the new building programmes. In May 1940 there were six fewer U-boats in service than when the war started, and the need for refit and repairs caused by the Norwegian campaign simply added to the problem. By January 1941 there were only eight U-boats on station in the Atlantic, the lowest point of the entire war. And, for the moment, the torpedo problems remained. Nonetheless, as Dönitz concluded, 'As long as there is the smallest prospect of hits, operations must continue…'. And so in June he sent his U-boats back to sea, primarily into the South Western Approaches to Britain where pack operations under local tactical control were tried once again. These proved, in the end, to be dismal failures; the convoys were tough to find, and once targets were located, torpedo problems undid much of the hard work. After three months – from March to May – during which the campaign of shipping was suspended, only sixty-three ships were sunk by U-boats in June 1940.

The slump in the war against shipping continued during the summer, but that quiet period was simply to be a portent of significant change. If Norway was a blow to Allied maritime power, the fall of France was an unmitigated disaster. The assault began on 10 May with a quick descent on Holland, followed by a thrust through Belgium and into northern France. By 21 May, German armoured spearheads had reached the sea at Abbeville, slicing the Allied armies in half. Italy entered the war in June, throwing her modern battlefleet and nearly 100 submarines into the Axis onslaught. On 25 June 1940 France capitulated and on that very day a long convoy of transports bearing torpedoes, stores, compressors and other essential equipment left Wilhelmshaven for the French naval base at Lorient.

The Germans understood full well the urgency of getting operational bases along the French coast. Not only would it be possible to base forces outside the narrow and dangerous passages into the North Sea, which were vulnerable to British blockading efforts, but the proximity to operational areas meant that time on station was increased. As a rough estimate, the French bases added about eleven per cent to the effective strength of the U-boat fleet, an important addition in a time of shortage. On 5 July the new base at Lorient was declared officially ready and the next day Klt Lemp – who had gained dubious fame for sinking *Athenia* on the first day of the war – brought U-30 into harbour, the first of hundreds to come. That month the first Italian submarines appeared in the Atlantic approaches to Gibraltar.

The surge of German power to the Atlantic littoral in the spring of 1940 changed the whole nature of the war at sea. From bases in France, Belgium, Holland and Norway, German forces, especially air power, made the English Channel and shipping routes along the east coast of Britain almost untenable – thus the essential traffic into the port of London was forced to move at night. This meant that many of Britain's key ports, such as London and Southampton, were soon closed to overseas traffic, which upset the whole careful pre-war planning for port and railway use, and the distribution of longshoremen and offloading equipment. By the late summer it was clear that only western ports, like Liverpool and the Clyde, were capable of receiving oceanic shipping. Railway timetables, manpower, cargo handling equipment and all the myriad things associated with Britain's import and export business had to be re-adjusted. This took time, and it is estimated that this process alone probably accounted for the greatest drop in British imports over the period. The Luftwaffe was also active in attacking British ports, which in turn helped to reduce handling capacity, occasioned delays in handling ships, reduced the carrying capacity of the fleet and resulted in losses of cargoes. All of this had little to do with the *Kriegsmarine*, and the U-boats in particular.

The loss of France also presented Britain with the threat of immediate invasion across the narrow straits at Dover, drawing the Royal Navy close to home on anti-invasion duty and stripping convoys of protection. Gone, too, was the large and very capable French fleet, which during the first nine months of the war pro-vided about half of the escorts in the South Western Approaches. Convoys crossing the Biscay were now more important than ever at a time when the numbers of escorts fell sharply. The arrival of the entire disposable strength of the tiny Royal Canadian Navy, four of the fleet's six modern destroyers, in early June was a wel-come addition and a portent of much greater help to come, but it was scarcely enough. Even air protection for convoys all but van-ished, as Coastal Command shifted its priority to home defence.

The long-term solution to this problem was the surge of emer-gency wartime escort construction in the offing: by spring 1940 nearly 300 small destroyers, sloops and corvettes were building in British, Canadian and French yards. HMS *Gladiolus*, the first of 269 corvettes that would carry much of the burden of the war against the U-boats, was still undergoing trials in April 1940; by the end of the year seventy-seven were in commission. These hastily built 'whale catchers' were designed primarily for inshore auxiliary work, including ASW, but they had the range and sea keeping ability to roam the Atlantic. They also filled in numbers to augment the core of escorts provided by the more complex – and numerically smaller – programmes of sloops and Hunt class destroyer escorts.

The Canadians, too, were building auxiliary warships frantically by the summer of 1940. By late 1940, the RCN had over a hundred on the stocks, seventy of these corvettes. To man them the Canadians needed to double the size of the navy, adding over 7,000 officers and men. As late as November 1940 none of these men had even been enlisted, the schools and depots required to train them had not yet been built, and in most cases the necessary land had not even been acquired. As the Chief of the Canadian Naval Staff commented to his British counterpart, on the matter of rapid wartime expansion, the RCN was 'making bricks without straw.' The ships and men would be there when they were needed most, but it would be some time before they reached an acceptable standard of efficiency.

The need to find a large number of escort vessels quickly in the high summer of 1940 drove the British to request the sale or lease of destroyers from the United States. On 1 September an agreement was signed handing over fifty aged 'four-stack' destroyers in exchange for base leases in the British Caribbean. This was the famous 'destroyers for bases' deal, the 'fifty ships that saved the world'. The first eight of these First World War vintage destroyers arrived in Halifax, Canada, within a week, with the first five arriving in the UK by 26 September. In the end, six were formally transferred to the RCN, and the Canadians manned two others. Most of the balance of the fifty ships were in Britain by the end of the year. Much-needed refits and the fitting of modern equipment delayed their introduction into service, however, until the crisis of 1940 was largely past. Thus, although it is hyperbole to suggest that these 'ships saved the world', the Town Class – as the RN dubbed them – did yeoman service for the next two years.

In the meantime, while the RN drew its force home, while the ex-American destroyers were being acquired and before all the new construction could arrive, the Germans enjoyed some of their most dramatic successes of the war. Dönitz knew in the summer of 1940 that he was being presented with a unique opportunity to deal Britain a knock-out blow, but he also knew that he had too few U-boats to actually do it – even if their torpedoes had been reliable. In fact, Dönitz was unable to persuade his superiors in 1939 and early 1940 that a crash programme of massive U-boat construction was needed. By early 1940, even the modest plan for twenty-five new U-boats per month was falling behind, as easy German victories on the continent suggested that Britain, too, would succumb. Dönitz was not convinced that the British would ever quit, and appealed for a substantial increase in the U-boat pro-gramme. 'The build-up of a powerful U-boat arm,' Dönitz wrote in his memoirs, 'simply failed, then, to take place. Our policy in this respect conferred enormous advantages on our British adversaries and they could not understand our decision.' As it turned out, the German emergency U-boat construction programmes did not begin until 1941 – much too late.

The deployment of twenty-six Italian submarines to the North Atlantic in late summer provided a welcome increase – at least until the Germans discovered that their allies were ill-suited in design, equipment, training, doctrine and temperament to the Atlantic campaign. And so, while the surface fleet patched-up the damage from the Norwegian campaign, Dönitz took advantage of his new French bases to resume operations against British convoys.

The fall of France forced the British to re-route all shipping through the North Western Approaches, using the North Channel between Ireland and Scotland as the main thoroughfare. By mid-August Dönitz had concentrated nine U-boats in the area bounded by the Hebrides, Faeroes, Ireland and the tiny pinnacle of Rockall. The use of Norwegian bases also allowed him to deploy the short-ranged Type II 250-ton U-boats into the inshore approaches to the North Channel, where these tiny submarines enjoyed considerable success. Packed as they were into the focal point of all British trade, the U-boats had little problem finding shipping. Independently routed vessels still abounded, while individual submariners were able to launch successful attacks against convoys moving virtually without naval or air escorts – which were concentrated in the south because of the invasion threat. Through August and September, as the Battle of Britain was being fought, skilled and daring U-boat captains, like Prien, Schepke, Kretschmer and Lemp, prowled offshore, attacking as targets presented themselves, sinking independents and convoyed shipping in equal measure (about twenty-five of each per month), while Dönitz tried to mount pack attacks on fleeting targets during their brief transit of the danger zone.

Finally, in late September, the Germans were able to put it all together. On 20 September, Günther Prien, down to one torpedo and deployed into the mid-Atlantic to provide weather reports in support of the Luftwaffe during the Battle of Britain, intercepted HX 72 while it was still well to the west. Five U-boats were ordered to intercept, and they arrived just as the convoy's ocean escort, the AMC *Jervis Bay*, departed. The first to arrive, Otto Kretschmer in U-99, found the convoy before the anti-submarine escort joined, and sank one ship and damaged two – which he and Prien finished off the next day. The arrival of the four-ship escort proved totally incapable of stopping Schepke from slipping unseen into the convoy and sinking seven ships in the night. Bleichrodt in U-48 sank two others, bringing the toll to twelve of the forty-one ships in HX 72.

Worse followed in October when two inbound convoys were intercepted well to the west and packs were able to form around them. The first to suffer was SC 7, one of a new series of slow transatlantic convoys begun from Canada in mid-August to include ships in the seven-and-a-half to eight knot range. For the next two years these slow and often unruly convoys were the easy targets in the Atlantic war. Bleichrodt in U-48 intercepted SC 7 on 16 October north-west of Rockall, reported it, and then attacked and sank two ships before being driven off by a long-range air patrol the next day – a novel and disturbing experience to occur that far out to sea. By then a pack had been deployed across SC 7's path east of

Rockall and the convoy stumbled into it the next night. The three escorts were no match for what followed, as the cream of the U-boat fleet nearly annihilated the convoy in a single wild night of action. Kretschmer in U-99 sank six and disabled a seventh, U-101 sank three and disabled two more, U-123 sank two and hit two others, U-38 hit one, U-48 sank two, and U-46 sank two. Kretschmer's log for 19 September captures some of the chaos:

> 00:15. Three destroyers approach the ship [which U-99 has just tor-pedoed] and search the area in line abreast. I make off at full speed to the south-west and again make contact with the convoy. Torpedoes from other boats are constantly heard exploding. The destroyers do not know how to help and occupy themselves by constantly firing star shells, which are of little effect in the bright moonlight. I now start to attack the convoy from astern.

Even the Germans found it difficult to determine who actually sank what and when. When it was over U-99, U-101 and U-123 had fired all their torpedoes, and twenty ships were gone from SC 7: the single largest loss of any convoy during the war to U-boat attack, and the most in a single night of furious battle.

The next day the U-boats from the battle around SC 7 and some who failed to make the interception turned their attention to HX 79. This one, too, had been first located by Prien 200 miles west of Rockall, with the aid of the German radio inter-ception service, *B-Dienst*. U-28, U-38, U-46, U-48 and U-100 made contact just as the anti-submarine escort of the outward-bound convoy OB 229 joined HX 79 to take it home. On this occasion the escort was large: two destroyers, four corvettes, one minesweeper, three trawlers and a submarine. But this inexpe-rienced and ad hoc group were up against Prien, Schepke, Bleichrodt and a new ace in U-46, Endrass. They poured uninhib-ited through the escort screen, sinking twelve ships in another night of carnage. All the U-boats engaged exhausted their torpe-does on the convoy and were forced to return to base to reload.

What they would have been capable of had the magnetic pistols worked we can only guess.

In three devastating attacks – on HX 72, SC 7 and HX 79 – in barely a month the Germans had sent forty-three ships to the bottom of the ocean, only slightly fewer than the average of sinkings by U-boats over the previous four months inflicted on just three convoys. Not surprisingly, these halcyon days were remembered for the seeming invincibility of the U-boats, with the period of July to October being dubbed the 'Happy Time' by those who lived to recall it. For the Germans, the ineffectiveness of the convoys' escorts seemed inexplicable, especially the strong one around HX 79. Small escorts saved U-boats from prolonged pursuits to be sure, but the depth charges seemed woefully inadequate and the escorts themselves were unable to erect a successful screen around the convoys at night. In part the problem was that many of the escorts were operating at the limit of their endurance in conditions they were never designed for. The practice of taking outbound convoys to a dispersal point and then picking up inbound convoys worked close to shore. But as the dispersal point moved westwards to cover the increasing range of U-boat attacks, many short-ranged ships were unable to stay with the inbound convoys. In addition, the new corvettes, designed as inshore jacks of all trades with short forecastles and in some cases auxiliary minesweeping gear aboard, were poorly suited to oceanic operations, and lacked the accommodation needed for long voyages. Only air power, increasingly oppresive inshore by autumn 1940 as Coastal Command began to shift back into the Atlantic following the British victory in the Battle of Britain in September and the ebbing of the invasion threat, had an impact on German operations. In particular, the long patrol times and ranges of Sunderland flying boats, their heavy bomb loads and tenacious pursuit of contacts made the immediate approaches to the North Channel untenable for the Germans by October.

Both sides learned valuable lessons from the battles around SC 7 and HX 79. The British now understood that their escort forces needed to be properly organised and dramatically increased in size.

Now that the threat of invasion had declined, many of the destroyers held in southern ports were reassigned to convoy escort duty in the North Atlantic, a powerful accretion of strength in the battle against the U-boats. In addition, it was clear that permanent escort groups needed to be established, with proper leadership and training in both convoy defence and ASW. Moreover, radar for small escorts was a priority. A search radar was already being fitted to Coastal Command aircraft, and so a set small enough for escorts – the ASV Mk I – was made available. Introduced into the RN as the type 286, the metric wavelength radar began to enter service in early 1941. Although the antenna for the 286 was fixed to the masthead and was therefore not trainable, and its 1.5-metre wavelength made it difficult to detect small targets like submarines, this first escort radar soon made a significant difference in the Atlantic war. In the meantime, improved illuminants, eventually named 'snowflakes', were being developed to turn night into day during convoy battles. The routing of convoys was also shifted further north, to move them away from the French bases.

While the RN scrambled to get its escort system in order, the air force did much to shape the development of the war at sea during the latter stages of 1940. Airborne radar, the type ASV Mk I, was in production by the autumn of 1940, as was the much improved Mk II set with increased ranges (up to twenty miles at 2000 feet) and better discrimination of targets on the sea. Many of the obsolete Anson aircraft that made up the bulk of Coastal Command had been replaced by the American Hudson bomber, a modern aircraft with a 350-mile operational range, by 1940, and once freed of anti-invasion duty they made the inshore untenable for U-boats. Further out seaward – out to some 600 miles – the lumbering Sunderlands plied their trade. They carried the modified naval depth charge, a powerful explosive much feared by German submariners and delivered with considerable determination by Coastal Command aircrew. Following the attacks on SC 7 and HX 79, Coastal Command concentrated much of its flying in direct support of convoy movements, harrying U-boats, clearing the lanes and helping the ships avoid the enemy. In the end, it was effective air patrols that by November had pushed the U-boats well out to sea, and therefore complicated the Germans' search and attack problems.

The Germans, too, learned lessons from their autumn campaign against convoys in the near approaches to the North Channel. The pack attacks on convoys confirmed the wisdom of that strategy and Dönitz worked to refine the operational concept in the autumn of 1940. Prien's example of shadowing convoys provided the model for the shadowing U-boat. This was normally the first to gain contact, and its job now became to provide contact reports every hour to *Befehlshaber der U-boot* (BdU), the U-boat headquarters, who would then co-ordinate the deployment of the pack (taking over formally from the earlier attempts to use a tactical commander at sea). The Germans understood that this routine and rather extensive radio traffic was susceptible to interception and being plotted by 'direction finding' (DF), but it was a risk well worth the benefits. U-boats were already required to broadcast a noon position report and to signal reports of any contacts, as well as weather reports on demand. These could all be DF'ed by British shore stations anyway. The Germans did not believe that it was possible to miniaturise DF equipment for shipboard use.

With the formalisation of Wolf Pack tactics in late 1940, BdU became the controlling authority, operating its fleet of submarines by the long tether of radio communications. Patrol lines were deployed on the basis of the latest intelligence, often provided by Germany's radio interception service, the *B-Dienst*, which until June of 1943 read the British convoy cypher routinely and plotted the routes of many convoys. Once a U-boat made contact, its shadowing reports – and, as requested, medium-frequency homing beacons of the type used for normal commercial navigation – were used to move other U-boats into position. Once the pack had assembled and permission was granted to attack, the leash was slipped and each 'Sea Wolf' was on its own. After attacks were made, packs were usually reformed against the same convoy or put onto the trail of another by BdU.

Thus were the foundations of the great battles of the Atlantic war in 1941-1943 laid. What followed over the winter of 1940-41 was a sharp decline in the effectiveness of the U-boat fleet, a dramatic increase in the effectiveness of British countermeasures, and the last gasp of the German surface threat in the Atlantic. The latter began in October, when the pocket battleship *Admiral Scheer* slipped into the Atlantic. The first the British learned of this was when Captain Fogarty Fegen, RN, of the old liner *Jervis Bay*, acting as sole ocean escort to HX 84, signalled that he was under attack. HX 84 scattered while the *Jervis Bay* charged headlong at *Scheer*. The AMC was reduced to a battered and sinking wreck before she even got within range of her guns. But that bought HX 84 time to disperse and *Scheer* had to settle for only six of the convoy's thirty-eight ships. Fegen was awarded a posthumous VC. HX 84 re-assembled as it approached Britain and received excellent support from Coastal Command, including help from a radar-equipped Sunderland, which used its ASV Mk I set to locate one of the U-boats trying to establish contact – the first airborne radar contact with a U-boat.

Not all U-boats were prevented from attacking convoys. Schepke in U-100 found SC 11 and sank seven ships all on his own in late November. But as a rule, the U-boats were unable to locate convoys far enough westward to mount an attack before the ships moved in under excellent air cover. The German U-boat history records the period from November to January as the lowest point in the war, with the smallest number of U-boats at sea (only eight in January) and few interceptions. In fact they got one in December, HX 90, which was attacked west of Ireland on the night of 1-2 December, after the ocean escort had left and before the A/S escort arrived. During that unopposed night of 'battle' nine ships were hit, three of which sank immediately. An attack the next day by the Italian sub *Argo* – before the escort arrived – failed, following which the escort then drove off the Italian *Tarantini*. While Kretschmer and others trolled in the wake of HX 90 sinking disabled ships, U-94 penetrated the screen in daylight on 2 December and sank two more, bringing the final tally to eleven ships.

The ineffectiveness of the Italian submarines *Argo* and *Tarantini* in the battle for HX 90 was, for Dönitz, simply confirmation that they were not up to the rigours of the Atlantic war. Much of this he already knew when the Italians arrived at the Biscay bases in the late summer, and for that reason he had deployed them further to seaward, well beyond range of British aerial reconnaissance, as additional 'eyes'. In this they also proved a dismal failure. 'Not on one single occasion,' Dönitz wrote of their mid-ocean patrols in October and November 1940, 'did the Italians succeed in bringing their German allies into contact with the enemy.' They fared no better in early 1941 and were eventually reassigned to distant operations where they enjoyed considerable success.

In fact, the battle for HX 90 was an anomaly. Most of the losses during this period along the northern routes consisted of a steady drain from attacks by lone submariners or from convoys attacked just beyond the limit of their ASW escort. Throughout much of December action shifted south, to the South Atlantic convoy routes where other forces could assist in the attack. One of these was *Kampf Geschwader 40* (KG.40) of the Luftwaffe, which operated the FW 200 Condor, four-engine, very long-range (VLR) maritime patrol bombers from bases in France. Although slow and vulnerable, the Condor could range into the Atlantic as far as Iceland and carry four 250-kilogram bombs. They had already proven their potential in the Atlantic by bombing the Canadian Pacific liner *Empress of Britain* on 26 October, just seventy miles west of Donegal. She survived the bombing only to be sunk by U–32 two days later. At over 42,000 tons, the *Empress of Britain* was the largest troopship lost during the war. The other addition to the German assault in late 1940 was the heavy cruiser *Admiral Hipper*, which slipped into the Atlantic unseen in mid-December in an attempt to locate HX convoys. Unable to make contact south of Iceland, *Hipper* shifted into the mid-ocean where, on Christmas Day 1940, she stumbled onto the Middle East troop convoy WS 5A. The convoy was heavily defended by three cruisers and the old aircraft carrier *Furious*. The strength of the escort proved a nasty shock to

Hipper's captain, who was driven off easily and took refuge for the moment in Brest – the first major German warship to do so.

As things turned out, more large raiders were on the way and so was some promised air support. In early January 1941, Dönitz obtained operational control over KG.40 and its Condors, and set them to work looking for convoys west of Britain. The idea was that the aircraft would locate the convoys and draw the U-boats in. Early efforts were not successful. Aerial navigation was, compared to that of ships, poor at best, and the aircraft could not shadow convoys discretely nor for long. Usually the U-boats homed the Condors to the convoys. That's what happened on 8 February 1941, when U-37 sighted the home bound HG 53 off the southern tip of Portugal – well outside the area where German aircraft had so far operated. U-37 attacked that night, sinking two ships, and then homed six Condors onto the convoy the next day. Their bombing attacks sank a further five ships. Meanwhile, *Admiral Hipper*, which was once again at sea, this time near the Azores, was diverted to intercept HG 53. She managed to find only a straggler and then was dispatched on the basis of a radio intercept to attack SL(S) 64, a slow convoy making its way home from Sierra Leone and still without an escort. *Hipper* came upon the convoy on 12 February, and sent seven of its nineteen ships to the bottom.

Operations against HG 53 and SL(S) 64 marked the first – and in the broad Atlantic the only – time that combined surface, subsurface and air forces operated against convoys. But that was not for want of trying. At the end of January, under the cover of the long northern winter nights, the battle cruisers *Scharnhorst* and *Gneisenau* sailed for the Atlantic. The RN's Home Fleet, alerted to their departure, sortied to intercept them. The British cruiser *Niad* made fleeting contact north of Iceland on 28 January, but the Germans slipped away, avoiding the British fleet by only a few miles, and steamed through the darkness of the Denmark Strait and into the Atlantic on 4 February. Four days later they were in contact with HX 106, escorted by the old battleship *Ramillies* whose presence was enough to turn them away. A two-month chase throughout the central

North Atlantic followed, as Admiral Gunther Lutjens, in command of the German task force, disrupted convoy routes, sank independents and stragglers, and played cat and mouse with British patrols.

Meanwhile, KG.40 increased the range and tempo of its reconnaissance of the mid-ocean, flying circuits from France out into the Atlantic, then to Norway, where they refuelled. These efforts resulted in the only serious convoy battles of the winter since HX 90 in early December, when aircraft located the outward bound OB 288 on 23 February 1941 near the Faeroes. The Condors attacked, damaging two ships, and then the first U-boats to arrive sank three on the first night. Now deep into the Atlantic and without anti-submarine escort, the convoy scattered the next day allowing five U-boats and an Italian submarine to each sink a ship, bringing the final tally to ten. OB 289, also headed into the Atlantic and now without escort, was located and attacked. U-552's efforts were completely foiled by torpedo failures, but U-97 managed to sink three and damage a fourth. A more infamous fate awaited OB 290, which was located by Prien in U-47 on 25 February. This convoy was routed well to the south of the U-boat concentration that attacked OB 288 and OB 289, which made it impossible for the U-boats to redeploy in time. So, while others were called to the scene, Prien attacked repeatedly and sank two ships. No other U-boats ever made contact with OB 290, but KG.40 did. Six Condors attacked the convoy to the west of Ireland during 26 February, sending seven ships to the bottom with bombs: the greatest single success achieved by German aircraft in the main Atlantic campaign.

The success of the Condor attack on OB 290 well out to sea, the depredations of the U-boat concentration between Britain and Iceland, and the simultaneous cruise of two battlecruisers along the convoy routes made February and March 1941 one of the most complex and anxious periods of the war for the British. Finding the two phantom capital ships required great resources and a measure of luck: the British just missed them repeatedly. Lutjens, for his part, understood that his primary task was to pull the lion's tail,

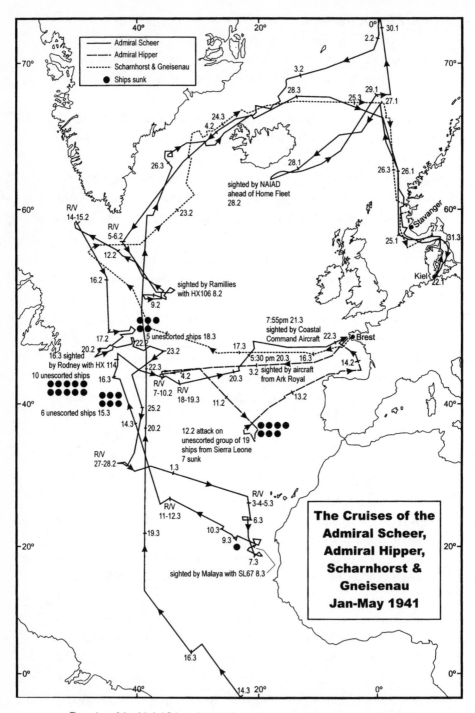

The cruises of the *Admiral Scheer, Admiral Hipper, Scharnorst*, and *Gneisnau*, January-May 1941.

not sink shipping, and he did that job superbly. *Scharnhorst* and *Gneisenau* slipped into Brest harbour at the end of March to a hero's welcome. The last-minute redeployment of British forces from the north to the Biscay to intercept them facilitated the successful passage of *Scheer* and *Hipper* through the British blockade and back to Germany for refits. It was magnificently orchestrated, the high point of the Atlantic war for the *Kriegsmarine's* capital ships. The British, stunned by the German success, swore that they would not let it happen again.

But the Germans did not have it all to their own liking in the Atlantic in early 1941. In fact, the tide in the U-boat war was about to turn markedly in Britain's favour – and not just because the fairer spring weather and longer days eased their task, although these were always crucial factors in the Atlantic war. In early February 1941, Western Approaches Command, which was responsible for trade defence and anti-submarine warfare, was moved to Liverpool and steps were taken to consolidate all aspects of the anti-U-boat war under it. This included not only training establishments, which had been working on the U-boat menace intensely since the previous summer, but beginning in mid-April operational control over Coastal Command as well. As part of this initiative, at the end of February the British Chiefs of Staff approved a major transfer of resources into the Atlantic campaign, including six squadrons of Hudson patrol aircraft and more escort vessels, and hastened airfield construction and the delivery of the American Catalina flying boats. And finally, efforts were stepped up to open an advanced refuelling base for escorts in Iceland, and base Coastal Command aircraft there. When Icelandic facilities – little more than a relay point at this stage for naval vessels – were ready in April, it was possible to extend the range of anti-submarine escort of convoys out to thirty-five degrees west, covering the area south of Iceland where U-boats attacked unescorted shipping.

By early 1941 the Americans were also increasingly involved in the war. The signing of the lend-lease agreement between Britain and the US, which became law on 1 March 1941, ensured that

Britain would receive what she needed to fight: from now on whatever she could not afford would simply be 'leased'. To make sure the supplies arrived safely, the US became an active 'neutral' in the Allied cause during 1941. It began in April with the extension of America's self-declared 'Security Zone' from sixty degrees west to twenty-six degrees west, including all of Iceland. American naval and air forces were now to patrol actively within this zone, supported from bases recently leased in Newfoundland and – by mid-year – Iceland as well. The idea was to secure the western Atlantic and free British forces to deal with the German threat in the so-called 'War Zone' of the eastern Atlantic.

While it took time for all these measures to come fully into place, it was clear by late winter 1941 that the British intended to tackle the problem of the North Atlantic. On 6 March Prime Minister Churchill publicly declared British resolve. 'We must take the offensive against the U-boat and the Focke-Wulf wherever and whenever we can,' Churchill proclaimed. 'The U-boat at sea must be hunted, the U-boat in the building-yard or the dock must be bombed. The Focke-Wulf…must be attacked in the air and in their nests…' Having persevered through six months of aerial assault, Churchill now declared that the Battle of Britain was over, but that 'the Battle of the Atlantic has begun.' The memorable phrase, intended for a discrete phase of the war at sea, quickly came to encompass the whole Atlantic war.

Churchill soon had much to crow about. On the very day his 'Battle of the Atlantic Directive' was issued, Günther Prien made contact with OB 293 200 miles south-east of Iceland. The first two U-boats called to the scene had some modest success, but were counter-attacked mercilessly by the escort of two destroyers and two corvettes acting as a well-oiled team. Kretschmer in U-99 narrowly escaped, but U-70 succumbed after three hours and over 100 depth charges. Prien stayed in contact and when, on 8 March, he moved in to attack, U-47 was sighted on the surface, driven down and depth charged for four hours. U-47 then surfaced briefly, so close to the destroyer *Wolverine* that she could not fire at the sub, before diving again. *Wolverine* surged in and delivered one final depth charge attack, which resulted in the most spectacular underwater U-boat destruction of the war – a rending explosion which produced a bright orange glow deep in the sea, which some witnesses claim pierced the surface with flame. No one escaped from Prien's U-boat: the Germans were so shocked that they waited until the end of May to announce his death.

On 15 March Lemp, now in command of a new U-boat, U-110, sighted HX 122 300 miles north-west of Scotland and called in a pack which included the Aces Kretschmer and Schepke. The escort, under the able leadership of Commander Donald Macintyre, RN, who would earn a reputation as one of the best escort commanders of the war, consisted of three destroyers and three corvettes. Like the group that had just killed Prien, Macintyre's group knew what they were doing. Schepke in U-100 was the first to attack, and initially the U-boats had it all their way. Kretschmer attacked on 16 March, sinking six ships in his first encounter and leaving the scene bathed in flames from stricken tankers and the escort's desperate illumination flares. Using this artificial light, Macintyre ordered his own destroyer, *Walker*, to sweep outside the convoy hoping to catch the next U-boat sliding in; it happened to be Schepke. U-100 crash-dived just as the first depth charges from *Walker* exploded around it. The destroyer lost contact in the disturbance that followed, while Schepke regained control of his boat and brought it to surface and slipped away. He had not gone very far when the destroyer *Vanoc* obtained a contact on her new type 286 radar – a first in the Atlantic war – found U-100 and rammed it, crushing Schepke against the periscope as the destroyer rode over the U-boat. Only six men were saved.

Meanwhile, at about the same time Macintyre was rewarded in his search around HX 122 by a contact with another U-boat that just happened to be U-99. A single six-charge pattern drove Kretschmer's U-boat down to nearly 700 feet – well beyond its designed maximum depth – before he was able to stop it and surface amid a hail of fire from *Walker*. One valiant signalman was able to send 'We are sinking' from U-99, which stopped the firing and allowed all but an engineer to be rescued. Among the survivors was Otto Kretschmer who, before U-99 sank, calmly signalled BdU, 'Two destroyers – depth charges – 50,000 tons sunk – Kretschmer.' A British officer who later interrogated the quiet, mild-mannered and well-educated young U-boat captain observed, 'I sincerely hoped that there were not too many more like him'. Kretschmer spent the rest of the war in Canada and later rose to flag rank in the West German navy, serving alongside his erstwhile enemies.

The loss of their three top U-boat aces in barely a week was a shattering blow to Dönitz and his fleet, and there was fear that the British had introduced some miraculous new sensor or weapon. The remaining U-boats were redeployed well south of Iceland, and for all practical purposes out of the convoy lanes, until well into April. To some extent Dönitz's fears were justified. *Vanoc*'s attack on U-100 was the result of a search radar having been fitted to a small ship, something new, which would ultimately prove to be a decisive weapon in the Atlantic war. But training, able leadership, permanent escort groups, new radio telephones (which allowed rapid voice communications within the escorts group), improved air support, the switch from a five charge pattern to a ten charge pattern for depth charge attacks – in fact a welter of little things, not the least of which was audacity and a certain lack of respect for British escorts – all contributed to the death of the Aces in March 1941. The first 'Happy Time' was indeed over and, as Churchill observed, the Battle of the Atlantic had really begun.

3
The Allies Strike Back
April–December 1941

The death of the U-boat Aces in March 1941 marked the end of an era in the Atlantic war. The increasing involvement of the US as an 'ally' of Britain in early 1941 put the goal of a decisive strategic result in the Atlantic out of reach for the Germans. The U-boats' first happy time was over, and worse was to follow during that momentous year. In May the spell of invulnerability enjoyed by large surface raiders in the Atlantic was also shattered. More significantly, despite an almost four-fold increase in the number of U-boats available for mid-Atlantic operations, the effectiveness of the submarine campaign declined so much during mid-1941 that Dönitz was forced to redeploy his U-boats in response to events in Russia and the Mediterranean. By mid-November virtually all German naval operations in the Atlantic had ceased. Although the pressures of an expanding war account for some of this change in fortune, much of it was wrought by the British, who tackled the

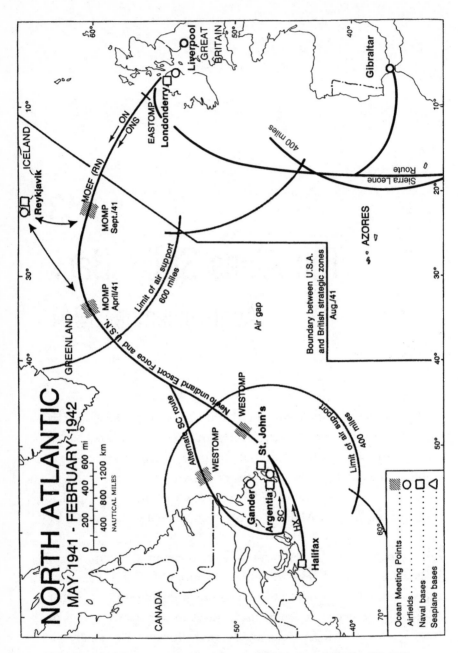

Principal convoy routes, air support and major air bases in the North Atlantic during May 1941-1942.

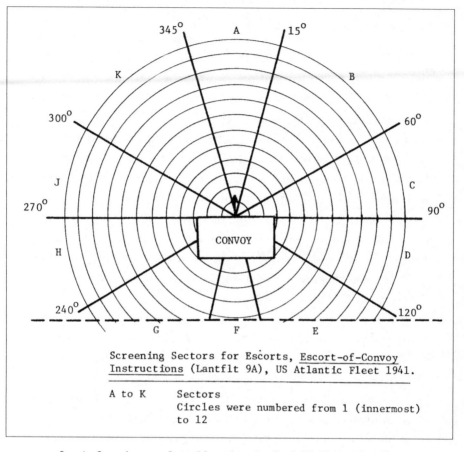

Screening Sectors for escorts, Escort-of-Convoy Instructions (Lantflt 9A), US Atlantic Fleet 1941.

problem of the Atlantic war with a determination and skill that impressed friends and enemies alike. In the end, during 1941 they and their allies achieved a solid – if fleeting – operational and tactical victory in the Atlantic.

At the core of the British Atlantic victory in 1941 lay sound organisation, strategy and doctrine. The consolidation of all anti-submarine naval and air escort operations under Western

Approaches Command, and its relocation to Liverpool in February as part of a new Area Combined Headquarters, brought all the key elements together under one roof and one commander, as of February 1941 – Admiral Sir Percy Noble, RN. Over the winter the British had also worked on escort tactics and doctrine. These were refined, tested and issued in April 1941 as the *Western Approaches Convoy Instructions (WACIs)*, a set of orders which formed the basis of Allied escort operations for the balance of the war. The central tenant of *WACIs* was laid out in the first line of the first section: 'The safe and timely arrival of the convoy at its destination is the primary object of the escort'. Evasion of the enemy was always to be the first course of action – just as it was in the larger sphere of convoy routing by shore authorities. It was, of course, the escort's duty to fight the enemy should he appear, but *WACIs* admonished that this must be done 'without undue prejudice to the safety of the convoy'.

WACIs also outlined convoy screening systems for both day and night, and pre-arranged countermeasures to execute in the event of an attack. Screening plans were formulated to provide the best possible coverage under different conditions and escort types for a target that usually covered more than twenty square kilometres of ocean. This was no easy feat. The typical convoy was made up of a series of short columns of four to six ships, with about 600 metres between each ship and 1,000 metres between columns, like a rectangle. A nine-column convoy, for example, had a frontage of eight kilometres and a depth of about two. The idea was to present as small a broadside target as possible to attackers while keeping the formation compact. The short flank of the convoy, where the sides of vessels overlapped in a solid wall of potential targets, could be covered reasonably well by a couple of escort ships. Effective screening of the face of the convoy was tough because of the greater distances, but there was compensation in the poor targets provided by the slender bows at the head of each column.

Generally, *WACIs* screening diagrams concentrated escorts ahead of the convoy by day to discourage submerged attacks, and on

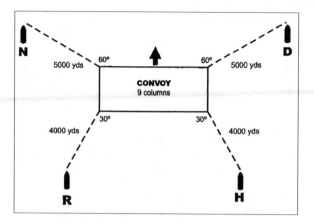

Typical Western Approaches night escort plan – NE4.

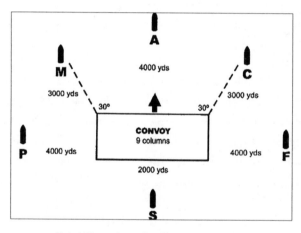

Typical Western Approaches day escort plan – PE6.

the flanks at night to try to prevent surfaced attacks. Given the limited range of asdic, theoretically 2,500 metres but in practice more like 1,500, the primitive state of radar and the problems of night vision, none of these deployments could provide a complete and impenetrable screen around any convoy in 1941. Radar offered a solution to the establishment of an effective night barrier, but the set in service in 1941, the type 286, was long wavelength (1.5m) and

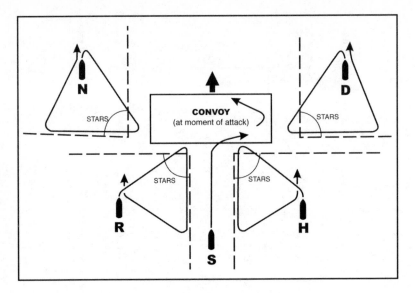

Operation 'Raspberry', illumination procedure for a convoy under attack at night.

was not usually able to locate a submarine on the surface in any kind of sea. In addition, the early type 286 was fixed to the mast-head and was not trainable; the radar operator could only see what lay directly ahead – provided that it was big enough. The solution to this problem was a high definition (centimetric wavelength) set with a full 360-degree automated sweep. In May 1941 HMS *Orchis* was at sea conducting trials on just such a set, the 10cm wavelength type 271, which British escorts soon began to fit. The early type 271 had to be trained by hand and displayed its information on an 'A' scan screen – like a modern heart monitor (automated sweeping and a modern 'plan position indicator' screen were not in wide-spread service until 1944), but even the earliest 10cm radars soon became crucial weapons in the war against the U-boats.

Countermeasures were also provided in *WACIs* to both disrupt attacks before they could be completed and to punish successful attackers. These consisted primarily of pre-arranged illumination and search procedures designed to turn night into day and, in some cases, conduct a sweep behind the convoy following an attack. Reflecting the British penchant for a little whimsy in war, most of these new countermeasures were given rather innocuous names, like 'Artichoke' and 'Raspberry'. The advent, by 1941, of radio telephones (VHF voice radio) in escort vessels was a key to the conduct and co-ordination of these measures. Prior to its introduction, all orders had to be passed either by visual means – flags or lights – or by fully encoded and encrypted wireless signals. In a fast moving convoy battle these were not efficient means of co-ordinating the escort. VHF could travel vast distances under the right conditions, it could be intercepted by the enemy, and uncoded voice traffic could be easily understood. But once the first torpedo exploded, or the first U-boat was sighted near the convoy, the senior officer of the escort (SOE) could safely assume that the Germans knew where he was. The tactical advantages of breaking radio silence then greatly outweighed the dangers of its free use. Thus by spring 1941 the SOE need only bark 'Raspberry, GO!' into his R/T to have his permanently established and well-trained escort group leap to action.

Some key developments in April and May 1941 further solidified the British grip on the Atlantic war. The establishment of bases in Iceland and the increase in range and effectiveness of air support in the eastern Atlantic made the waters east of twenty degrees untenable for U-boats. On 8 May, Dönitz ordered his subs to operate further into the Atlantic, between twenty-five and thirty-five degrees, which further complicated the problem of interception of convoys. Strengthening defences (U-boats now reported as many as eight escorts with convoys) also led to the loss of Lemp and his new U-boat U-110. Lemp had already gained notoriety for sinking *Athenia* on the first day of the war, and for taking the first U-boat into a French port. Now he would gain the misfortune of allowing all the key coding and encryption systems of the U-boat fleet to fall into enemy hands.

On 9 May, while attacking OB 318, U-110 was damaged by depth charges from the corvette *Aubretia*, and then smothered in gunfire from the destroyers *Bulldog* and *Broadway* when it surfaced, during which time Lemp was killed. As the U-boat's crew took to the sea *Bulldog*'s captain, Commander Baker-Creswell, alertly called off the ramming and sent a boarding party onto U-110. They recovered U-110's code books, confidential books and its Enigma coding machine. Until now the British had only sporadically cracked the U-boat codes. The documents and machine from U-110, coupled with the concurrent introduction of a giant computer at the British Government Code and Cypher School at Bletchley Park, plus other coding information recovered by HMS *Petard* in the Mediterranean, meant that for the balance of the year the British intercepted and read all the wireless communications of North Atlantic U-boats, with devastating effect on German fortunes at sea.

May 1941 then started with a British coup in the Atlantic. It also ended with one. While the RAF watched and bombed the two battlecruisers at Brest, British intelligence tracked the westward movement of German's latest capital ship, the 50,000-ton battleship, *Bismarck*. Units of the Home Fleet were deployed to secure the route into the North Atlantic and bring her to battle if she tried to break out. *Bismarck*'s sortie on 22 May, along with the heavy cruiser *Prinz Eugen*, was a bold and perhaps foolhardy move. The British were still smarting from Admiral Lutjen's winter cruise of the Atlantic with *Scharnhorst* and *Gneisenau*, but given the long spring nights in northern latitudes Lutjens could expect little cover except bad weather this time. Moreover, the British now had more radars at sea and in the air, and the Americans were actively patrolling their 'security zone' in the western Atlantic, ready to push back any raider.

Still, this was no average raider. Intercepted in the Denmark Straits between Greenland and Iceland, *Bismarck* and *Prinz Eugen* shot their way out. HMS *Hood*, the ageing pride of the British fleet, was despatched after a few salvoes, disappearing in a catastrophic explosion that left the sea littered with wreckage and woodchips from her deck covering. Her consort, the new battleship *Prince of Wales*, was sent packing. But not before the British got a hit on *Bismarck*'s fuel tanks, and she was forced to make for Brest, hounded and dogged the whole way by radar-equipped cruisers and aircraft. What finally sealed her fate was another strike by a torpedo delivered by a lumbering Swordfish carrier-based biplane, which struck *Bismarck*'s rudderpost while she was turning to avoid the attack. The rudder jammed and *Bismarck* was left to steam in endless circles until the British fleet arrived to pummel her into a wreck on 27 May. The lion had caught the jackal. *Prinz Eugen*, turned loose after the action in the Denmark Straits, arrived in Brest with engine problems on 1 June. No major German warship cruised the Atlantic again.

While the Home Fleet and Coastal Command worked to settle the problem of heavy raiders in the North Atlantic, the British also moved to establish complete transatlantic anti-submarine escort of the main convoys. When naval and air bases opened in Iceland in April, the British were able to push their own escort forces out to thirty-five degrees west. What remained by May was a gap in A/S escort between thirty-five degrees west and the Grand Banks of Newfoundland, the easterly limit of escorts operating from the Canadian ports. On 20 May the British asked the burgeoning Royal Canadian Navy to fill the gap.

The RCN was only too happy to do so. By the spring of 1941 it had eighty corvettes either in service or building. Ten of these were already operating from British bases, alongside seven of its twelve destroyers. Seventy of the Canadian corvettes were of the early, short forecastle design, intended primarily for inshore jack of all trades duty, and fifty-four were fitted with complete minesweeping gear. Over the winter of 1940-41 the British had begun to modernise their early corvettes to better suit them to oceanic escort duty. This included enclosing the forecastle to improve sea keeping, habitability and accommodation, and improving the bridges to carry heavier secondary armament and new equipment. The British also soon abandoned corvette building altogether, switching to the new, much longer, 'twin screw corvette' (a type of vessel later dubbed a 'frigate' by the Chief of the Canadian Naval Staff, a term which stuck) designed for ocean-escort duty. The Canadians were aware of these changes, and of the new designs. But to delay the completion of their corvettes to modernise them meant that the gap in A/S escort of convoys would not be filled. They also knew that their crews were untrained and that the corvettes lacked much essential equipment. The Admiralty advised the Canadians not to be concerned. Completing the convoy system provided a measure of protection out of all proportion to the tactical limitations of the escorts. Besides, the Americans would soon be engaged in the escort of convoys west of Iceland; the Canadian commitment was therefore simply a stopgap. Before the year was out the Canadians would have reason to regret their enthusiasm.

The first corvettes of the Newfoundland Escort Force (NEF) left Halifax for St John's on 23 May. The Canadian destroyers and corvettes released from the Clyde Escort Force reached St John's in early June, bringing with them Commodore L. W. Murray, RCN, as commander of the new force. Murray and the NEF were subordinate to Western Approaches Command, organised along WAC lines into groups of four vessels, normally a destroyer and three corvettes under a permanent SOE, and were to conduct operations in accordance with *WACIs*.

With the establishment of the NEF, end-to-end anti-submarine escort of transatlantic convoys was complete. As Admiral Sir Percy Noble observed, 'The Royal Canadian Navy solved the problem of the Atlantic convoys'. And so it had. The sudden and fortuitous addition of a fleet of over fifty fully manned – if indifferently equipped and trained – ocean-going escorts was something no British planner had foreseen. Starting in June the Canadians, under the overall control of Western Approaches Command, therefore took over primary responsibility for escort duty between the convoy assembly ports in Nova Scotia to the 'Mid-Ocean Meeting Point' (MOMP), south of Iceland. At the MOMP, HX and SC convoys were handed over to British groups operating in relays to and from Iceland. As the British escorts headed east to the snug harbours and excellent facilities of home, NEF groups took brief refuge in barren and windswept Hvalfjordhur, drawing fuel and a bit of succour from a depot ship. They then returned to MOMP to join a westbound convoy for the long beat to windward and the comparative comfort of the tiny cleft-like harbour of St John's. The plan – and the ambition of most Canadians – was to turn this duty over to the Americans as soon as possible and redeploy the fleet to the war zone in the eastern Atlantic.

To aid in the escort of convoys in the western Atlantic in May, the British also diverted nine of their much-cherished American-built Catalina flying boats to the Royal Canadian Air Force. They augmented the fifteen Douglas Digbys of No. 1 Group, RCAF, already flying over the Grand Banks from Newfoundland bases. Some general support was possible from the USN Catalinas and US Army Air Force Digbys and B-17 Flying Fortresses flying from new American bases in Newfoundland, although with the US still officially neutral, their efforts were not co-ordinated with convoy movements. By summer 1941, air support from Newfoundland reached 400 miles into the North Atlantic. This was significantly shorter than the 600-mile range achieved by their RAF counterparts in the east with similar aircraft. But Newfoundland-based aircraft faced strong and steady headwinds on the way home, turning a return flight from a patrol 400 miles out to sea into a six-hour marathon. Alternate landing sites were few and the best available were on the mainland – hundreds of miles from Newfoundland. Plagued by incredibly poor weather, almost perpetual fog, contrary winds and towering icebergs, operational flying from Newfoundland remained an enormous challenge throughout the war.

Meanwhile, on the eastern side of the Atlantic, the growing power of Coastal Command coupled with the intelligence coup from the capture of U-110 dramatically increased the effectiveness of air patrols. By mid-1941 the RAF operated some 200 maritime patrol aircraft from British and Icelandic bases. Most of these were now modern American-built aircraft: eighty Hudsons, thirty-six Catalinas and ten powerful four-engine B-24 Liberators, which were to be converted to very long range. They, and the British-built Whitleys, Wellingtons and Sunderlands, earned their keep primarily by harassing surfaced U-boats and forcing them to sub-merge. It was not entirely what airmen preferred. After flying over 55 million air miles and making 587 attacks in the first two years of the war, Coastal Command claimed only a handful of U-boat kills. And so it remained until 1943, since the lumbering aircraft lacked the sensors and weapons to kill effectively. However, their efforts in protecting shipping were enormous, and guided by special intelligence, Coastal Command made U-boat operations within range of its aircraft untenable by autumn 1941.

German fortunes in the Atlantic therefore went from bad to worse in May 1941. Most attacks on convoys were limited to indi-vidual U-boats, which happened on them by chance. Only HX 126 was found by a pack, this time at forty-one degrees west, the fur-thest west yet for a convoy interception. Nine ships were lost as HX 126 and four other convoys were diverted to avoid an even bigger problem, the *Bismarck*. But the success against HX 126 was the last the Germans would enjoy for three months. By June con-voy routing in the broad ocean was based on special intelligence, making the German search problem all but impossible. Dönitz was already suspicious of his high volume of radio traffic, believing that the Allies were DFing U-boat locations. They were, but these fixes were never so accurate as the U-boats' own estimates and BdU's deployment orders. To make matters even worse, on 18 June the British raised the upper limit for ships required to steam in convoy from thirteen to fifteen knots, dramatically reducing the number of unescorted targets and cutting the monthly average of independ-ents sunk from nearly thirty-five to barely twelve. Frustrated by the sudden lack of success, Dönitz ordered the U-boats east in July, where they were to work with KG.40 once again. Over the next three months only four transatlantic convoys were attacked and the Germans reported that 'British anti-submarine forces had increased to an astonishing degree'.

While the waters to the north-west of Britain proved a largely barren hunting ground for U-boats over the summer months, they fared much better along the southern routes where excellent co-operation was afforded by KG.40. The Axis had agents watching over Gibraltar from Spain, who reported all departures. In addition, the *B-Dienst* radio intercept service retained its ability to read the British convoy cypher until mid-1943, and provided routing information. This combination, plus the deployment of both German and Italian submarines along the UK–Gibraltar route, produced some of the most sustained action of 1941.

By 18 July Dönitz had assembled a force of some twenty U-boats west of Ireland, supported by Italian submarines patrolling the Gibraltar route further south. The Italians began the action by intercepting HG 67 shortly after it left Gibraltar. While the Italians pursued, four U-boats were ordered south to help but the convoy evaded them all. On 24 July *B-Dienst* got a fix on both OG 69 and SL 80; eight U-boats were despatched to attack OG 69, and six to intercept SL 80. The next day Condors from KG.40 established contact with both convoys, and their homing beacons were received by the fifteen U-boats. The search for SL 80 was abandoned the next day when contact could not be re-established, but the Condors relocated OG 69 and the first U-boat arrived on the scene on the 26 July. Dönitz now committed seven U-boats and three Italian submarines to the battle. Over the next three days, in a running fight supported by aircraft, Axis submariners claimed thirteen ships had been sunk and three damaged. In reality, seven ships were lost, which for the Allies was bad enough.

The Germans were able to concentrate in force again around SL 81 in early August, but this battle did not happen exactly as they anticipated. Once again *B-Dienst* provided the crucial initial intelligence on 1 August that led to the interception of the convoy west of Ireland by U-204 the next day. By 3 August, ten more U-boats were in contact. SL 81's escort was strong: three destroyers and eight corvettes. They also had one-shot air support from the Catapult Armed Merchantship (CAM ship) SS *Maplin,* which carried one worn-out Hurricane fighter on a rocket-assisted catapult. So when the first Condor appeared over SL 81 on 3 August it was promptly shot down. The same day the escort also sank U-401, one of the first U-boats to approach the convoy, and prevented any successful attack from developing that night. Round one therefore went to the escort, and the convoy was fast approaching safety. When two Condors returned the next day, however, the anti-aircraft guns of the escort could not prevent them sinking one ship, and that night four U-boats penetrated the screen and sank six more. On 5 July the escort, now supported by land-based air power, succeeded in driving off the last shadowers.

As convoy battles went in 1941, the struggle for SL 81 was something of a draw – one U-boat and one Condor exchanged for seven ships. Following SL 81, operations against HG 68 and HG 69 failed, and it was not until 17 August that they got their teeth into another one. This convoy, OG 71, was detected by KG.40 early, while still west of Ireland, so there was ample time to concentrate. Additional air patrols and U-201 maintained contact until the night of 18–19 August, when three U-boats attacked sinking the escort *Bath* and four ships. During the day on 19 August the remaining escorts of EG 5, a sloop, five corvettes and a trawler, drove off the shadowers. The next day two destroyers arrived to reinforce the screen, and on 21 August another destroyer arrived, just as KG.40 re-established contact. The U-boats failed to locate OG 71 until 22 August, when five more ships and the corvette *Zinnia* were sunk, bringing the tally to two escorts and nine ships. No U-boats or aircraft were lost.

What surprised the Germans about their August 1941 U-boat operations was not their success, but their inability to locate even more convoys and the inability, in many instances, of U-boats to penetrate the screen around convoys and press home their attacks. For while operations along the Gibraltar and Sierra Leone routes enjoyed some success, the massive concentration of U-boats south of Iceland in August, some twenty-one boats, enjoyed none at all. Time and again U-boats were unable to get into the convoy because of the strength and effectiveness of the escort. BdU now suspected that the British had some form of long-range radar which, in combination with air patrols, allowed convoys to skirt

U-boat patrols. Although they were sceptical that small vessels were fitted with surface warning sets (when they were actually starting to fit the second generation of radar), U-boat captains were alerted to watch for mysterious masthead antennae. Whatever the reason, as the German history observed, 'Three weeks of battles against the Gibraltar convoys showed that – apart from their greater effectiveness, probably owing to radar – enemy A/S forces had increased to an astonishing degree'. Dönitz now had to devise a scheme to cope with this much-improved defence.

While the U-boats tackled the Gibraltar convoys over the summer, the US finally got involved in the war at sea. Much behind the scenes work was already complete when Roosevelt and Churchill met at Argentia, Newfoundland, in August to settle the task of fighting the Axis. They agreed to divide the Atlantic into American and British strategic zones, either side of roughly thirty-five degrees west. With this agreement the US assumed both strategic and operational control of the western Atlantic to the MOMP, although for the time being control of convoys, diversions and the NCS remained a British Commonwealth responsibility. The new zone fell under the USN's Atlantic Fleet, which was to establish 'Support Force' (soon renamed Task Force 4 and then TF-24), with fifty destroyers operating from their new Argentia base. The Americans were to escort all convoys west of Iceland, except those in the approaches to Canadian shores, employing a pool of US flag shipping deployed over the summer to Halifax to support the fiction that these were really American convoys with friendlies attached.

The agreement reached at Argentia essentially assigned Canada – a belligerent country – to the strategic care of a neutral state, but no one was going to object to drawing the US deeper into the war. In fact, both the Canadians and the British had already worked hard to integrate the Americans into the war. Since 1939 the Commonwealth partners had operated a 'clandestine' naval control of the shipping network throughout the United States. Following the signing of the Lend-Lease agreement in March 1941, this NCS network was formally opened to the USN. Confidential books and special publications were distributed from Ottawa, and liaison officers were exchanged between the two North American capitals to train the Americans in the system. The operational arrangements did, however, pose serious command and control problems that would affect the war at sea. Under the new system, Western Approaches Command's writ no longer extended west of Iceland; that area now belonged to Rear Admiral A.L. Bristol, USN, Commander of Support Force. Bristol issued his 'orders' to the Canadian naval and air forces under his command as requests, and the Canadians always complied. US Army Air Force B-17s based in Newfoundland did not; they went their merry way, flying long patrols looking for raiders and invaders. It was also agreed that, until the full USN force arrived, Bristol's few destroyers would escort fast convoys (the HX series), while Murray's slower corvettes escorted the SC series. It was a temporary division of labour that, as things turned out, survived for a very long time.

Quite apart from the strategic importance of drawing America into the war on the Allied side, the agreements reached at Argentia eased the growing demands on the escort forces of the RN. The American take over of escort duty in the north-western Atlantic would eventually free the Canadian escorts of NEF to redeploy to the 'War Zone' in the east, and thus provide the British with much-needed reinforcement. This was particularly opportune in August, as the RN began to run convoys into the Arctic to help Britain's new ally, Russia.

While the sleek and powerful USN destroyers of Support Force moved into place, Dönitz sought desperately to change his luck. Frustrated by the interception problem, at the end of August BdU introduced a new system for U-boat deployments in the Atlantic. Instead of fixing groups to a specific zone, Dönitz adopted a system of moving concentrations, which would drift back and forth across the Atlantic as battle and circumstance required. Four concentrations were assigned to the transatlantic routes, and two smaller ones to the Gibraltar convoys, totalling some thirty-five U-boats.

In the first week of September, 'Movement No. 1' found the chink in the armour where the convoy lanes narrowed south of Greenland.

Squeezed north by other diversions and heavy weather, the slow eastbound convoy SC 42, escorted by the four Canadian warships of EG 24, was located by U-84 on the afternoon of 9 September near Cape Farewell. By then it had been clear for some time that SC 42 was in danger, and Commodore Murray had despatched two corvettes of his training group under Cdr James 'Chummy' Prentice, RCN(R) to reinforce EG 24. But five poorly equipped and largely untrained corvettes and one destroyer were no match for the dozen U-boats sent to attack. EG 24 lacked just about everything needed to provide an effective defence, including R/T, radar, proper training and even illuminants. The groups' captains had perhaps read *WACIs*, but it did not guide their actions and the SOE had had no time to impose the necessary standards of discipline and training. In fact, no one really expected EG 24 to do as well as it did, and the corvettes sent out to help surprised U-501 near the convoy and destroyed it. But in the long Arctic night, wave after wave of U-boats penetrated the convoy. Over two days SC 42 lost fifteen ships in the worst battle of this period. Most of the U-boats who participated in the battle returned to base, their torpedo supply exhausted. Massive naval and air reinforcements, including air support at night for the first time, ended the battle on 11 September, west of Iceland. The Germans later confessed that they found the escort 'surprisingly strong' despite the distance from support.

After SC 42, the British asked the RCN to increase the size of NEF groups from four to six (still much smaller than the eight or nine escorts provided to the Gibraltar convoys), something they were just able to do as the destroyers of the USN began escorting HX convoys in mid-September. Better equipment for the struggling Canadian escorts was on the way, including a Canadian-designed-and-built equivalent of type 286 radar, the SW1C. But the RCN knew that the convoy system itself was the key and it had to be kept going, and so the NEF carried on without access to modern equipment, training, or repair facilities. The British and Americans helped when they could, and it was needed, since in September and early October the Germans keyed on the SC convoys. Murray could only agree. He had no training establishment, and his training group – the one which so successfully supported SC 42 – was abandoned in late September when MOMP was moved five degrees east to free British escorts for service on the embattled UK-Gibraltar/Sierra Leone route.

The decision to stretch the Newfoundland-based escorts even further stemmed in large measure from the arrival of the Americans on the scene. Admiral Ernest King, CinC Atlantic Fleet, issued the operational plan for Support Force on 1 September, and on 16 September five USN destroyers took over HX 150 from the Canadian local escort south of Newfoundland. Their first action came four days later, when five American destroyers were despatched to assist SC 44 and its Canadian escort, which were under attack by five U-boats east of Cape Farewell. By this time the battle was essentially over, four ships and the corvette *Levis* being lost in one night's furious action. But the USN was now in the shooting war.

With the North American navies now carrying the burden along the North Atlantic run, the British could afford to concentrate on the other trouble spot: the Gibraltar and Sierra Leone routes. There the threat was more serious and much more complex. On the same day that the USN reinforced SC 44, U-124 intercepted the Gibraltar-bound convoy OG 74 to the southwest of Ireland: twenty-seven ships escorted by one sloop and five corvettes of EG 36, plus a new type of vessel, the auxiliary aircraft carrier HMS *Audacity*. The need for air protection for convoys had been evident for some time, and the real solution was a small carrier with several fighters embarked. *Audacity* was the first converted to this purpose. Ironically, she was the ex-*Hannover*, a 11,000-ton German cargo-liner captured by the RN and RCN in 1940, and carried six Marlet (American Wildcat) fighters. *Audacity* therefore provided OG 74 and EG 36 with their own air defences, and they proved their worth. One Marlet and its escorts drove off the first attacker, U-201, to arrive on 20 September, although U-124 penetrated the screen that night and sank two ships. The next day the Condors arrived, one of which was promptly shot down by a fighter from *Audacity*. The combination of air patrols and aggressive action by EG 36, under the able direction of Captain Johnny Walker, RN – who was later destined to become the premier U-boat killer of the war – broke contact, and the Germans had to settle for sinking three stragglers.

The Germans also switched their attention to HG 73 coming north, which was intercepted by the Italian submarine J.8 on the 23 September. The convoy was heavily escorted by a destroyer, two sloops, eight corvettes and the CAM ship, *Springbank*. For the first two days the escort had good luck driving off the shadowers, and on the 24 September *Springbank*'s solitary Fulmar fighter drove off the first Condor to make contact. Over the next two days, however, the pack slipped through in a series of night attacks and sank nine ships. Between the two convoys, OG 74 and HG 73, the Germans accounted for fifteen ships. But they were unable to do more; all the U-boats had to return to France for more torpedoes, the enduring price of the failed magnetic pistol. Following the attack on HG 73, British reinforcements arrived from the mid-Atlantic – where the burden of escort was now borne by the two North American navies – and effective routing and bad weather foiled German operations. OG 75, sighted by aircraft while still north-west of Ireland, was pursued for most of the first two weeks of October without success, while the attack on HG 75 later in the month produced disappointing results: only four ships in return for a major six-day effort.

Operations in the north-western Atlantic during October went only marginally better for the Germans. SC 48, routed through the central North Atlantic, lost three ships while under RCN escort, but a further six after it was heavily reinforced by five British and American destroyers and one RN corvette. It was during this battle that the USS *Kearney* was torpedoed, the first US warship damaged by enemy action in the war: she made Iceland under tow. The USS *Reuben James* was not so fortunate. On 30 October U-552 sank the old four-stacker with a single torpedo south of Iceland while escorting HX 156.

By autumn 1941 the British had realised that pushing a slow convoy across the stormy Atlantic in the face of a waiting pack was courting disaster, especially in the mid-ocean gap between the ranges of land-based aircraft, the so-called 'Black Pit'. Progress was so slow that an enemy pack could easily form around an SC convoy, while its seven-knot speed made tactical evasion pointless. So fearful of such a situation were British authorities that, when SC 52 was actually intercepted south of Cape Race, Newfoundland, on 1 November – a new record for westerly interceptions – the convoy was sent back to Nova Scotia via the Straits of Belle Isle. This was the only convoy turned back by the threat of enemy action during the Atlantic war. Even so, the U-boats still sank four ships and two were lost when they ran aground in the Strait.

Massive air searches for U-boats that now operated virtually within sight of Newfoundland did little to deter the Germans. Weather on the Grand Banks is notoriously fickle and typically foggy. Persistent air patrols helped, but the crucial factor was effective routing, which allowed most convoys to steer very tight but successfully evasive courses around the U-boat lines. Under the existing weather conditions, heavy reinforcements helped to reduce the level of losses but could not stop them. Some Canadians wanted to withdraw their destroyers and form support groups, which could be hastily despatched to aid threatened convoys, something the British had already done periodically in the eastern Atlantic. But the RCN lacked the ships to operate both proper escort groups and free destroyers for support duty, and the idea died for the moment.

As it was, the decision at the end of September to reallocate British escorts to the southern routes by drawing USN and RCN escort operations further east soon pushed the Canadian effort in the mid-ocean to the brink of collapse. As early as mid-October the senior USN officer in Iceland warned that the NEF was near a breaking point. 'They arrive here tired out and their DD [destroyers] barely just make it...With winter coming on their problems will be more difficult. They are going to have breakdowns and ships running out of fuel.' In October 1941, RCN corvettes averaged twenty-eight out of thirty-one days at sea, and as winter weather set in things could only get worse. American sailors thought the short forecastle RCN corvettes spent so much time underwater that their crews ought to get submarine pay.

RN officers were also upset by what they saw of the fledgling RCN escort fleet in the autumn of 1941. As the British SOE of SC 45 complained, Canadians were sloppy at signalling, reckless in their use of lights and 'their convoy discipline is not good'. This was all true. Most RCN corvettes lacked single lamps, telescopes, qualified watch keepers and signalmen, and even enough duffel coats for the whole crew. But the convoys moved and the British apologised in November for their carping. To ease the problem, Murray was informed in mid-October that every available ocean-going escort in the RCN would be sent his way: by early December seventy-eight per cent of Canada's fleet was operating with the NEF.

By the late autumn of 1941 it seemed, therefore, that the burgeoning RCN was a permanent fixture in the north-west Atlantic. Although the USN's Support Force, now designated Task Force 4, was up to full strength by November, it had enough to do in escorting the fast convoys. That left Commodore Murray's NEF to escort the most vulnerable of targets – the slow convoys – through U-boat packs, while serving under a neutral admiral in a designated non-war zone. More importantly, perhaps, the isolation of the growing RCN within the US zone left it in a doctrinal wasteland. *WACIs* ostensibly governed the RCN as well, but Murray possessed no training staff or establishment to impose its methods and injunctions, especially the cardinal rule of safe and timely arrival of the convoy. And with NEF reaching only as far as Iceland, it never fell into the anxious clutches of WAC's own staff.

For their part, the Canadians naturally thought they had gone to war to fight the Germans. The RCN concentrated on their anti-submarine training, which was sound, and Canadian escorts displayed a real penchant for pursuing U-boats whenever they could. In this they mirrored their North American cousins, under whom they now served. The USN's *Escort of Convoy Instructions (Lantflt 9A)*, issued in November 1941, placed safe and timely arrival of the convoy last on the list of priorities. An escort's primary duty was to destroy the enemy. The staff at WAC were appalled. The USN they could do little about, but by November they were already trying to find ways by which they might get the Canadians back under RN control.

Fortunately for NEF and its Anglo-American allies, the effectiveness of convoy routing and developments elsewhere forced the Germans to abandon the mid-Atlantic in late November. The British army's 'Crusader' offensive in the Western Desert on 18 November was serious enough to force the redeployment of no fewer than twenty U-boats from the Atlantic into the Mediterranean. Given the steady inwards flow of the sea and the control of the Straits of Gibraltar by British radar-equipped forces, these U-boats were effectively lost to the Atlantic war; in fact, three were lost in passing the straits. And with the war in the east suddenly stalled in front of Moscow, Hitler grew anxious about a possible British descent on Norway and the opening of convoy routes to the Arctic. Dönitz was forced to redeploy six operational submarines to patrol lines in the Norwegian Sea. By mid-December the only U-boats left in the North Atlantic were the five patrolling the Atlantic entrance to the Mediterranean.

The German abandonment of the North Atlantic in late autumn 1941 constituted a significant – if transient – victory over the U-boats. In fact, the U-boat fleet declined sharply in efficiency as the year wore on, despite a dramatic rise in its size. The high point of the year was in May, when the 'tonnage sunk per U-boat day at sea' – Dönitz's measure of efficacy – peaked at 486: forty ships from convoys and sixteen independents. This was actually well down from the monthly average of 727 tons per U-boat day at sea in the last seven months of 1940; from May 1941 until the end of the year the average was 220 tons. What was particularly alarming to Dönitz was that while the average number of U-boats at sea was steadily rising – from twenty-four in May to thirty-six by August and thirty-eight by November – their success rates plummeted. The monthly average of tonnage sunk per U-boat day at sea from July to November 1941 was a paltry 124 tons, drawn down by an average of only sixty-six tons in November – over 900 tons less than the wartime peak of 976 in October 1940. It is unlikely that Dönitz would have been forced to redeploy U-boats to the Mediterranean and the Norwegian Sea if operations in the Atlantic had been demonstrably more effective.

By November, BdU had begun to suspect that perhaps the British had penetrated their codes and cyphers, but dismissed the idea as impractical. Even with the coding machines and necessary books, the number of permutations generated by the German system – in the millions – would make it unlikely that the British could use the information effectively. They failed to account for British ingenuity, for the breaking of other codes which might provide 'cribs' or keys to the daily settings, and to the computer at Bletchley Park which ran the possible solutions and generated a setting with considerable speed. It is estimated that the evasive routing provided by Ultra in 1941 following the capture of materials from U-110 saved the Allies about 300 ships. It certainly contributed to the sharp decline in the efficiency of the U-boat fleet in the Atlantic and its subsequent withdrawal in the late autumn of 1941.

To a considerable extent improvements in A/S defence of convoys also contributed to this fleeting Allied victory. The filling in of gaps in A/S escort, a significant increase in the number of escorts available from all sources, improvements in the range and number of aircraft, and key improvements in command, control, technique, equipment and training of escorts all made U-boat operations around convoys more precarious. Under the right conditions the

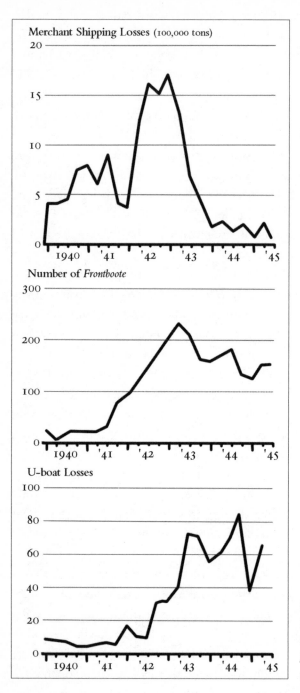

Merchant shipping losses (quarterly), number of U-boats operational in the Atlantic (Frontboote), and U-boat losses, 1939-45.

U-boats could still penetrate the escort screen and sink ships, but it took many more U-boats to ensure that would happen and so the slide in overall fleet efficacy could not be easily arrested. And the torpedo problem remained. By the autumn of 1941 the Germans were working on a new homing torpedo and a new proximity fuse, but for the time being they were limited to contact pistols. That meant two or more torpedoes per ship sunk, which cut the potential of the fleet by a half.

As 1941 drew to a close, Dönitz nonetheless had reason to be optimistic. The total size of his fleet doubled from April to the end of the year, and the number of *frontboote* tripled from twenty-eight in April to eighty-eight by December – and this despite the loss of twenty to enemy action over the same period. But it was also true that this rapid expansion diluted his cadre of skilled crews, just as the rapid expansion of Allied escort forces diluted their experienced personnel. New U-boats and their green crews took a long time to train and nurture. To some extent, the race in 1942 was to see who could learn the quickest. WAC already had this well in hand and British escort groups were already well equipped and superbly trained. The USN, by late 1941, had decided that the vile North Atlantic was no place to train crews and was already rotating their ships back to the US for rest and training. Only the Canadians were left to try to build an efficient escort force in the sub-Arctic winter, long nights, cruel seas and pitiful resources of the northwest Atlantic. But in early December even Commodore Murray was optimistic. He signalled his plans for a new training regime for NEF to Ottawa on 7 December 1941, just as the first Japanese bombs began to fall on the US Pacific Fleet at Pearl Harbor.

4
Carnage off America
January–September 1942

On the evening of 14 January 1942, Kaptainleutenant Reinhard Hardegen brought U-123 to the surface in Rhode Island Sound. What he saw astounded him. Germany and the United States had been at war for nearly six weeks, but here peacetime conditions reigned. After years of blackout conditions in Europe the shoreline looked like a carnival. Even the lights of the navigation system were all on. 'It is unbelievable,' Hardegen confided to one of his lookouts. 'I have a feeling the Americans are going to be very surprised...'. And so they were, for reasons which now defy explanation. Hardegen had already announced his presence by sinking the British steamer *Cyclops* south of Sable Island on 13 January. He now signalled his arrival on the American coast by sinking a tanker in Rhode Island Sound and another ship south of New York the next day. On 18 January, U-123 arrived off Cape Hatteras, where it slipped into a coastal shipping lane and sank four ships at leisure. 'It is a pity there were not...ten or twenty submarines [here] instead of just one. I am sure they would have found targets in plenty.'

In fact, U-123 was not alone. Four other U-boats were off the US coast with one, U-66, already hunting off Cape Hatteras on the 18 January, stalking a heavily laden tanker steaming north with all its lights blazing. Fregattenkapitän Richard Zapp knew that his torpedoes were precious, so he took four hours to get into position before hitting the *Allan Jackson* with two, ripping her apart and starting a huge fire that spread for half a mile around the stricken tanker. Betrayed by her own running lights, the *Allan Jackson* was an easy target, but familiarity with wartime conditions and running fully darkened did not save Zapp's second victim the next night. The small Canadian passenger liner *Lady Hawkins* steamed past Cape Hatteras like a black hulk while steering a zigzag course, the best she could do. But it was not enough. Zapp spotted her dark silhouette easily against the glow of lights along the shore. Liners, like tankers, were prime targets and once again Zapp took his time – six hours – before blasting away one side of the *Lady Hawkins* with two torpedoes. Only ninety-six survivors of the 300 passengers and crew were rescued from their boats five days later. There was ample reason for Zapp's cautious use of torpedoes. U-123 ran out on 19 January after sinking eight ships, although the resourceful Hardegen sank two more with his deck gun on the way home. Dönitz immediately awarded him the Knight's Cross. Zapp ran out of torpedoes on 23 January, but by then the second wave of attackers had arrived off what Allied seamen were already calling 'Torpedo Junction.' The U-boats' 'Second Happy Time' campaign off the US coast had begun in earnest.

Winston Churchill later claimed that the first sound sleep he enjoyed during the Second World War came the night after the Japanese attack on Pearl Harbor. The knowledge that America was finally in the war, and that Allied victory was now seemingly inevitable, allowed him to sleep like a baby. He might have slept less well had he known of the carnage that awaited Allied shipping in 1942. For Dönitz, war with the US offered a fertile new theatre of operations with untold possibilities – a chance for the U-boat fleet to redeem itself after the disappointments of 1941. Dönitz would not be entirely disappointed. Until the end of 1941 the Allies had lost an average of 2.1 million tons of shipping per year to all causes. During 1942, losses to Allied merchant shipping skyrocketed to some 7.2 million tons. In fact, the total tonnage lost in 1942 accounts for more than a third of over 19 million tons lost to enemy action around the world during the whole war. U-boats alone accounted for 6.1 million of this in 1942, mostly in the Atlantic, an average of almost half a million tons per month in the first half of 1942. All that said, the numbers fell far short of the 800,000 tons per month Dönitz estimated needed to be sunk to achieve decisive results. Nor was he able to bring all his strength to bear. Despite a fleet of over 300 U-boats by the spring of 1942, Dönitz was seldom able to keep more than a dozen off the US coast at any one time. The destruction they inflicted was nonetheless out of all proportion to their numbers and, as had been the case during the 'First Happy Time', only the limited numbers of torpedoes and the lack of an influence pistol kept the losses as low as they were. And, as in the case of 1940-41, sensible measures and sound organisation for the defence of shipping – this time on the part of the Americans – would have cut losses to a fraction of those which did occur.

The U-boats' descent upon the American coast was no surprise. In the autumn of 1941, U-boat packs probed south of Newfoundland, and with Germany's declaration of war on the United States on 9 December it was only a matter of time before they pushed further west and south. In the immediate aftermath of the Pearl Harbor attack, however, there were no U-boats in the broad Atlantic; they were all either in the Mediterranean, the approaches to Gibraltar or off Norway. The U-boats off Gibraltar launched the only real convoy battle for the next six months, when they intercepted HG 76 on 14 December, shortly after the convoy cleared the Straits. For the Germans, the battle for HG 76 suggested just how far British ASW and convoy defence had come. It was a rude shock and a portend of what lay in store when the battle against convoys was renewed later in 1942.

The Admiralty was well aware of the U-boat concentration off Gibraltar, and delayed sailing HG 76 until its escort could be properly reinforced. When the convoy departed its escort, EG 36 was led by the redoubtable Captain J.F. 'Johnny' Walker, RN, who would become the Allies' all-time U-boat killer; HG 76 marked the start of his remarkable record. His escort comprised his own EG 36 plus a support group of two sloops, three destroyers, seven corvettes and the auxiliary carrier *Audacity* (now down to just four Marlet fighters), which was further supported by a group of four fleet class destroyers deployed on anti-submarine duty – the latter of which promptly sank U-127 on 15 December. Many of Walker's escorts carried the new 10cm radar, making them a powerful and well-equipped escort.

Condors from KG.40 found HG 76 on 16 December, just as the first three U-boats to make contact were driven off. Three more U-boats were ordered to intercept and one of these, U-131, was attacked repeatedly by aircraft from *Audacity*. U-131 managed to shoot one down, but was so damaged that the submarine was scuttled before the surface hunters arrived to finish her off; the second kill by the escort and the convoy was barely out to sea. The next U-boat to make contact, U-434, was blown to the surface on the 18 December and sunk by the destroyers *Stanley* and *Blankney*, at about the same time that fighters from *Audacity* were shooting down the two Condors which made contact.

Thus, by 18 December, the escort of HG 76 had sunk three U-boats and shot down two Condors. The U-boats got a little of that back on the 20 December when U-754 put torpedoes into the destroyer *Stanley*, sinking her, only to be rammed and sunk by Walker's own *Stork*, the fourth U-boat to succumb. All this action left the convoy unguarded long enough for U-108 to force one ship out by shellfire, while *Audacity*'s Marlets shot down yet two more shadowing Condors, and chased U-boats trying to close on the surface. With that, HG 76's run of exceptional luck ended. The shadowing U-boat was able to bring up five others, and on the night 21-22 December they sank one steamer and *Audacity* herself. It was a heavy blow to the escort, but they redeemed themselves by sinking yet another of the attackers, U-567, which went down with all hands, including her skilled captain Endrass, Günther Prien's former first lieutenant. On 23 December, HG 76 was still some 700 miles out to sea, and normally a full day's steaming away from air support, when very long range (VLR) Liberators from 120 Squadron RAF arrived to help. They forced two U-boats, and possibly a third, to break contact, and naval reinforcements arriving the same day drove off a fourth, effectively ending the battle.

The struggle for HG 76 was an epic battle, and a terrible blow to the Germans. Large, powerful and well-equipped, Walker's escorts maintained a solid barrier around HG 76 for most of the passage, denying the enemy intelligence, forcing the shadowers off, shooting down four of his precious long-range reconnaissance aircraft and sinking no less than five U-boats. Flat calm conditions were credited with enhancing the importance of British radar, increasingly the modern 10cm 271 sets, and revealing U-boat bow waves and wakes to aircraft. As BdU concluded, 'Experience shows that Gibraltar convoys are more difficult to attack than the Atlantic convoys. This is because of the relatively short distance from Gibraltar to Britain, which enables the enemy to concentrate his available A/S forces'. Air power and good radar now made trolling around a convoy a very dangerous business. In exchange, the British lost two merchant ships, a destroyer and *Audacity*, not a bad exchange rate. The loss of *Audacity* was a serious blow, but she had proven the concept of small ASW carriers beyond doubt. Escort carriers were nearing completion in American yards and the tactics simply needed fine-tuning. Air power, radar, and a large and well-trained escort were clearly the keys to not only defending a convoy, but to punishing the attacker as well.

With the prospect of easier targets off the American coast, Dönitz soon abandoned attacks on convoys in the eastern Atlantic and, on 2 January 1942, ordered the first wave of five U-boats into the area between the Gulf of St Lawrence and Cape Hatteras. They were to operate south of Newfoundland and, according to weather and traffic conditions, were at liberty to move south. Hardegen, Zapp and the others soon found cause to push right through to the American coast. Winter weather conditions off Canada and Newfoundland were brutal, the worst in the war at sea outside of the Russian convoy route. The chill waters of the Labrador Current spilled over the Grand Banks of Newfoundland and down the Nova Scotia coast, while winter cold fronts bearing temperatures as low as minus thirty-five degrees poured across eastern Canada. Four hundred miles out to sea the Gulf Stream, which warmed Iceland and northern Europe, changed conditions tremendously. But the arctic winter of Canada and most of the Allied shipping hugged the coast, and most of the ships – the Germans discovered – already travelled in convoys. Eastbound trade from the assembly ports of Halifax and Sydney, the HX and SC series of convoys, was hard to find and difficult to attack. The only success the Germans enjoyed was against independently routed shipping, especially that from the westbound convoys which were still dispersed on or south of the Grand Banks. But this was little compensation for the brutal arctic conditions inshore.

The lure of warmer American waters was enormously enhanced by the myriad of undefended targets and peacetime conditions of navigation, which made the shipping lanes and targets easy to locate. Indeed, the targets were so plentiful and conditions so lax that the Germans reserved a high proportion of their precious torpedoes for tankers: seventy per cent of the tonnage lost during the first two weeks. In March fifty-seven per cent of losses by tonnage were tankers. 'Some of the details of these sinkings, especially of the tankers, are pitiful to relate,' S.E. Morison, the USN's official historian, wrote of this period. 'Oil scum ignited by signal flares on life preservers, men knocked out by cork life preservers, attempting to swim in a heavy viscous layer of fuel oil, and ducking to avoid flames.' U-boats operated with impunity and, on occasion, with deliberate brutality. As Morison went on:

The loaded tanker *Gulftrade* was torpedoed and sunk two miles off Barnegat, only 300 yards from a Coast Guard cutter.... A tugboat and three barges, shelled by U-574, sank the night of 31 March-1 April off Cape Charles and there were only two survivors from the tug; the same night, tanker *Tiger* was sunk off Cape Henry when manoeuvring to pick up a pilot; on the following night, between Cape Charles and Cape Henlopen, the unarmed collier *David H. Atwater* was sunk by a submarine's gunfire at a range of about 600 yards. Her crew of twenty-seven, given no opportunity to abandon ship, were riddled with machine-gun fire: only three men survived.[1]

In February U-boats sank seventy-one ships, more than any previous monthly total during the war. Sixty-one of these were independents, most in the American zone. These also included two ships alongside at Port of Spain Trinidad on 18 February, sunk by U-161. Italian submarines appeared off Brazil in March, when things only got much worse. Like some virulent infection the losses spread south faster than anyone expected. By mid-February U-boats were operating off Florida and pushing into the Caribbean and into the Gulf of Mexico, and off Trinidad. In March ninety-two Allied merchant ships were sunk by U-boats. Only three were travelling in convoys. U-161 repeated its bold foray of February by slipping into the port at St Lucia and sinking two ships that were lying, brilliantly lit, in the inner harbour. As Dönitz later declared, 'Our submarines are operating close inshore...so that bathers and sometimes entire coastal cities are witness to the drama of war, whose visual climaxes are constituted by the red glories of blazing tankers'.

Nothing the Americans did in early 1942 stopped the tide of U-boat-inflicted carnage. The British pressed from the outset for the introduction of coastal convoys as the basis for a sound defensive system. The Americans refused because they claimed that they lacked the necessary escorts – essentially destroyers – to make the

[1] P 133 Morison, Samuel Eliot, *History of United States Naval Operations in World War II: volume I: The Battle of the Atlantic, September 1939-May 1943* (Boston: Little, Brown, 1954).

system work. There is truth to that claim. Not only was the US eastern seaboard under attack, but much of the USN naval and air strength was committed to the Pacific. There the tide of Japanese victories seemed unstoppable too, and the US was the major player in this new war in an ocean that dwarfed the Atlantic by a large measure. Destroyers, among other proper naval vessels, were in high demand, and the US had not yet begun any crash programme of wartime emergency construction of small auxiliary vessels.

In the absence of proper escort vessels, the Americans could not be persuaded in the winter of 1942 to establish even a rudimentary convoy system in their own waters. 'It should always be borne in mind,' the USN's Board on the Organisation of East Coast Convoys reported in March, 'that effective convoying depends upon the escort being in sufficient strength to permit their taking offensive action against attacking submarines...'. This at least was in keeping with USN doctrine as promulgated in the autumn of 1941, which specified that the primary duty of the escort was to destroy attackers and not simply to get shipping safely through. Moreover, the Board's assessment of the need for a strong escort was certainly true of slow convoys operating deep in the Atlantic beyond the range of air power in the face of pack attacks, something the USN had experienced in the autumn of 1941. But the Board's conclusion did not square with Anglo-Canadian experience, especially with the doctrine that the primary duty of the escort was to ensure 'safe and timely arrival of the convoy'. Nor did it square with the reality of coastal convoys operating under an air umbrella in the face of lone attackers. The convoy under a general air umbrella was the key. U-boats operating in the Canadian zone in 1942 generally found shipping hard to locate because it sailed in escorted convoys, which also made it more difficult to attack. The essence of the convoy system – even with thin escorts – according to British reasoning in early 1942, was not that it would stop all losses, but that it would reduce them dramatically and would encourage U-boats to go elsewhere. In early 1942, the Americans would have none of this. Even the first destroyers released for duty in the Eastern Sea Frontier in February were committed to offensive patrols, which the USN admitted were useless but that it had to adopt because of public and political pressure.

The establishment of a convoy system along the American coast required an effective naval control of shipping organisation and a modest infusion of escorts. What galled the British about the American delay was that the NCS organisation was already in place and the rudimentary escorts could be found. Since 1939, a complete Anglo-Canadian NCS organisation had operated, initially clandestinely but since March 1941 in collusion with the USN, throughout the continental US. British 'Consular Shipping Agents' shed their civilian clothes after Pearl Harbor, donned their uniforms and continued to operate as British Routing Liaison Officers alongside their USN counterparts. All the necessary confidential books and special publications had been supplied from Canada, while all the tracking and routing of convoys and independents in the western Atlantic north of the equator was run (until July 1942 when the USN was ready to assume the duties) from the RCN's headquarters in Ottawa. With some rudimentary escorts – old yachts, trawlers, and the like – and willingness on the part of the USN an effective convoy system could have been operating off the US east coast in early 1942.

It was inevitable, given the global demand on American resources, that Allied escorts would follow the U-boats south-westwards – if only until the Americans sorted out their defences. That process began in earnest in February when the USN reduced its operational role in the north-west Atlantic to a nominal five escort groups, all buttressed by a leavening of Canadian and British corvettes. To free these escorts, Iceland was eliminated as a relay point and the escorts responsible for convoys between the Grand Banks and Ireland were reorganised into a new Mid-Ocean Escort Force (MOEF). 'B' (British) groups now used the excellent USN base at Argentia, Newfoundland, as a western terminus, while the Canadian groups exchanged windswept Hvalfjoirdhur, Iceland, for the welcoming embrace of Londonderry, Northern Ireland, as their eastern terminus. That also put the Canadians back within reach of the scions of WAC tactical orthodoxy, although the Americans refused to allow re-extension of Western Approaches Command to Newfoundland. What did not change in the introduction of MOEF was that the Canadians still escorted the bulk of the slow transatlantic convoys.

Mid-ocean escort forces were further squeezed and pared throughout early 1942 as more were shifted south. As early as March the USN's role in MOEF was reduced to a single notionally American group, A.3, typically two or three destroyers or Coast Guard cutters ably supported by a clutch of Canadian or British corvettes. Also in March five Canadian corvettes were withdrawn to help run the Canadian-escorted Halifax to Boston convoys – the first convoys established along the American seaboard. Given the fairer weather of spring the increased strain on MOEF was bearable, but these and later reductions impaired the tactical and operational flexibility of mid-ocean groups and, in time, setting up a crisis there in the autumn. For the moment, Admiral Murray at St John's helped the stretched escorts of MOEF by re-establishing the Canadian training group and using it for support operations in the fog-shrouded waters of the Grand Banks.

In the spring of 1942, the possibility of future problems in the mid-ocean took a back seat to those that were already unfolding, and the demand for escorts proved relentless. In April the British sent one of their MOEF groups to the Caribbean to run oil convoys between Aruba and Trinidad, as the toll amongst large and valuable tankers continued unabated. By then the British had also sent twenty-four anti-submarine trawlers and one Coastal Command squadron to the US east coast, and assigned ten of their newly constructed corvettes to the USN. In the absence of a proper convoy system, this did little to stop the carnage. By 1 April, the Commander, ESF, had roughly eighty small inshore patrol vessels of his own and there were now over 160 naval and army aircraft in the zone. In addition, the Americans had established a Civil Air Patrol of private aircraft flown by volunteer pilots who searched the inshore. By British or Canadian standards, this was ample to commence a system of coastal convoys, with solid naval and air escort. But by the end of April there were still no convoys, other than those that had come north from Boston escorted by the Canadians. A 'Bucket Brigade' of short inshore hops along the coastal waterway north of Georgia proved ineffective, while the routine of useless destroyer patrols made life comparatively easy for the hunting U-boats.

As U-boat attacks spilled into the Gulf of Mexico in May, shipping losses simply went even higher. The Gulf Sea Frontier, formed in early February with virtually no resources whatever, had little more by May when the attacks began in earnest. In the end, May and June 1942 proved to be the most successful months of the war for the U-boat fleet. Operations peaked during this period with as many as nineteen U-boats operating in the American zones. This increase was made possible by the deployment of the first U-boat supply tanker, the 'milchkuhe', U-459, to a position 600 miles north-west of Bermuda on 21 April. By 6 May she had discharged 600 tons of fuel to fourteen U-boats, which allowed even the small type VII submarines to penetrate the Caribbean. In May they sank no fewer than 115 ships, 101 of them independents and about half of those in the Gulf of Mexico (and about half of those tonnage tankers). In June the figures peaked at 122 ships, all but fourteen of them steaming independently and most in waters under USN command.

By mid-May, with both the British and Canadians operating successful convoy systems in the American theatre, the first US coastal convoy system finally began between Key West and Hampton Roads. Admiral Ernest King, Commander in Chief of the USN, now petitioned the British to sent him another fifteen or twenty corvettes to allow the Americans to do more. Finding them was the tough part, not least because the British were fearful by May that their weakened forces along the transatlantic route were now more vulnerable to attack, especially when beyond the range of air support. ON 67 was mauled by U-boats in transit to the US coast in February. More importantly, on 1 February the Germans introduced a fourth rotor for the coding machine used by Atlantic U-boats, ending the long run during which the British were able to read U-boat signals on a daily basis. The new settings were not solved until December, leaving transatlantic convoy routing to more conventional – and much less precise – means, like land-based direction finding. As it turned out, this intelligence gap had no influence on the carnage off the US coast. Conventional intelligence tracked German deployments well enough, and the 'flaming datums' of explosions, wreckage and wireless fixes marked the operating sites of U-boats on station.

There was reason, therefore, for the British to be anxious about the main convoy routes in the spring of 1942. Convoy routing was less accurate and the drastically reduced size of MOEF forced convoys to cleave fairly tightly to the Great Circle route. As if to remind them of this problem, Dönitz cobbled together group Hecht in early May, the first deliberate pack operation in the North Atlantic since the previous November. On 11 May, Hecht intercepted ONS 92, escorted by A.3 (a USN destroyer and a US Coast Guard cutter and four Canadian corvettes) and a four-day battle ensued. The escort lacked modern equipment, especially radar (only HMCS *Bittersweet* was fitted with type 271) and shipborne high frequency direction finding (HF/DF) sets which were first used successfully in February. ONS 92 lost seven ships without exacting any retribution from the enemy. Attempts to mount attacks on two British-escorted convoys failed, largely because of fog and poor weather. Meanwhile, on the Gibraltar route another U-boat group took a swipe at HG 84, sinking five ships before retreating once again in the face of much improved defences.

In early June Hecht got its teeth into ONS 102, another convoy escorted by A.3. This time its senior officer Captain Paul Heineman, USCG, handled the escort well and had some better resources to work with. In addition to his two cutters, Heineman had four RCN corvettes, one of which was *Bittersweet* with her modern radar, and the Canadian destroyer *Restigouche* which, thanks to the initiative of her captain, was the only RCN destroyer fitted with HF/DF in 1942. Admiral Murray also despatched his training group under Cdr James Douglas 'Chummy' Prentice, RCN(R), to operate in support. Hecht made contact on 16 June. That day the HF/DF set off *Restigouche* detected each U-boat as it made its contact report, and A.3 drove them all off, damaging two. Meanwhile Prentice's 'striking force' provided distant cover as the convoy crossed the Grand Banks. Only U-124 penetrated the screen, in a submerged daylight attack, and sank one ship. Everyone on the Allied side had reason to be pleased with the battle for ONS 102. Dönitz put the failure down to effective anti-submarine radar, but introduced a few small changes to radio procedure just in case HF/DF – which the Germans believed was too bulky to mount on ships – was a problem.

While Hecht was chasing convoys in the mid-ocean, more resources slipped away from that theatre. In May the RCN began a series of convoys between Nova Scotia and Quebec City, 1,000 miles up the St Lawrence. At the same time, in the absence of American action, the Canadians established direct tanker convoys between Halifax and Trinidad, through the embattled Eastern Sea Frontier. The escorts to run these two systems, thirteen Canadian corvettes, were released from the C groups of MOEF. The first Canadian oil convoy sailed on 22 May and they ran right through the embattled US coastal zone without loss until the end of the summer, despite at least one German attempt to intercept them with a pack operation. With two B groups already serving in the Caribbean, the British and Canadians responded to further requests for help from the US by simply trimming the operational size of MOEF groups from eight to six (of which at least two ought to be destroyers). With that, MOEF was at full stretch, spending twenty-four of every thirty days at sea with no margin for tactical manoeuvre or escorts that failed to sail.

The British made these adjustments on the assumption that everyone was worked equally hard, but they managed to keep fully one third of their escort fleet allocated to refitting, re-equipment and training. This was something that paid them enormous dividends in the long run, but not everyone enjoyed that luxury.

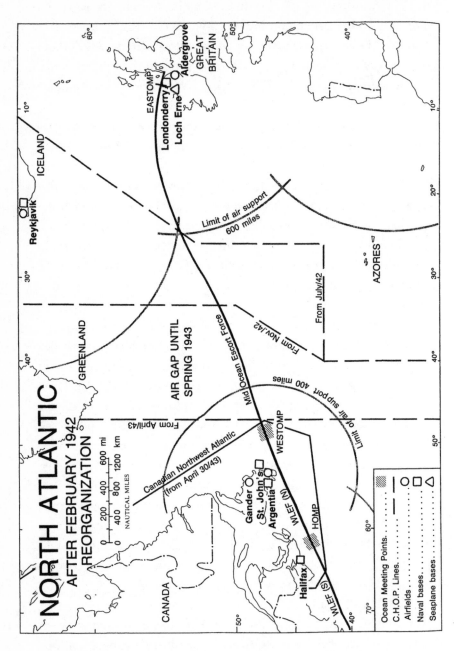

Principal convoy routes, limit of air support and major air bases in the North Atlantic after February 1942 reorganisation.

1 The battlefleet lay at the core of British sea power – and defence of the Atlantic – in the inter-war years. Battleships like *Nelson,* seen here, simply could not be improvised in times of crisis. Moreover, the older ones, like the R class, required extensive modernisation during the inter-war period.

2 Between the wars the Royal Navy held a reserve of about eighty ageing First World War vintage 'S', 'V' and 'W' class destroyers, similar to HMS *Viscount,* seen here. Most were assigned to escort duty in 1939 and many, like *Viscount,* had distinguished wartime careers.

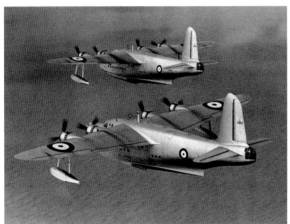

3 *Above:* The Avro Anson, the aircraft which equipped ten of RAF Coastal Command's eleven General Reconnaissance Squadrons in 1939. With a top speed of only 144 knots and an operational radius of barely 200 miles, the Anson could not even cover the distance between Scotland and Norway.

4 *Left:* The only modern maritime patrol aircraft in RAF service in 1939, the Short Sunderland. It had a range of nearly 600 miles and could carry a ton of ordnance. Two of Coastal Command's six flying boat squadrons were equipped with this aircraft.

5 The immediate threat in 1939: pocket battleship *Admiral Graf von Spee,* steaming in Montevideo harbour after the battle of the River Plate on 12 December 1940. When the ship was scuttled off the harbour five days later, the German steamer *Tacoma,* in the background of this rare picture, took off her crew.

6 Convoy escorts in the early days: a Supermarine Stranraer flying boat of 5 Squadron, Royal Canadian Air Force, and the Armed Merchant Cruiser HMS *California* – a 16,792-ton liner converted to carry eight six-inch guns, seen here entering Halifax harbour in early 1941. The Stranraer, which equipped several RAF and RCAF squadrons early in the war, had an operational radius of 300 miles carrying 1,000 lbs of bombs – all at the genteel pace of 104 knots.

7 Oceanic escort for convoys in the early years was often provided by the RN's smaller and ageing battleships, like HMS *Royal Sovereign* seen here in early 1940, to guard against German surface raiders.

8 The latent threat in 1939: U-96, a type VIIC U-boat, the mainstay of the Wolf Pack campaign, hits the water at the Germaniawerft, Kiel, 1 August 1940. She survived in service until 30 March 1945, when she was destroyed by American bombers at Wilhelmshaven.

9 The youthful Kaptlt. Otto Kretschmer, one of the most successful U-boat captains of the war, on the bridge of U-99 returning from a patrol in 1940.

10 A damaged picture of HMS *Gladiolus*, the first Flower Class corvette commissioned into the Royal Navy. She was also among the first to have her forecastle extended – as seen here recovering survivors from U-556 in June 1941 – to make her a better ocean escort.

11 Happy days: the crew of U-201 poses with Reichsführer and Head of the SS Heinrich Himmler on their commissioning day, 25 January 1941. U-201 was sunk by HMS *Fame* south of Greenland in February 1943.

12 *Above left:* Loading depth charges onto throwers aboard the Canadian corvette *Mayflower* in 1941, hard and dangerous work on a slippery and heaving deck. The charge being handled here is a 'heavy' one; the crewman in the white cap has his hand on the weight added to make it sink a little faster.

13 *Above right:* Lt Joachim Schepke, in the white hat and standing in the bridge where he died, takes U-100 to sea.

14 The FW 200 Condor. Built as an air liner, the Condor had an operational radius of 1,000 miles. Thirty were deployed to France in the summer of 1940 for maritime air patrols; Churchill called them the scourge of the Atlantic.

15 The killer of two U-boat Aces in March 1941, HMS *Walker*, seen here all bright and newly equipped following a refit in July 1943.

16 *Left:* Admiral Karl Donitz, the architect of the U-boat war, meets some of his submariners.

17 *Below:* A damaged picture of *Scharnhorst*, worn by the sea but unbeaten, cruising in the mid-Atlantic on 7 March 1941.

18 The first modern land-based aircraft in the Allied struggle at sea: the Lockheed Hudson, 230 knots and an operational radius of 350 miles. The RAF and RCAF each had one squadron in service by 1939. The Hudson seen here is from 11 (Bomber Reconnaissance) Squadron, RCAF, in 1940: note the dark colour scheme.

19 The mainstay of Allied medium-range air patrol in the Atlantic: the Consolidated Catalina flying boat, in this case one from 240 Squadron, RAF, in late 1940 or early 1941. The type had an operational range of 600 miles.

20 *Bismarck* steams out to meet her fate, May 1941: seen from *Prinz Eugen*.

21 A rare view of the mainstay of the Wolf Pack campaign in the mid-ocean: the type VIIc U-boat.

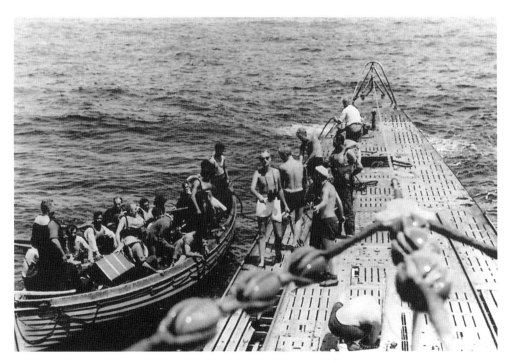

22 The operations of large U-boats in remote parts of the Atlantic still offered opportunity for acts of civility in 1941. Here Kaptlt Günther Hesseler, in the white shorts, passes a course to the African coast – some 200 nautical miles away – to the survivors of U-107's latest victim, the Dutch steamer *Marisa* on 17 May.

23 Closing the gap: the Canadian corvette *Orillia* seen from *Chambly* as the first corvettes of the Newfoundland Escort Force make passage to St John's, 24 May 1941.

24 The key North Atlantic convoy escort relay point in 1941 and early 1942: Hvalfjordhur, Iceland. Oilers, an R-class battleship and an AMC lie to the right, a depot ship, four destroyers and two corvettes to the left.

25 USS *Gleaves*, one of the powerful and modern destroyers deployed by the USN into the northwest Atlantic for escort duty in late 1941.

26 Americans serving in the north-west Atlantic thought that the crews of British and Canadian corvettes ought to receive submarine pay. HMCS *Battleford,* with a convoy in November 1941, shows why – and why forecastle extensions were so important to the early corvettes. Note the antenna for the Canadian 'SW1C' metric wavelength radar at the masthead.

27 *Left:* Roosevelt and Churchill at the historic meeting in Argentia, Newfoundland, in August 1941 that drew the USN into the war – and into the Battle of the Atlantic. The head of the USN, Admiral Ernest King, is standing behind Roosevelt.

28 *Below:* The Hunt Class destroyer HMS *Exmoor* in company with HMS *Malaya* on the Sierra Leone-Gibraltar route, February 1942. *Exmoor* played a key role in the early stages of the battle for HG 76 in December 1941, helping to sink U-131 before she had to part company. Note the type 286 radar at the masthead.

29 Defence of the Sierra Leone-Gibraltar convoys in the fall of 1941 was aided significantly by the deployment of powerful and well-equipped escorts, like the Black Swan class sloop *Stork* (seen here in 1943). *Stork*, the flagship of Capt. Johnny Walker's EG 36, shared in the destruction of U-131 and sank U-574 around HG76 in December 1941. By then she was fitted with the first sea-going 10cm radar, the type 271, seen here on a lattice mast on the stern.

30 A better solution to the problem of range and speed: the ex-American four-stacker HMS *Stanley*, newly converted to a Long Range escort, Devonport, England, September 1941. Her forward boilers have been removed and additional storage and bunkers added, a totally new bridge has been built, weapons modernised and the latest type 271 radar fitted in the lantern just above the bridge. As a member of EG 40 *Stanley* fought in the battle around HG 76, helping to sink U-131 and U-434, before being sunk herself by U-574 on 19 December.

31 Few corvettes survived a torpedoing long enough for the crew to get off, let alone have their photograph taken. The Free French corvette *Alysse* was one. She had her bow severed by a torpedo from U654 on 8 February 1942 while escorting ONS 61 in the mid-ocean.

32 A merchant vessel of the 'Liberty' class under fire from the deck gun of an unknown U-boat.

33 US escort forces, like the auxiliary vessel USS *Zircon* seen here in 1943, were slow to develop. Note the radar at the masthead and the 'Mousetrap' mortar — the smaller version of the British hedgehog developed by the USN — on the bow.

34 U-123, the type IXb U-boat in which Kaptlt Hardegen conducted two highly successful patrols in American waters in the first four months of 1942.

35 Merchant seamen rescued from ships lost in the battle for convoy ONS 92 in May 1942 crowd the upper deck of HMCS *Shediac*, happy to be alive, now out of work and, from the moment they abandoned ship, unpaid, too.

36 Tankers remained the targets of choice for U-boats throughout the inshore campaign in 1942, in part because of the oil they carried but really because of their size. The *Robert Tuttle*, seen here off Cape Henry on 12 June after being torpedoed by U-701, was nearly 12,000 tons – about twice the size of the average dry cargo steamer.

37 Replenishment of U-boats at sea was key to the German campaign in 1942; in this damaged picture U-459, the tanker whose presence off Bermuda in May sustained the assault along the American coast, gets ready to transfer supplies.

38 By 1942 most British destroyer escorts, like the old Town Class *Churchill* of group C 4 seen here, were fitted with the type 271 10cm radar and, atop the short mast at her stern, the shipborne HF/DF.

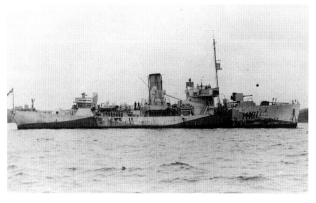

39 HMCS *Sackville* in mid-1942, about the time she fought three U-boats in the fog around convoy ON 115: still short forecastle with a full suit of minesweeping gear aft, a secondary armament composed of .50 calibre machine guns on the bridge wings and Lewis .303 machine guns aft, and the Canadian SW1C metric wavelength radar at her masthead. *Sackville* is now preserved in Halifax, NS, as the National Naval Memorial of Canada.

Over the summer of 1942 the RCN – pulled ever deeper into covering for the USN in the North Atlantic – seldom had less that ninety per cent of its fleet operational. It was only able to cover its responsibilities by assigning all of the burgeoning Bangor class minesweeping fleet to escort duty in May 1942. Even so, by June the four C groups of MOEF were three destroyers and eighteen corvettes short of the number needed to maintain their operational strength of six ships. The RN helped the struggling Canadians by assigning ten aged short-ranged destroyers in the spring of 1942 to the RCN's Western Local Escort Force to help bring westbound convoys, previously dispersed near the Grand Banks, right into Nova Scotia ports. By September, as the assembly point for all transatlantic convoys shifted from Nova Scotia to New York, WLEF assumed responsibility for escort duty for one third of the whole transatlantic passage. Fortunately for WLEF's motley collection of ships, that whole section was under effective air support.

The U-boat campaign in American waters in early 1942 forced the Americans to address the problem of escort and ASW in a systematic fashion for the first time, and some crucial steps were taken. In many ways the biggest impediment to rapid and effective reaction to the U-boat assault was the anglophobic head of the USN, Admiral King himself, who felt that the British had nothing to teach the USN, who clung to the inappropriate USN command structure in the Atlantic and who tended to centralise authority. By 1942 there were three separate USN commands in the Atlantic, CINCLANT, who commanded the fleet units and was responsible for TF-24 at Argentia, and two sea frontier commanders, Eastern and Gulf (of Mexico). All three reported directly to King, who was supposed to co-ordinate their activities. King also retained responsibility for the development of ASW doctrine and disse-mination of essential tactical pamphlets – even as he fought a desperate campaign against the Japanese in the Pacific. In March an Atlantic Fleet Anti-Submarine Warfare Unit was established by CINCLANT in Boston to tackle the ASW problem. However, despite the tremendous pressures of the global war, King continued to act as operational commander for the anti-submarine campaign in the Atlantic, trying to maintain tight control without the staff, resources and time to do a proper job. This meant that until May 1943, when the problem was finally resolved, CINCLANT and the USN sea-frontier commanders were free to make up their own tactics and doctrine. The result was a patch-work. In 1942 the USN did not even have a standard depth charge attack procedure. During 1942, the Americans learned old lessons the hard way.

Increasingly, the key to the whole Allied defensive – and offen-sive – system was radar-equipped air power. It was air power that largely defined the nature and pattern of the U-boat war. This was because Germany's U-boats, like other contemporary submarines, were not true submarines. Rather, they were really submersibles. Although their primary design feature was the ability to operate submerged and to deliver an attack from periscope depth, their diesel-electric propulsion system was air breathing. Diesels gave the U-boat its mobility and range, while air drawn down through open hatches gave life to the engines that propelled the boat and allowed its small bank of batteries to remain charged. On the sur-face the type VII U-boat, the 750-ton mainstay of the Atlantic war, could cruise comfortably at ten knots for 10,000 nautical miles. Forced to rely on its electric motors, however, a sub could move at only a walking pace for a day or so, at most. If forced to sprint (at up to nine knots) while submerged, a U-boat would exhaust its bat-teries in little more than an hour.

For tactical, operational and strategic reasons, then, Dönitz depended on the surface manoeuvrability of his U-boats. Indeed, apart from the complicated business of trying to get ahead of a convoy for a submerged attack, all the aspects of pack operations against convoys – in fact, all attacks on trade that hoped to meet Dönitz's target of 800,000 tons of shipping sunk per month – relied entirely on rapid and reliable surface movement, from location of targets, to assembly of the pack, and even the final attack. The great value of air power was that it determined where and when U-boats could move freely on the surface. It was the combination of convoy and air power that made the eastern Atlantic unsuitable for pack operations and, because of the vast areas through which oceanic convoys could be routed, difficult for individual submariners to find convoys let alone attack them. Inshore, the combination of air power and convoys tended to reduce the threat to manageable proportions, and ensured that if the convoy was attacked, the naval escort had only one U-boat to deal with.

This principle of the combination of air power and convoy was applied off Canada with great success in 1942 using an odd assemblage of trawlers, armed yachts, minesweepers, corvettes and worn-out destroyers. Among the oceanic convoys off Nova Scotia, it reduced losses to a single ship during the year (while losses to independently routed vessels over the same period were nearly 100, most in the first few months of the year when ON convoys were still being dispersed on the Grand Banks). The simple fact was that a U-boat captain, hundreds or thousands of miles away from home across a sea dominated by hostile naval and air forces, could not risk damage to his pressure hull. An inability to submerge meant certain destruction. The danger of air power to air-breathing submarines is perhaps best demonstrated by the American use of blimps for ASW and convoy escort throughout the war. These non-rigid airships even dove on U-boats, forcing them into a weary submergence lest the blimp get in a luck shot or call up help.

By the end of 1941, the RAF's Coastal Command was good enough to ensure that most pack operations ceased inside its range from bases in Britain and Iceland – effectively 600 miles. For the nine Liberator Mk I VLR aircraft of 120 Squadron RAF, no spot in the mid-ocean was beyond reach and effective patrol. The good news for the Germans, for the moment, was that the under-strength No. 120 Squadron was the sole VLR squadron in the North Atlantic. Aircraft ranges from Newfoundland and Canada using the same aircraft were, as noted earlier, rather less effective because of weather and wind conditions, leaving a funnel-shaped mid-Atlantic air gap through which convoys had to pass and

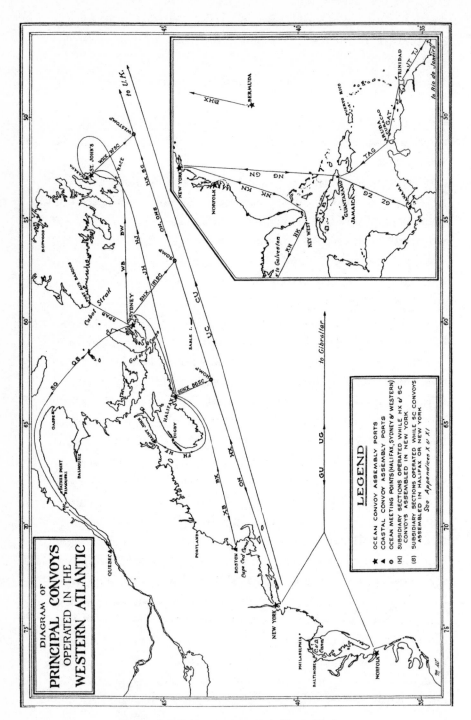

Diagram of principal convoys operated in the Western Atlantic.

within which U-boats could still operate with impunity. The almost perpetual fog of the Grand Banks also allowed pack opeations to penetrate to within a couple of hundred miles of Newfoundland, while aircraft patrolled harmlessly above. Until Newfoundland-based aircraft received modern radar – one that could discriminate between a ship and towering icebergs, a problem unique to the Grand Banks area – no flyer would plunge down through the murk to check out a suspicious contact. But where the weather was good and aircraft were present, U-boats had to hunt alone and, so long as convoys were operating, that made the location of targets and the attack problematic. At the very least, it sharply reduced shipping losses.

By 1942, after over 55 million miles of wartime flying and over 600 attacks on U-boats – resulting in only five U-boat kills – airmen began to solve the problem of sinking subs. When the U-boats abandoned the main Atlantic in late 1941, Coastal Command switched to a more aggressive patrolling of the transit routes through the Bay of Biscay and the northern entrances to the Atlantic. As with previous offensive operations and their occasional attacks on fleeting U-boats, no submarines were either sunk or damaged by these transit patrols in the first five months of 1942. Aircraft radar, the ASV Mk I and Mk II, were long wavelength and generally did not reveal a U-boat by day before it was seen by the naked eye, by which time the U-boat could also see the aircraft. Moreover, attack altitudes were too low – right in the natural line of sight of a U-boat's lookout – and the tendency to retain dark RAF camouflage schemes made the aircraft easily visible. Radar was naturally more important at night, or in poor visibility. But the early sets were so crude that the target was lost about a mile away, and so at night it was not possible to complete an attack. As a final point, only the large flying boats, like the Sunderland, and the bigger bombers like the Wellington and Liberators, could carry the converted 450lb naval depth charge. And even the hydrostatic fuse settings on these were limited to a minimum of fifty feet, based on the assumption that they were to be dropped on a U-boat which had submerged. But most attacks were on U-boats taken by surprise and still either on the surface or very shallow. The fifty-foot setting on the depth charge usually bathed the U-boat in spray or gave it a good shaking; it seldom killed.

In early 1942 all of this was about to change. New radar, a 10cm set with very high definition, was about to enter service. Aircraft colour schemes were changed to white – like the belly of a seagull – and patrol altitudes were raised to make the aircraft harder to spot. And a new 250lb aerial depth charge with a twenty-five foot setting entered service in May 1942. All of these would provide aircraft with the means they needed to become very serious U-boat killers in the second half of 1942. Some inkling of this came in early June, when the first RAF squadron fitted with special search lights – Leigh Lights, named after the RAF officer who invented them – entered service in the Bay of Biscay transit patrols. On 4 June the large Italian submarine *Luigi Torelli* was slipping quietly along the southern reaches of the Bay of Biscay under a dark, moonless sky when all of a sudden the conning tower was illuminated in a blaze of light. A Liegh Light Wellington of 172 Squadron RAF, flown by S/L Jeaff Greswell, had picked up the sub at six miles on radar, made its approach and at one mile switched on the powerful light. Nothing was seen from the flight deck of the aircraft until much too late, but on the bridge of the *Luigi Torelli* pandemonium ensued. Uncertain of what was going on, the sub's crew fired off recognition flares, which allowed Greswell to cue his second attack. At three quarters of a mile and 250 feet off the sea the Wellington's powerful searchlight came on again, illuminating the Italian submarine, and Greswell straddled it with four depth charges set to thirty-five foot intervals, inflicting serious damage. *Luigi Torelli* made port in Spain.

But that was not the end of the story. Forbidden by international law from staying for more than twenty-four hours, *Luigi Torelli* put to sea again the next day and was attacked by two Sunderlands of 10 Squadron, RAF, who straddled her again with depth charges. Again the sub was damaged, but refused to sink. After a brief internment in Spain (and an official transfer to the Spanish Navy) the *Luigi Torelli* escaped to France.[2] Post-attack assessment revealed that the failure of aircraft to sink the sub stemmed from the charges sinking too fast and carrying down with them an air bubble, which delayed the action of the fuse. The solution quickly adopted was to fit a nose and tail cone, which caused the charge to hit broadside and slowed its sinking, producing a genuine twenty-five foot depth setting which was lethal to U-boats caught on the surface. With that, aircraft – after nearly three years of war – finally had an effective weapon. On 12 June Dönitz ordered U-boats transiting the Bay to remain submerged by day until twelve degrees west. This was the first tangible victory in the long Biscay offensive, and it had an impact on the time in which U-boats could stay on station.

And so, in early 1942, Allied aircraft starting killing submarines, slowly at first, and then in time by the score. British flyers doubled their wartime score in the first six months of 1942, when land-based aircraft sank five U-boats. Three more succumbed to naval aircraft, two of these claimed by land-based USN Hudsons flying out of American airfields. Two other kills were shared with naval escorts.

The Allies needed to start killing U-boats as 1942 wore on. The bitter winter of 1942 seriously delayed the first wave of new U-boat construction that Dönitz was relying on. In the first quarter of the year only thirty-nine new U-boats became operational, a rate of thirteen a month. Twenty-six of these were despatched to the arctic to attack the Russian convoys, and two went straight to the Mediterranean: over the same period twelve were sunk. The net gain in the Atlantic was therefore not appreciable until June. After that the construction and commissioning bottlenecks were gone and Dönitz could expect to receive twenty new operational submarines a month: 120 before the end of the year. By December his operational strength reached nearly 350 U-boats. From Dönitz's perspective it was now a race between his growing fleet and the development of Allied countermeasures.

[2] She survived the war, serving briefly as both a German and Japanese submarine in the Far East before being taken over by the Americans and scuttled in 1946.

The U-boat fleet also needed new torpedoes and radar detectors if they were to remain viable. And they needed to sink shipping much faster. In June Dönitz learned through German intelligence that the Allies were already building several millions of tons of new shipping in 1942, an estimate that proved to be correct, and an estimated 10 million tons (actually 14 million tons) in 1943. If that was so, then his target needed to be 900,000 tons per month to make an impact, about double the rate for June, which turned out to be the best month of the war. Dönitz's only real hope, and one nearly realised, was that tanker losses would paralyse the Allies' shipbuilding industry.

By early July, four U-boats were still slaughtering shipping in the Gulf of Mexico and the Caribbean – thirty-three ships during that month – but the establishment of a convoy system there and an end to the carnage was only a matter of time. USN forces had already hunted U-157 down in the Florida Straits and sank her on 13 June in a well-organised and systematic search. Minefields increasingly restricted movements, air patrols grew more oppressive and the U-boat's luck could not hold. As Roskill observed, by early July 'most of the U-boats were working cautiously on the perimeter of the Caribbean'. With operations now reaching well beyond the easy range of his smaller submarines, and sensing a possible weakening of defences closer to home along the transatlantic route, by mid-1942 Dönitz decided it was time to renew attacks in the mid-ocean.

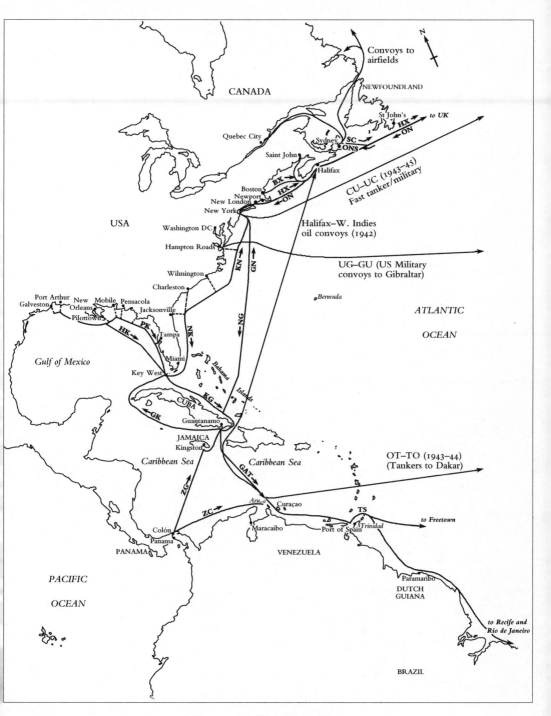

Convoy system in the Western Hemisphere.

5

Mid-Atlantic Confrontation

July-December 1942

In mid-1942 the U-boat war in the Atlantic reached the peak of its effectiveness. In June, Dönitz's submariners sank 136 ships of some 637,000 tons, the highest monthly score of the war and the highest rate of tonnage sunk per U-boat day at sea, 359, ever achieved. Although his fleet was in the throes of a major expansion, what worried Dönitz by the summer of 1942 was that his U-boats' success since 1939 was largely the result of exploiting weaknesses in the enemy's defence. The type VII and IX U-boats were essentially improved First World War designs which succeeded only because of new tactics and command and control systems, and because they attacked the gaps in the evolving convoy and escort system. The one important technological improvement in submarine warfare since the First World War, an influence detonator for torpedoes, had been a dismal failure. Only bold new tactics and a reliance on surface manoeuvrability for all phases of the campaign, coupled with

successful efforts to extend the operational range of U-boats, accounted for the remarkable success to date. Every new Allied convoy
system, every extension of air power, forced this fragile weapon further and further afield in search of easy targets. By the high summer
of 1942, the U-boat was just about at the end of its reach. To achieve
decisive strategic results it now had to mass closer to its bases in
France, and into a direct confrontation with Allied ASW forces.

Dönitz also knew that he was losing the technological battle.
Apart from new torpedoes, new detonators, radar detectors and
heavier anti-aircraft weaponry – all on the way in 1942 – there
were no radically new developments looming in the U-boat fleet.
He was still dreaming of an air-independent U-boat, the Walter
boat driven by hydrogen peroxide, but that was in the early stages
of development. Newer type VII and IX had stronger hulls, which
allowed diving to depths of 600 feet or more, but these were
simply a variation on a theme. Meanwhile, Allied anti-submarine
countermeasures were – by 1942 – moving at an alarming pace.
Not only were convoy systems spreading, but radar-equipped naval
and· air escorts were stripping away the cloak of invisibility
enjoyed by U-boats, and would soon eliminate surface manoeuvrability entirely. The presence of very long-range Liberators on
extensive patrols in the very depths of the Atlantic suggested that
there would soon be no place left for the kind of free-wheeling
Dönitz's U-boats required.

All of this Dönitz knew full well, but there was much more besides
that he had no inkling of. British escorts had begun to fit a new
A/S weapon called 'hedgehog', which threw a pattern of small
contact-fused bombs ahead of an attacking ship. The ability to retain
asdic contact and stand-off while attacking a submerged U-boat
promised a dramatic increase in lethality. More importantly, A/S
aircraft were about to receive a new array of weapons and sensors.
The Americans were working on Magnetic Anomaly Detectors
(MAD), which picked up the change in the earth's magnetic field
caused by the presence of a large ferrous metal mass – like a submarine – and could detect submerged U-boats from the air.

Roto-bombs fired backwards from the MAD-equipped aircraft allowed it to attack the contact. Small disposable air-launched sono-buoys also went into production in the US in late 1942, as did an air-launched acoustic homing torpedo code-named Fido for sono-buoy-equipped aircraft. Meanwhile, the British began to fit their Hudson and Swordfish A/S aircraft with rockets fitted with a solid warhead designed to punch holes in submarine pressure hulls. All this and more was waiting in the wings in the summer of 1942. The days of the great U-boat offensive in the Atlantic were numbered.

Evidence of the changing situation came throughout July in sev-eral ways. On the night of 5 July, U-502 was transiting the Bay of Biscay en route to her home port after a successful cruise off the US when it was suddenly illuminated by a 179 Squadron Wellington. Pilot Officer W. Howell, an American serving in the RAF, conducted a textbook approach and attack on the U-boat and sank it, the first victim of the new Leigh Light. Eight days later Howell seriously damaged U-159 under similar circumstances. On 16 July Dönitz reversed the previous practice for Biscay transits of submergence during the day and free running at night – which simply resulted in a sharp rise in the number of U-boats sighted and attacked during the day. It was time to put a radar-warning device into service.

Two days after P/O Howell sank U-502 in the Biscay, a US Army Air Force patrol off Cape Hatteras sank U-701 – the first kill by the USAAF. A week later it was the USN's turn, as one of its air-craft damaged U-576 and called up a patrol vessel to finish the job. Including U-215, destroyed by HMS *Tigre* off Nantucket on 3 July, that meant three U-boats sunk off the US east coast in a little more than two weeks. Two others, U-87 and U-404, were heavily dam-aged by air attack and forced to return. 'These losses,' *The U-boat War in the Atlantic* records, 'representing one third of forces engaged, were not commensurate with the results.' From 'mid-July, nearly all our boats were being attacked from the air', that same history observes. Indeed, they were. On 17 July, Coastal Command aircraft sank U-751 off Portugal, and on the last day of the month the Royal Canadian Air Force added U-754 to the score south of Nova Scotia. Anti-submarine aircraft had begun to find their teeth.

But that was not all. As the expansion of the convoy and escort system pushed U-boats further south and towards the edges of the Caribbean, Dönitz decided to renew pack attacks along the main transatlantic routes. Based on his experience with group Hecht in May and June, Dönitz knew that the greatly reduced escorts of the main convoys forced them to travel closely to the Great Circle Route. That, and the tremendous success enjoyed by *B-Dienst* in penetrating the British Convoy Cypher, meant that these crucial convoys were easy to find and attack. They also passed through the mid-ocean air gap, which was still largely free of Allied aircraft. There, in the mid-Atlantic, the medium-sized type VII U-boats that composed the great bulk of his fleet were still free to roam. Moreover, the main transatlantic convoys were a target of unquestionable strategic importance.

And so in mid-July a pack of nine U-boats, all commanded by new captains, was deployed 600 miles west of Ireland. By 24 July, with the help of *B-Dienst*, Group Wolf had located the westbound convoy ON 113, thirty-three ships escorted by C.2 composed of the two Town Class destroyers, *Burnham* (RN) and *St Croix* (RCN), and three RCN and one RN corvette. Faced with a building pack, the SOE sent the two destroyers on distant sweeps around the convoy, during which *St Croix* found and sank U-90 on the 24 July. Once the convoy crossed into the American strategic zone (roughly twenty-seven degrees west) USN authorities, who took over routing of convoys in their zone from the Canadians on 1 July, ordered a course change which the SOE knew would bring ON 113 back into danger. The SOE and the convoy commodore affected a compromise, but the result was that ON 113 turned a completed circle in the mid-ocean and ran into the U-boat pack anyway. Without modern radar the Canadian escorts were unable to prevent U-boats penetrating the screen on the night of the 24 July and ON 113 eventually lost three ships.

As the battle for ON 113 ended, ON 115, escorted by C.3, was intercepted mid-ocean by U-210 of Group Pirate on 29 July. In the absence of shipborne HF/DF equipment, the SOE of the Canadian group sent his destroyers on sweeps directed by interception of the U-boats' MF/DF homing signals. These earned C.3 nothing except the approbation of senior WAC officers, who preferred HF/DF directed sweeps – something the Canadians, who lacked shipborne HF/DF in all but one escort, simply could not do. However, the maintenance of a distant forward screen by destroyer *Skeena* and the corvette *Wetaskiwin* produced a contact with U-558 in the early hours of 31 July. U-558 went deep – very deep by existing standards, more than 600 feet – which made attacking it extremely difficult. Eventually, *Wetaskiwin* stood off, maintained asdic contact and acted as directing ship while the destroyer delivered the depth charges on her orders. The attack was evidence of how much Canadian training had improved, and it worked superbly; boats were lowered to gather the human remains needed to confirm a kill. The loss of U-558 brought to eleven the number of U-boats killed in July, the worst month of the war so far.

In fact, things might well have been even worse. When the battle for ON 115 slipped into the fog of the Grand Banks of Newfoundland both attacker and attacked groped for one another in poor visibility. One Canadian corvette, HMCS *Sackville*, was originally thought to have sunk two U-boats on the night of 2 August, blowing one into the air with her depth charges and hitting another with a shot from her four-inch gun in a frantic action. But both eventually made port. As the Admiralty's assessment observed, 'Sackville's two U-boats would have been a gift if she had been fitted with RDF type 271'. As things turned out, the Germans got the best of the poor visibility on the Grand Banks, sinking two ships and damaging a third from ON 115 in waters where reinforcements – both naval and air – ought to have ended the battle sooner. WAC's A/S officer lauded Canadian and American flyers for setting out for the Grand Banks 'under conditions which would be regarded as quite impossible elsewhere.' But until both naval and

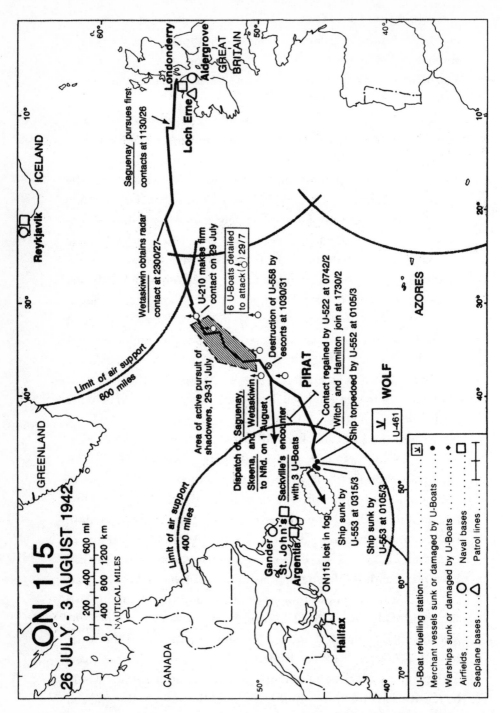

ON 115: principal convoy routes, limit of air support and air bases during the period of 26 July–3 August 1942.

air escorts had modern radar, convoy battles would both begin and end virtually within sight of Newfoundland. And, of course, the nagging problem of the air gaps – in the mid-Atlantic, east of the Azores and near the Canary Islands – remained, and it was there that the U-boats began once again to concentrate by August 1942.

In the mid-Atlantic, where the most serious gap in air support remained, the problem was further complicated when the USN's Convoy and Routing Section in Washington took over from the Canadians in the western hemisphere on 1 July 1942. Now only about one third of the Atlantic passage – the least dangerous eastern portion, which enjoyed excellent air support from both Britain and Iceland – was under British control. Differences in command philosophy in the two zones were immediately apparent. WAC followed the principle of providing the man on the spot with as much information as possible, and leaving him to fight his own battles. In July 1942, Washington's new Convoy and Routing Authority demonstrated more hands-on control, as the battle for ON 113 indicated. The British held Washington completely responsible for the subsequent losses to the convoy. Admiral Brainard, the USN's new Commander, Task Force-24 at Argentia, agreed. The British Admiralty's tinkering with the Arctic convoy PQ 17 in early July 1942 reinforced this point. When, based on its own intelligence appreciation of the danger to the convoy from *Tirpitz* and against the recommendations of the SOE, the Admiralty ordered PQ 17 to scatter, it was slaughtered by U-boats. This, the British official historian observed, was entirely out of keeping with the stated philosophy of the RN. After ON 113 it seems Washington, too, was content to pass along intelligence to SOEs and let them fight their own battles.

The fiasco over ON 113 also provided the British with more leverage in their struggle to re-assert WAC's control westward. This was accomplished in stages over the next ten months. In September WAC replaced its *WACIs* with the new *Atlantic Convoy Instructions*, which were adopted as the basis for all transatlantic trade convoys. CTF-24 endorsed the adoption of *ACIs*, which included American

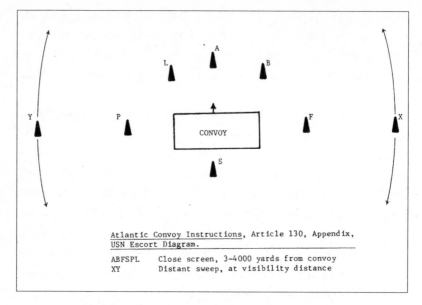

Atlantic Convoy Instructions, Article 130, Appendix, USN Escort Diagram.

screening diagrams and other elements, making *ACIs* the first joint Allied operational and tactical manual in the Atlantic war. Problems of a different phonetic alphabet remained, and so too did lingering differences in pre-arranged escort tactics between the token American group in the mid-ocean (A.3) and all the others who followed British procedures. For example, a British Senior Officer Escort could not assume that an attached American ship would know what to do when a 'Raspberry' was ordered. By the same token, a British ship parachuted into A.3 would have to wait to see what everyone else did when the order 'Zombie Crack' was heard over the radio.

American assumption of full operational control over convoys in their strategic zone on 1 July occurred only after most American naval forces had been withdrawn from the north-west Atlantic. The preponderance of British and Canadians along the transatlantic route by mid-1942 – roughly ninety-eight per cent of the escorts –

allowed the British to influence the conduct of operations there, even if the formal command was American. But the command problem in the north-west Atlantic remained an increasing impediment to the Allied war effort, with no fewer than nine separate commands split between two countries and four services involved in escort and anti-submarine operations. Naval headquarters in Ottawa was even forbidden to transmit operational intelligence directly to its own forces operating just outside Canada's three-mile territorial limit – although they did it anyway – and by July CTF-24 was carping about the 'freelance operations' of Admiral Murray's training group, which the Canadians used to support convoys on the Grand Banks.

It would take much time and effort to sort out the now-muddled command and control situation in the Atlantic, but in the meantime the war at sea went on. The intensification of the battle in the mid-ocean is usually acknowledged to have begun with the passage of SC 94 in early August. This thirty-six-ship eastbound convoy escorted by C.1 was intercepted in the fog of the Grand Banks on 5 August and an eight-day ordeal ensued. With only one destroyer, the Canadian *Assiniboine*, modern radar in only one of his three RN corvettes and no shipborne HF/DF, Lt Cdr A. Ayer, RNR, the SOE, was hard pressed to keep the U-boats at bay. It got harder still on the 6 August, when *Assiniboine* pursued and rammed U-210 in heavy fog, and was so damaged that she had to return to St John's. Ayer was now down to six corvettes as SC 94 pushed out into the air gap. Over the next three days he kept most of the inexperienced U-boat captains away, until an unexpected and nearly simultaneous submerged daylight attack from directly ahead hit five ships. C.1 got a little of that back on 8 August when the British corvette *Dianthus* blew U-379 to the surface and sank it by ramming, the second U-boat kill by the escort, and the first British kill around a transatlantic convoy in nearly a year. The arrival of two British destroyers – fitted with HF/DF – just as SC 94 reached the edge of Coastal Command range on 9 August brought relief to Ayer's struggling corvettes, but the U-boats still managed to pick four more ships from the convoy on the final night, bringing the total losses to eleven.

In the end, Ayer and C.1 had done well. Until the reinforcements arrived on the 8-9 August Ayer kept losses to seven and killed two U-boats. With two destroyers, HF/DF and modern radar, he might have done better. Such was the case with ONS 122, the first B-group escorted convoy to be seriously attacked in the mid-ocean since the renewal of the campaign in July. The core of B.6 was, in fact, a clutch of Norwegian corvettes, all modernised, all fitted with the latest radar, and all manned by tough, well-trained and professional seamen. B.6 was ably led by Lt Cdr J.V. Waterhouse, RN, in the old destroyer *Viscount*: old, but nonetheless fitted with modern radar, HF/DF and the new A/S mortar 'hedgehog'. Waterhouse used his HF/DF to locate shadowers and U-boats as they made the contact reports, sending out mostly corvettes to drive them down, while B.6's modern radar formed a barrier around ONS 122. On one occasion he used *Viscount*'s speed to sweep around the convoy and drive off every shadower. But Waterhouse was careful not to exhaust the destroyers' fuel and leave his group without tactical speed and its crucial HF/DF equipment. Despite all his efforts, however, by the evening of 24 August the situation 'was somewhat grim.' Nine U-boats were in contact, but only four could be accounted for. That night three U-boats slipped through the screen and sank four ships.

Nine U-boats were still in contact with ONS 122 on the morning of 25 August, however, they soon lost the convoy in heavy fog and the battle ended. Four ships were lost in exchange for two U-boats being heavily damaged. WAC staff were pleased with the results. No fewer than thirteen attacks on the convoy had been foiled by modern radar. The lack of U-boat kills was at least partly attributed to Waterhouse's insistence on driving U-boats down and getting back to the convoy, not on hunting submarines. Good intelligence provided by excellent equipment allowed Waterhouse to make sensible tactical decisions: he usually knew how many U-boats were in contact and where they were. Most were driven off. The Norwegians, for their part, acted superbly. 'It was a pleasure to see (and hear) the Norwegians go into action,' Waterhouse reported; 'Raspberry went like clockwork and whenever, during the night, the cry of "Tally ho" was heard on the scram, I had only to check the bearings'. Although it was their first serious battle, B.6 had done very well indeed.

British groups operating in the other air gap, near the Azores, enjoyed similar success with similar equipment and much better weather. The six U-boats of Group Iltis pursued SL 118 west of the Canaries from 16-20 August, but were kept at bay by the escort. Like the U-boats probing around SC 94, those of Iltis had their greatest success by submerging ahead of the convoy and making surprise daylight attacks. Very long-range air support from Cornwall, operating 780 miles from base, ended the battle on the 20 August. Bit by bit the system was coming together for the Allies.

But not all the escort groups that were operating in the North Atlantic in 1942 enjoyed the benefits of good tactical intelligence provided by modern equipment. Canadian and American convoy battles in July and August 1942 revealed serious deficiencies in equipment and in tactical speed among their larger ships. The Coast·Guard Cutters of A.3 were too slow to conduct effective sweeps around their convoys, and so A.3 was reduced to maintaining a distant screen during the day in an attempt to drive lurking U-boats down. No American ships were yet fitted with 10cm radar or HF/DF. Canadian MOEF groups had a nominal strength of two destroyers, but the aged British destroyers that were assigned, which were usually fitted with HF/DF, were often unable to sail owing to defects. C groups tried to fill the tactical information gap by looking for the shadowing U-boat's MF/DF homing beacon, but this signal was more diffused and less useful for tactical purposes. Finally, Canadian escorts of MOEF lacked the modern radar that the B groups used to such good effect. By the end of August the Canadians had proven themselves proficient U-boat killers in the mid-ocean – responsible for four of MOEF's five kills over July and August – but there was already serious doubt about the ability of the Canadians to defend convoys in the air gap.

The situation only got worse by the end of August, for a number of reasons. Perhaps most importantly, the Germans put their new radar receiver *Metox* into service. This crude but highly effective device was designed to give U-boats warning of airborne metric wavelength radar. The combination of Leigh Light and radar had made the Biscay night unsafe for German submariners, forcing them to run the gauntlet of Coastal Command's daylight patrols and resulting in a dramatic jump in daytime attacks on transiting U-boats in August. By September *Metox* made it safe for U-boats to run on the surface at night again; only two night contacts were made by Coastal Command aircraft on U-boats crossing the bay that month. The deployment of KG.40's long-range JU88c fighters into the Bay to prey on the lumbering anti-submarine aircraft flying daylight patrols in late September, finally forced Coastal Command to abandon its Biscay offensive entirely in October. For the moment, *Metox* won the battle of the transit routes.

This much, historians have long known. But the *Metox* receiver also picked up the radar transmissions of naval escorts still using metric wavelength radar. In late 1942 that meant the Canadians, who provided thirty-five per cent of escorts operating in the mid-ocean. *Metox* not only warned U-boats that Canadian escorts were near, it allowed them to home in on the convoys they prote-cted. The fact that the Canadians escorted the bulk of the slow transatlantic convoys simply made the German task of finding them that much easier. In the autumn of 1942, then, the RCN bore the brunt of German attacks, with weak and poorly equipped escort groups protecting the most vulnerable targets and relying on a radar which betrayed their presence.

If that were not enough, the strength of the C groups of MOEF continued to dwindle as the summer wore on. In August the RCN committed sixteen of its best corvettes to the upcoming invasion of North Africa, Operation TORCH. In early September the RCN was stretched south when the western terminus for transatlantic convoys shifted from Halifax to New York and the Canadians assumed responsibility for the additional leg. With this, the interlocking system in the western hemisphere was complete, and RCN corvettes escorting Canadian oil convoys from the Caribbean were reassigned to help the USN run their main convoys south of New York. These corvettes, like those assigned to North Africa, were among the best in the Canadian fleet and were sorely needed mid-ocean by autumn of that year.

By late summer 1942, the RCN was over extended, with no slack for training, refits and modernisation of vessels, or for the augmentation of the embattled mid-ocean. This profoundly affected events over the next year. In fact, to meet the new commitments the RCN accepted a tactical defeat at the St Lawrence River in September 1942, where – in the face of renewed attacks – it shut down Canada's great ocean waterway and caused a storm of protest in the Canadian Parliament. The only way Admiral Murray in Newfoundland could possibly cope was to once again transfer his training group to operations, which he did at the end of August. And as losses to RCN destroyers mounted through the last months of 1942, C groups continued to loose tactical speed and hitting power. The decision to over extend and run the fleet hard was a conscious one by the Canadian Naval Staff. It was taken in the midst of crisis in 1942 in the certain knowledge that the RCN could not, by itself, win the war at sea, but it could help its larger Allies to do so. Indeed, the ability of the RN in particular to refit, re-equip and train its escort fleet in 1942 is silent testimony to the willingness of the RCN to drive its own men and ships to the limit of their endurance.

As a result of all this, the highly vulnerable slow transatlantic convoys escorted primarily by Canadians became the prime targets of German operations in the mid-Atlantic during the last months of 1942. Slow convoys were incapable of effective evasive action once the enemy made contact, and they took longer to cross the air gap. A full strength MOEF group, with two destroyers available for HF/DF directed sweeps and the latest equipment, was essential for pushing a convoy through the increasingly larger packs waiting along the North Atlantic run by the autumn of 1942. The solution to the problem was to eliminate the air gap and reinforce threatened convoys as required. Unfortunately, the new auxiliary carriers designed to fill the role so ably pioneered by *Audacity* were syphoned off to provide air support to the forthcoming North African landings. So, too, were the 'support groups' established by WAC in the eastern Atlantic in September. For the time being the only help available in the depths of the Atlantic came from occasional support by the nine Liberators of 120 Squadron RAF. The Allied air forces desperately needed more VLR aircraft.

Until the problem of the air gap was solved, Mid-Ocean Escort Groups had to push their convoys through with little help. Reductions in the size and number of groups over the year forced these convoys to adhere closely to the Great Circle route, while the continuing gap in reading German radio traffic made the precise location of waiting U-boat packs difficult. Only the increasing use of refuelling at sea by late 1942 allowed many MOEF escorts to stay with their convoys. To make matters worse, the *B-Dienst* still routinely read the British convoy cypher, which revealed routing, and occasionally the Admiralty's daily U-boat estimates. Meanwhile, the North Atlantic gradually filled up with the waves of new U-boats entering service. By early November, Dönitz had over ninety at sea. Some twenty-three of these were the larger type IX submarines, which still enjoyed enormous success in southern waters of the eastern Caribbean, the Atlantic 'narrows' between Brazil and Africa, and off South Africa. These few submarines continued to account for the lion's share of the sinkings through the late summer and early autumn, as they took a terrible toll of independently routed shipping – 179 during August, September and October. In contrast, the fifteen pack attacks on convoys over the same period produced only twenty-two per cent of overall losses. But how long that could last was anyone's guess. By early November, Dönitz had over forty U-boats in the central North Atlantic, and the air gap there was literally filling up with submarines. If they could not be avoided, they had to be fought and the situation promised to get much worse before it got better.

The importance of tactical proficiency among escorts in this stage of the Atlantic war was revealed in another combination of battles in September and early October 1942. This round began when ON 127, escorted by C.4, ran into the U-boat pack Vorwarts on the edge of air cover on 10 September. The first knowledge the Canadian escort had of U-boat contact came when U–96 hit three ships in a submerged daylight attack. No escort group was large enough to form a complete asdic barrier in front of a convoy, and there was little C.4 could have done. Acting Lt Cdr A.H. Dobson, RCNR, the SOE in the old four-stacker *St Croix*, used his two destroyers to sweep aggressively around the convoy, but he lacked HF/DF to make the sweeps effective and apart from the British corvette *Celandine*, whose set was defective, none of his escort had modern radar. When all was said and done,

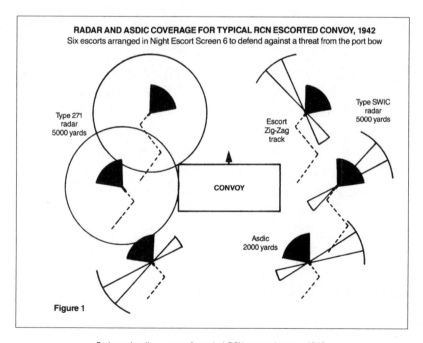

Radar and asdic coverage for typical RCN escorted convoy 1942.

ONS 127 lost seven ships, four were damaged and the Canadian destroyer *Ottawa* was sunk. Although the British were generally unimpressed by Dobson's conduct of the defence, they put the problem down to lack of modern radar and the inscrutable problem of surprise submerged attacks. Dönitz had reason to be happy. Only one U-boat was damaged, and ONS 127 earned the distinction of being the only convoy during 1942-43 against which all U-boats deployed fired torpedoes.

ON 127 also brought an end to the RCN's tremendous string of good fortune in the mid-ocean. During the summer of 1942 Canadian ships were the premier U-boat killers in the mid-Atlantic, with four. Whenever a Canadian-escorted convoy was bitten, the escort had bitten back. But a combination of *Metox* and increasingly poor weather put an end to that. And with *Ottawa* sunk and *Assiniboine* under repair, C groups were now desperately short of destroyers in addition to all the other problems they faced.

Meanwhile, unable to catch the British escorted HX 206, the Germans turned their attention in late September to SC 100 escorted by A.3 – two US Coast Guard Cutters and one RN and six Canadian corvettes. Through a combination of tight screening and aggressive patrolling A.3 kept twenty U-boats at bay for four days, while the German operation became entangled with a convoy of Hudson River steamers, which they mistook for troopships. Both SC 100 and RB 1 slipped through with minimal losses. It was not until 11 October that the Germans were once again able to concentrate a pack around a convoy and launch a concerted attack. As it was, SC 104 almost slipped neatly around the edge of the waiting pack, until U-221 made firm contact on 12 October. The escort was B.6: two fully equipped British destroyers and four superb Norwegian corvettes. They had already proven their mettle on the battle for ONS 122. However, B.6's excellent training, equipment and professionalism were put to the test in a battle with serious losses on both sides.

Poor weather favoured the attackers in the early stage, and B.6 could not stop the intrepid Kapitänlieutenant Trojer of U-221 from pressing home his attack in a howling wind and crashing seas on 12 October, sinking three ships. The next day Trojer homed-in four other U-boats, but as each made its contact report the HF/DF sets of B.6 located the U-boats and drove them down. Pursuit of these newcomers left SC 104 open to Trojer and he attacked again on the second night, taking advantage of continued bad weather to sink two more ships. A chance encounter with the destroyer *Viscount* nearly ended in a ramming of U-221, but Trojer escaped. Poor weather also allowed three other U-boats to penetrate the screen around SC 104 and sink another three ships.

Finally, on 14 October, the weather moderated and B.6 got the best out of its modern equipment. When U-619 closed in to attack SC 104, *Viscount* found it on radar and sank the U-boat by ramming. *Viscount* left for repairs, while all six further attempts to attack SC 104 that night were foiled by radar. By daylight the next day, the SOE, Cdr S. Heathcote, RN, pushed his remaining escorts out on HF/DF directed sweeps, while Liberators from Iceland drove off shadowers. The following night was therefore quiet, and dawn on 16 October brought a relay of air support, while Heathcote's own destroyer, *Fame*, blew U-353 to the surface and sank it by ramming. The escort, now down to the four Norwegian corvettes, used its radar to stop the only attempt to penetrate into the convoy that night and the Germans finally abandoned the chase on 17 October. Despite the loss of eight ships, WAC considered the battle for SC 104 a heartening success. The losses were explicable by the early bad weather. That said, Heathcote left his convoy open to attack on several occasions, and WAC officers would have been less charitable had he been a Canadian. But good tactical intelligence allowed Heathcote to make sensible battle plans, and he also got two U-boats. Despite the losses, WAC was pleased; B.6's had balanced the score by sinking subs. These were, in fact, only the second and third kills by the RN along the main transatlantic convoy routes since September 1941.

If there was contentment at WAC over the success of B.6's defence of SC 104, there was also ample reason for concern by early November. Losses to shipping through 1942 had been unprecedented, and although Dönitz effectively lost the tonnage war in November 1942 when new construction finally outstripped losses, the morale of merchant mariners was in a precarious state by late 1942. Their losses through the year had been the heaviest yet of the war, and with the Russian convoys about to recommence for the winter there was grumbling about refusals to sail into dangerous waters. Dönitz now hoped to win at sea by pushing merchant seamen to the point of mutiny. The British were equally determined to ensure that this did not happen. Moreover, the bulk of Allied shipping losses were still suffered by the British and their import situation was, in the words of the RN's official historian, 'never tighter'. The Allied landings in North Africa, Operation TORCH, which commenced on 8 November, plunged the British shipping and import crisis to new depths. To find the escorts for the assault and follow-up convoys, the whole trade convoy system in the eastern Atlantic, the SL, OS and HG-OG series, were suspended. SL 125, the last to arrive in the UK until April 1943, was also heavily attacked and lost eleven ships. Starting in October, ships travelling from Britain to the South Atlantic and back were routed through the interlocking convoy system off North America. This circuitous route cut the overall carrying capacity of the British merchant fleet, and the demands of the North Africa campaign soon outstripped planner's estimates. This was especially true of oil, which was drawn from UK reserves, and its decline alone precipitated a crisis. The temporary abandonment of the eastern Atlantic also meant that the only way into and out of Britain for trade was now the embattled North Atlantic run.

Just as that route became Britain's sole lifeline, deteriorating weather, longer nights and increasing numbers of U-boats combined to increase the likelihood of German success. By late October the Germans regarded the onset of winter weather 'as difficult for the enemy's surface and submerged detection devices and favourable to our U-boats'. That was certainly the case when the twelve U-boats of group Puma pursued HX 212 across the air gap between 26-29 October. The eight ships of MOEF group A.3 all lacked modern equipment and could not stop the annihilation of the convoy's entire seventh column – seven ships – and two stragglers. Only a rapid transit made possible by the convoy's speed and a routing well to the north, where the air gap narrowed, ended the battle quickly. The SOE, Cdr Lewis, USCG, complained that the promised auxiliary carrier had failed to show up to help him through the air gap; it was getting ready for TORCH.

A.3 was nonetheless fortunate that HX 212 was intercepted late and its passage was fast. SC 107 was intercepted while still south of Newfoundland on 29 October and faced nearly two weeks of danger from U-boats. Dönitz mustered a pack of seventeen to attack it even before SC 107 had cleared the fog of the Grand Banks. The escort, C.4, comprised the destroyer *Restigouche*, with HF/DF, the British corvette *Celandine*, which carried modern radar, and five poorly equipped RCN corvettes. The rescue ship *Stockport* was also fitted with HF/DF, so the SOE, Lt Cdr D.W. Piers, RCN, could get good fixes on transmitting U-boats. But shortages of escorts meant that C.4 was essentially a scratch team, and with only one destroyer Piers could not take full advantage of his HF/DF equipment. Piers, so junior that he was paid less than his ship's doctor, had been SOE on at least seven previous occasions and never lost a ship; his luck was about to change. German naval intelligence had intercepted SC 107's routing signal, and, although an RCAF aircraft sank two U-boats around the convoy on 30 October, the convoy ploughed smack into the middle of group Veilchen the next day, only 300 miles off the Newfoundland coast.

From noon on 1 November until the next day, no fewer than twenty-five U-boat signals were plotted in *Restigouche* and *Stockport*. Piers drove all of them off but three, but they proved to be more than the escort could handle that night when eight ships were lost. Apart from a surprise submerged attack on 2 November, the extremely poor weather gave SC 107 a welcome respite, while HMS *Vanessa*, a destroyer, joined from HX 213. When the weather improved the next day, SC 107 was found clinging steadfastly to its original course. The two destroyers pushed U-boats aside all day with HF/DF directed sweeps, but they could not account for them all. Further losses followed the next night before VLR Liberators arrived on 5 November, while SC 107 was south of Greenland. Piers directed the aircraft using HF/DF bearings, and S/L Terence Bulloch's Liberator sank U-132. By the time the battle ended on 6 November with the arrival of powerful rein-forcements and air support, SC 107 had lost fifteen ships; the worst losses to a transatlantic convoy since SC 42, fourteen months earlier. On 18 November, to ease the problem of convoy battles – like SC 107 – developing in the fog off Newfoundland, the British and Americans formed the Western Support Force, a group of short-legged destroyers withdrawn from Halifax and based at St John's to do what Admiral Murray's defunct training group had done over the summer.

As if to highlight the problem of the Canadian MOEF groups, the intrepid Norwegians of B.6 fought ONS 144 through the air gap in mid-November with minor losses. Operating without their destroyers *Fame* and *Viscount*, damaged in the battle for SC 104, the five corvettes of B.6 lost only five ships from their small convoy and the corvette *Montbretia* in a five-day running battle with nine U-boats, one of which was sunk. Lt Cdr Monsen, RNorN, kept a tight rein on his group, using their modern radar to establish a fighting screen at night and the HF/DF of the rescue ship *Perth* to push shadowers off during the day. WAC had nothing but praise for B.6's efforts, but the captain of the corvette *Rose* put his finger on the key source of success: '*Rose* came from a long refit a couple of months ago [September] and I like to add that I do not believe all these good attacks could have been made without all the improvements we got during that refit'. *Rose* was also given a full month to work up following her refit. Canadians could only look on in wonder. While the RCN had been driven to the brink of collapse, the RN used the opportunity to modernise ships and concentrate on training. In the autumn of 1942 that crucial differ-ence began to show in the mid-ocean.

ONS 144 was also spared an overwhelming attack because in the aftermath of the TORCH landings, most of the Atlantic U-boats were deployed to the Gibraltar area in a futile attempt to attack the follow-on convoys. Although nine U-boats were enough for the corvettes of B.6 to deal with, C.4 had to contend with seventeen in the battle for SC 107. In its next major battle B.6 enjoyed the same luck. The Canadians, as things turned out, were not intercepted again until the U-boats returned in numbers late in December.

The looming crisis in the mid-Atlantic had much to do with the appointment of Admiral Sir Max Horton, RN, to the post of CinC, WA on 19 November. A skilled submariner and a tough, uncompromising commander, Horton's task was to whip WAC into shape and get a handle on the U-boat problem. It helped that Noble had assembled a superb staff at Western Approaches Command and they, as much as Horton, shaped the victory that

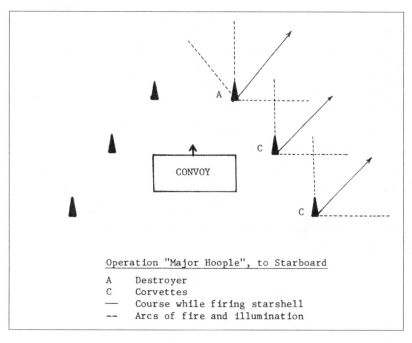

Operation 'Major Hoople', to starboard.

followed in early 1943. Training and effective leadership were the keys to Horton's scheme and it did not take long for his critical eye to fall sharply on the struggling Canadians. To the British, the leadership and standards of efficiency of Canadian groups in the mid-ocean had always been suspect, and the valiant but ultimately unsuccessful attempt by young Cdr Piers to defend SC 107 with a scratch group seemed to confirm that. Canadian SOEs, in the absence of modern radar and HF/DF, seemed unable to make good tactical decisions, while those they did make seemed to increase the risks to their convoys. A tactic developed by C.3 to compensate for the lack of modern radar, Operation Major Hoople, which was a form of pre-emptive illumination based on a best guess of when the U-boats might be closing for a night attack and first used around SC 109, illustrated the problem. So too did an operational research study completed on the problem by the end of November, which suggested that the disparity between well-led and well-trained groups and those which apparently were not had cost the British sixty ships in recent convoy battles.

By early December the solution was clear, and so too was the need. November had been a singularly disastrous month for shipping losses, with 128, making it the worst month since June and the third worst of the war. Most were independents lost in the Atlantic narrows between Brazil and Africa, or off South Africa. The thirty-five ships that had been lost in convoy were only a slight increase over previous months, but nearly half of these came from SC 107 alone. With increased demands resulting from TORCH, and dwindling oil reserves, the carnage had to be stopped somewhere, and in Horton's command he quickly fixed on the Canadians and Americans of MOEF.

40 *Above:* A gallery of notable RCN officers on the corvette *Chambly* in St John's harbour, 7 August 1942: RAdm. L.W. Murray, on the left, Adm Sir Humphry Walwyn, Governor of Newfoundland, Cdr James D. Chummy Prentice, the captain of *Chambly* who has just received his DSO for sinking U-501, and Mrs Prentice. Just behind Prentice, with the beard, is LCdr Guy Windeyer, RCNR, who sank U-588 a week earlier and was later Senior Officer of the ill-fated convoy ONS 154.

41 *Left:* U-210, seen from HMCS *Assiniboine*, during their furious action in a Grand Banks fog, 6 August 1942. The chase ended when the destroyer rammed the U-boat.

42 The B-24 Liberator, in the new white scheme of Coastal Command: the appearance of such aircraft from 120 Squadron, RAF, in the mid-Atlantic in the summer of 1942 came as unwelcome news to the Germans. With a cruising speed of more than 200 knots and a radius of action in excess of 700 miles, the Liberator was able to operate in the heart of the mid-Atlantic air gap.

43 HMS *Viscount*, one of the key components of B.6. She sank U-619 in the battle around SC 104 in October 1942 and U-69 in February 1943. Note the 271 radar and HF/DF.

44 *Above:* HMS *Snowflake*, typical of British corvettes on the main convoys routes in 1942: forecastle extended, bridge improved, heavier secondary armament and type 271 radar – in this case rather curiously offset on the starboard side.

45 *Left:* Adm Sir Max Horton, Commander in Chief, Western Approaches Command from November 1942. Horton is usually seen as the architect of the Allied victory of early 1943, but the credit for that really goes to the superb staff he inherited from Adm Sir Percy Noble.

46 *Below:* Waiting for the depth charges: the crew of a U-boat pays the price for an attack on a convoy.

47 U-175 succumbs to pounding from the US Coast Guard Cutter *Spencer*, 17 April 1943, during the battle around HX 233.

49 *Above:* A damaged picture of the USS *Bogue*, the first anti-submarine aircraft carrier to operate in the mid-ocean as part of a support group EG 6 in the spring of 1943. She is seen here in late June while operating in the central North Atlantic as part of the USN offensive.

48 *Left:* The winter of 1943 was the worst of the war, and it beat the St John's-based Western Support Force into complete submission. This is HMS *Mansfield* alongside on 30 January.

50 The British contribution to carrier air support in the mid-ocean in the spring of 1943, HMS *Archer*. Her Swordfish bi-planes were the first to sink a submarine, U-752, with rockets on 23 May 1943.

51 An effective U-boat killer in 1943: the acoustic homing torpedo 'Fido', in the background with the propeller, seen here in this damaged picture with depth charges in the bomb-bay of an Avenger, aboard USS *Mission Bay* in February 1944.

52 The American carrier offensive begins; USS *Santee* providing cover for UGS 10 en route to North Africa, June 1943.

53 A new kind of anti-submarine warfare: the Combat Information Centre on *Santee* plots the movements of her aircraft, the carrier's supporting destroyers and enemy, November 1943.

54 Ultra intelligence in action: bombs from Lt Sallenger's Avenger (off the USS *Card*) explode around the tanker U-117 at its rendezvous with U-66, 7 August 1943.

55 The Merchant Aircraft Carrier *Empire MacAlpine*, with two Swordfish on her deck, provides cover for a North Atlantic convoy in 1943.

56 Several RAF Coastal Command squadrons flew the B-17 Flying Fortress in the Biscay offensive of 1943. This one is seen waiting at Montreal to be ferried overseas: note the ASV Mk II radar under the wings.

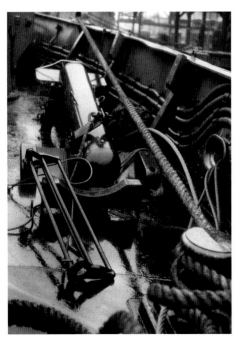

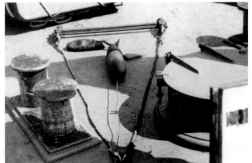

58 *Above:* The elegantly simple Canadian Anti-Acoustic Torpedo (CAT) gear: two pipes and a wire yoke, seen here with a depth gauge attached for trials and a leather mitten to indicate scale.

57 *Left:* Foxer, the complex British solution to the acoustic homing torpedo. The noisemaker (with its two rattling pipes in the centre) lies in the foreground. The torpedo-shaped paravane was used to pull it away from the ship. Another set of Foxer gear would be found on the other side of the ship.

59 Dark days for the U-boat fleet: U-249 slides quietly into Kiel harbour, 23 October 1943. A type VIIC, she is already obsolete. Note the false deck to hide her from Allied aerial reconnaissance, and the bomb damage to the building sheds.

60 The growing complexity of modern anti-submarine warfare is revealed in this shot of the asdic hut of an unidentified corvette. This is the type 144, which also provided automated fire control for the Hedgehog mortar.

61 Captain Johnny Walker, RN — sandwich in hand and ready to boil the ocean with depth charges — lines up an attack from the bridge of *Starling*.

62 A rare image of the Black Swan class sloop *Wild Goose*, a stalwart member of Walker's EG 2. She shared in nine of the group's twenty-three U-boat kills, and was second only to Walker's own *Starling*.

63 The River class frigate HMS *Spey*, of EG 10, supporting a North Atlantic convoy in early 1944. In mid-February she used her superb modern asdic equipment to kill U-406 with one depth charge pattern, and blow U-386 to the surface — where it was finished-off — with another.

64 U-625 succumbs to attacks by Sunderland 'U' of 422 Squadron, RCAF, 10 March 1944. As the crew took to the life rafts someone on U-625 signalled 'Fine bombish!' to the circling Sunderland. None of these men were ever found.

66 *Above:* The end of the second longest hunt of the war: U-744, shattered and sinking, wallows in a rising sea as a boarding party from HMCS *Chilliwack* tries to salvage her. Note the white ensign on the conning tower over the shell holes.

65 *Left:* Sonobuoys in the bomb-bay of an USN Avenger. In late March 1944 aircraft from USS *Croatan* used them to track U-856 off Sable Island until destroyers arrived to finish the job.

67 U-505, a type IX U-boat captured by USS *Guadalcanal*'s task group on 4 June 1944: the submarine is now on display in Chicago.

68 *Above left:*: Hunting U-boats in the English Channel, July 1944. Bridge personnel of HMCS *Ottawa* check their watches as a pattern of hedgehog bombs strikes the water.

69 *Above right:* Flying Officer John Cruickshank, RAF, whose attack on U-347 on 17 July 1944 earned him seventy-two wounds and a Victoria Cross.

70 U-347 as seen from Cruickshank's 210 Squadron Catalina. Note the heavy anti-aircraft armament. The narrow slot on the port side of the conning tower housed the new 'Hohentweil' air search radar.

71 HMS/M *Seraph*, with a very streamlined hull and increased battery storage, was the key to the development of tactics for dealing with the type XXI U-boat. Trials began in October 1944 and Allied hunters trained on her for the balance of the war.

72 *Left:* Rear Admiral Jonas Ingram, CinC US Atlantic Fleet, the architect of the last and largest Allied hunter killer operation of the war, Operation Teardrop in April 1945.

73 *Middle:* USS *Stanton*, DE247, typical of the destroyer escorts that made up the bulk of Ingram's striking forces. She worked with *Croatan*'s group in the first barrier of Teardrop.

74 *Bottom:* The USN did not have it all their own way during Operation Teardrop: the USS *Frederick C. Davis* was torpedoed and sunk by U-546 on 24 April 1945.

75 *Above:* Right to the bitter end, the U-boat remained a young man's business. Lt Werner Meuller, twenty-two, and Lt Ernst Glenk, twenty-one, were both three year veterans of the Atlantic war by the time U-190 surrendered to the RCN in May 1945.

76 *Left:* The end: surrendered U-boats lie alongside the Captain class frigate HMS *Conn*, on the left, and the Loch class frigate HMCS *Loch Alvie* in Loch Eriboll Scotland, May 1945.

77 The type IX U889 surrenders at Shelburne, NS, May 1945. Note the schnorkel arrangement.

78 The crisis that never was: type XXI U-boats – U-2502, U-3514 and U-2518 in the foreground – at Lisahally, North Ireland, 1945. U-2502 has its schnorkel mast raised. Note the streamlined hull form and the fully enclosed anti-aircraft guns in the turret.

In early December, B.6 once again proved what could be done if all the parts worked effectively. *Fame* was back for this battle, along with Heathcote as the SOE. The Polish destroyer *Burza* joined to give the group two, while the three remaining Norwegian corvettes were augmented by one of the RN. The destroyer *Montgomery* of Western Support Force helped the convoy, HX 217, across the Grand Banks, and diverted the first four U-boats to make contact by staging a pyrotechnic show astern of the convoy as she departed for St John's. By 7 December HX 217 was in the depths of the air gap with five U-boats in contact when S/L Bulloch arrived in his Liberator, 800 miles from his Icelandic base, and drove them all off. Most regained contact as dusk fell, but they were repeatedly detected by B.6's radar and by the innovative use of asdic as a hydrophone. Liberators arrived the next day and the pattern repeated itself, with HX 217 losing only one ship the next night. By 9 December HX 217 was well within range of Coastal Command, but poor weather allowed the U-boats to press home their pursuit. That night B.6 intercepted every attempt to penetrate the screen, and on 10 December the weather cleared and the sky was full of aircraft. B.6 brought HX 217 home with only two losses. 'Fame was the master,' the Admiralty assessment observed. Air power in the depths of the mid-ocean helped enormously, as did the fact that HX 217 transited the narrowest portion of the air gap in barely thirty-six hours. Indeed, Heathcote used his resources superbly, pushing aside U-boats, maintaining a tight screen and seeing his convoy safely through. It was perhaps the best defence of a convoy during the war.

HX 217 also demonstrated, once again, what a well-led and trained – not to say equipped – escort group could do. By 15 December the Admiralty petitioned Churchill to seek the removal of both the Canadians and the Americans from the mid-ocean. 'Recent heavy losses in transatlantic convoys have shown that the Canadian and American groups are not nearly so well trained...as British groups,' the Admiralty claimed. They proposed to remove the North Americans from MOEF and run it with eight

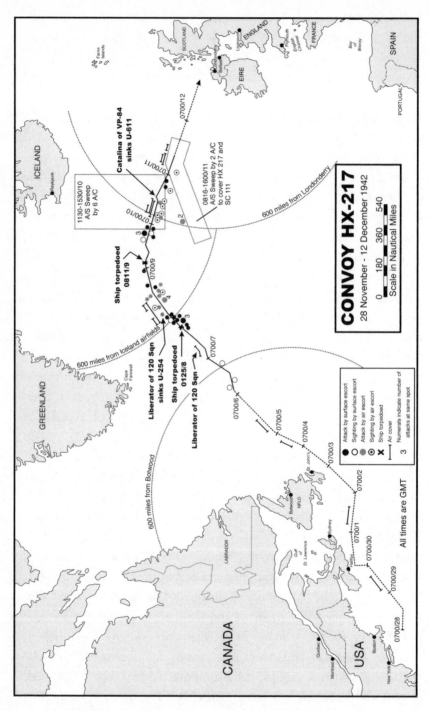

Convoy HX-217: convoy routes, air attacks and sea-battles, during the period 28 November–12 December 1942.

B groups. The case against A.3 was thin at best; it was consistently well trained and led. Its record was comparable to the C groups – but so was its equipment. So on 17 December Churchill petitioned only the Canadian government to remove its escorts from the mid-ocean, blaming the problem on the RCN's too rapid expansion and consequent lack of efficiency.

Canadians were incensed that the problems in the mid-ocean were now laid at their door. The Staff Officer A/S in Ottawa, an RN officer on loan and a recent arrival from St John's, reported that lack of modern equipment and a shortage of destroyers were responsible. While the RCN argued its case and waited for a WAC staff officer to arrive to explain the plan, ONS 154 escorted by C.1 was routed through the widest portion of the air gap through the tail end of a hurricane and into the embrace of twenty U-boats. British cryptanalysts had just solved the riddle of the fourth rotor in the U-boat coding machine, but not in time to save ONS 154. Unlike the good fortune enjoyed recently by B.6 – a northern routing through the narrowest portion of the air gap, a fast convoy, a small number of U-boats, and the hope of air support – C.1 drew the short straw on every count: a five-day passage well to the south, beyond any hope of air support (the battle took place closer to Portugal than any other landfall), and fighting without modern equipment against a pack which outnumbered C.1 almost four to one. The result was a catastrophe. C.1 sank a U-boat early in the battle, although that was not confirmed until after the war, but then the escort was overwhelmed. The captain of the corvette *Shediac* reported that, 'torpedoes were so numerous…that the officer of the watch remarked, "there goes ours now, sir"…as if next week's groceries were being delivered.' By 30 December, ONS 154 had lost thirteen ships. On that day the SOE watched as most of his escort, unable to refuel because the designated tanker had been torpedoed, departed for the Azores. Down to 'only four escorts to take the bowling', he expected that night would see ONS 154's 'final carving'. But the U-boats were exhausted, too, and had lost contact. When Heathcote arrived on 31 December to take over,

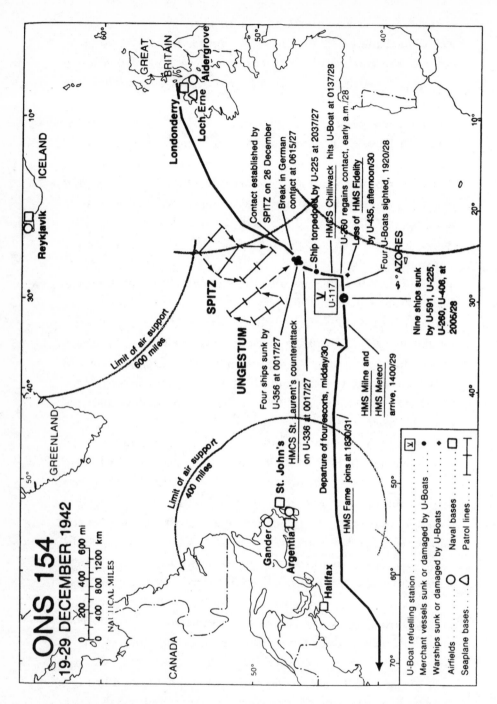

ON 154: principal convoy routes, limit of air support and air bases during the period of 26 July-3 August 1942.

the Canadian SOE, who had 'begun to see torpedoes at every turn' was put to bed by his doctor.

In early January 1943 the Canadians agreed to the temporary removal of their escorts from the mid-ocean to Britain for training and – the Canadians having won their case – re-equipping. As the Admiralty's *Monthly Anti-Submarine Report* for January observed, 'The Canadians have borne the brunt of the U-boat attack in the North Atlantic for the last six months, that is to say, of about half of the German U-boats operating at sea'. And so they had – eighty per cent of losses to transatlantic convoys from July to December 1942 were suffered by those escorted by the RCN. The British were quick to attribute those losses to uniquely Canadian problems, especially training and leadership. But the real problem, apart from lack of equipment, was trying to bring slow convoys across an ocean that was filling up with U-boats. The British would soon discover that problem themselves, when they tried to run transatlantic convoys alone. Unfortunately for the Germans, though, the British found the resources to resolve the mid-ocean problem, and to inflict a decisive defeat on the Wolf Packs.

6

Crushing the Wolf Packs

January-May 1943

'The great moments of naval history have to be worked for', Sir Julian Corbett wrote in reference to the Battle of Trafalgar. For Corbett, Nelson's triumph on 21 October 1805 was not a single act by a brilliant admiral. It was, rather, the culmination of a process of blockade and harassment, which forced the combined Franco-Spanish fleet into a battle they could not win. That same assessment applies to the Battle of the Atlantic in the first five months of 1943. For over three years Germany's fleet had pulled the lion's tail all over the Atlantic. Propagandists, and historians – 'greedy of dramatic effect', to quote Corbett again – focused naturally on the *Kriegsmarine*'s remarkable accomplishments. But while Germany built a huge fleet of U-boats which relied on unimpeded surface manoeuvrability to accomplish their goals, the Allies built a sound defensive system that progressively denied them that mobility. By 1 January 1943, Dönitz had the fleet he had longed for in 1939,

300 operational U-boats. By then, however, there was only one place left where the U-boat fleet could be used with impunity, the mid-Atlantic air gap. Like Admiral Villeneuve off Cape Trafalgar on that fateful day in 1805, in early 1943 Dönitz knew his U-boats now had to fight a battle that they, like Villeneuve's fleet, could not win. After over three years of war the U-boat fleet was 'fixed' for the decisive confrontation.

In late 1942 things had finally begun to go awry for the Axis. The Allied campaign in North Africa was enormously successful, with the Germans and Italians soon being driven back into a small pocket in Tunisia. The Japanese advance in the South Pacific was checked at Guadalcanal, and the German 6th Army lay besieged in Stalingrad, trapped by the embrace of Soviet armies and winter itself. The failure of the German surface fleet, now based in Norway, to sortie effectively against the renewed Russian convoys in late 1942 also provoked a serious crisis in the *Kriegsmarine*. On 6 January Hitler inflicted on Admiral Raeder, the head of the *Kriegsmarine*, a ninety-minute tirade outlining all the apparent failures of his service, followed by an announcement of Hitler's intent to scrap the entire surface fleet and rely exclusively on U-boats. Raeder offered his resignation, effective from 30 January.

For the Germans things did not go well in the Atlantic either in January 1943. The restoration of Ultra intelligence to British routing authorities allowed most transatlantic convoys to pass without serious attack, while operations against those intercepted were largely undone by atrocious winter weather. The 'elements seemed to rage in uncontrolled fury,' Dönitz wrote later of that winter, the worst of the war. During January, Dönitz had nearly 100 U-boats at sea, most in the mid-ocean air gap, but they accounted for just forty-four ships. Only ten of these were plucked from the ranks of convoys, and seven came from one battle. That battle developed around a special nine-tanker convoy, TM1, routed directly from Trinidad to Gibraltar to provide fuel for Allied operations in North Africa. German naval intelligence, generally superb during this period, failed to detect TM1, but the convoy stumbled onto U-514 west of the Azores on 3 January. British authorities immediately ordered a redirection that would have brought TM1 safely around the U-boats of group Delphin, which was operating in the area. The SOE of B.5 declined. He wanted the fairer weather of the mid-ocean so his escorts could refuel. As a result TM1 collided with the eight boats of Delphin on 7 January and the small escort of one destroyer and three corvettes could not prevent a catastrophe. Only two of TM1's nine tankers made it to Gibraltar, a loss-rate unparalleled in the Atlantic of 55,000 tons of shipping and 100,000 tons of fuel. General Von Arnim, holding on in Tunisia, sent Dönitz a personal telegram of thanks. The British tightened fuel rationing by another ten per cent.

TM1 was an explicable – and avoidable – calamity for the Allies. On the day the survivors arrived in Gibraltar, Roosevelt, Churchill and their senior staffs met in Casablanca to settle their plans. The ultimate objective was a major landing in France followed by a march on Berlin. But they soon discovered that nothing could be done – or even planned – until the Atlantic war was resolved. Even the build-up of American forces in Britain, code-named Operation Bolero, for the invasion of France was seriously in arrears. Only more convoys, larger ones, and fewer losses in the mid-Atlantic would allow the build-up to proceed so that a landing could be made in the spring of 1944. Thus, at Casablanca in January 1943 the western Allies identified the Atlantic war as their number one priority. Resources were to be committed until the problem was solved.

The way forward was obvious: eliminate the air gap, commit more naval escorts and increase the size and number of convoys. The famous British operational research scientist P.M.S. Blackett produced several reports in early 1943, one of which argued that some sixty-four per cent of all previous losses would have been avoided had mid-ocean convoys been given air support. Nearly a quarter could have been saved by simply increasing the size of escort groups from six to nine ships. And in another report Blackett demonstrated convincingly that big convoys – up to eighty or pehaps 100 ships, rather than the thirty to forty which was the current practice — suffered substantially fewer casualties. The average U-boat, Blackett argued, sank one ship per attack and so six U-boats attacking a thirty-ship convoy might be expected to sink six ships. But they would do no better if the convoy had ninety ships. Moreover, doubling or tripling the size of the convoy did not double or triple the area which the escort had to screen, so proportionately fewer escorts were required to screen significantly larger convoys. Fewer, but much larger, convoys was one way the average size of escort groups could be increased without finding more escorts.

While senior Allied staffs debated how best to proceed on the decisions taken at Casablanca and the fruits of Blackett's research, the Germans reminded them of the urgency of of doing so. At the end of January Dönitz became Chief of the *Kriegsmarine*. He managed to convince Hitler that scrapping the surface fleet would constitute a tremendous British 'victory', and that the continued success of the U-boats depended upon the surface fleet tying down British naval and air resources. He also retained personal control of the U-boat war. The Allies saw this development as something ominous. Dönitz now had a free hand to fight his war his way, and there could be little doubt over what method he preferred. What followed in February and March was the high point of the Wolf Pack campaign in the mid-ocean. Huge packs ably directed and receiving excellent intelligence finally connected with a series of convoys to achieve the highest interception and attack rates of the war, in what could be dubbed 'phase one of the final crisis of the Atlantic war'.

That final crisis began in earnest on 29 January, when U-boats of group Haudegen operating on the Grand Banks intercepted HX 224, escorted by C.4. Five U-boats were drawn onto the convoy in a heavy westerly gale. They sank only three ships before air power from Iceland ended the battle on 3 February, sinking U-265 in the process. However, intelligence gathered from a merchant seaman rescued by U-632 revealed a slow convoy coming up astern of HX 224, and so Dönitz turned his attention to this much more vulnerable prey. The convoy, SC 118, actually ran into group

Pfeil on 4 January anyway, and soon twenty U-boats were assigned to attack it. What followed was a major four-day convoy battle in which both sides suffered heavy losses.

SC 118, sixty-one slow moving ships, was escorted by B.2, one of WAC's best. But the regular SOE, Captain Donald Macintyre, RN, was absent while his ship was in refit. The interim SOE, Cdr F.B. Proudfoot, RN, was new to the job and to his ship, the destroyer *Vanessa*. Macintyre's destroyer had been temporarily replaced in B.2 by *Vimy* just prior to the previous crossing, and the old four-stacker *Beverly* had just been reassigned from B.4. Neither *Vimy* nor *Beverly* were fitted with HF/DF, but the rescue ship *Toward* and the US Coast Guard Cutter *Bibb*, hastily assigned to B.2 to increase its strength, were. Only B.2's two British corvettes were long-standing members of the group. Two Free French corvettes had joined just prior to SC 118, while two USN destroyers and the USCG cutter *Ingram* arrived on day two of the battle to round out the naval escort. By any description B.2 was a scratch team under inexperienced leadership.

The first phase of the battle for SC 118 went well enough for the Allies. On 4 February *Vimy* and *Beverly* ran down an HF/DF bearing provided by *Toward* and *Bibb* and sank U-187, and that night five shadowers were driven off. The next day U-boats sank one ship from the convoy and one straggler. The arrival of the US reinforcements that day helped to drive off the pack again, as did the arrival of Liberator 'X' of 120 Squadron in the depth of the air gap. Attempts that night and during the day of 6 February to press home attacks were largely foiled by the escort, and two U-boats were seriously damaged. After midnight that night U-402 finally penetrated the screen and sank six ships, including *Toward*. Later that night one straggler was sunk while the Free French corvette *Lobelia* rammed and sank U-609. On 7 February the naval escort and Flying Fortresses of 220 Squadron RAF pushed the pack back, and Fortress 'J' sank U-624. One more ship was sunk during the night of 7–8 February, before air power ended the battle, and badly damaged two more U-boats. By the time the battle was over,

SC 118 had lost eleven ships, eight of them from the ranks of the convoy itself (the rest were stragglers). In exchange, three U-boats were sunk and four damaged in what both sides considered one of the hardest fought battles of the Atlantic war.

Each side drew clear lessons from the battle. For Dönitz, they were ominous. Not only was the exchange rate unfavourable, but of the twenty U-boats sent to attack only a handful pressed home their attacks. Most of the kills were the work of one man, Von Forstner in U-402, who sank seven ships. In Western Approaches Command the meaning of the fate of SC 118 was also clear, that large and untrained escort groups, cobbled together at the last moment under temporary leadership, could not protect slow convoys in the mid-ocean when they were attacked by overwhelming numbers. This, of course, was precisely the 'problem' identified as uniquely Canadian in late 1942, and why the C groups were now being removed from the mid-Atlantic for refit and retraining. Admiral Horton's reaction in the aftermath of SC 118 was to finally do something about the problem. 'Although this is very terrible,' Horton confided to a colleague, 'it is all lending weight to my arguments and I believe I shall get Cabinet approval for forming Support Groups.'

The British cabinet was already mulling over the recommendations of the Casablanca conference and Professor Blackett's reports, but before they could act another convoy got into serious trouble. The situation developed in part because the Germans were now reading the Admiralty's daily U-boat position estimates, allowing them to anticipate routing and Allied countermoves in the increasingly congested mid-ocean. The first to suffer from this intelligence coup was ONS 166, a forty-nine-ship slow westbound convoy escorted by A.3. The core of A.3 had been together since the previous August – the US cutters *Spencer* and *Campbell*, and the Canadian corvettes *Rosthern* and *Trillium* – under steady and skilled leadership. The corvettes *Dauphin* (RCN) and *Dianthus* (RN) had been with A.3 for over two months. Only the corvette *Chilliwack* (RCN), returning to Canada for a refit, and the Polish destroyer

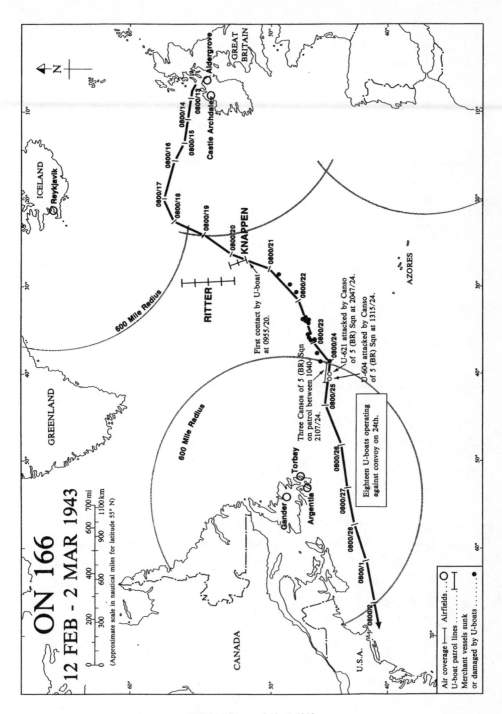

ON 166 12 February–2 March 1943.

Burza, which joined during the battle, were new to the group. All the escorts carried modern 10cm radar, and *Spencer* and the rescue ship *Stockport* had HF/DF. The SOE, Cdr Paul Heineman, USCG, and his stand-in, Cdr Lewis, trained A.3 hard prior to each departure. The only thing A.3 lacked was the tactical speed provided by destroyers, a problem Heineman complained about repeatedly. Unfortunately, ONS 166 also needed considerable luck to be able to push through eighteen expertly directed U-boats.

The battle for ONS 166 followed a now familiar pattern, but there was little familiar with the larger context in which it happened. Duelling intelligence agencies now shifted packs and convoys, in a grim game of cat and mouse. Most of the February convoys made it through safely, routed gingerly around waiting U-boat patrol lines, and increasingly supported by effective air patrols in the depth of the air gap. In particular, the last convoys escorted in the mid-ocean by Canadian groups prior to their transfer to the eastern Atlantic in February were almost invariably fast convoys and were carefully routed wide of danger.

But not all convoys slipped through and on 20 February U-604 intercepted ONS 166 as the convoy moved into the gap. As often happened, the first phase of the battle went well for the escort. U-604 was located by HF/DF and driven off, and on 21 February a Liberator from 120 Squadron sank U-623 while the combined naval and air escort drove off most U-boats. That night the first attacks penetrated the screen, sinking ships. As ONS 166 reached the depths of the air gap, the battle intensified. *Spencer* and *Campbell* both sank U-boats, but the poor weather, waves of attackers, the loss of the rescue ship, and the large number of damaged vessels littering the wake of the convoy made it impossible for A.3 to adequately defend ONS 166.

Aircraft from Newfoundland finally arrived on 24 February, with RCAF Canso amphibians (the Canadian version of the Catalina) of 5 Squadron flying beyond their normal range to reach 600 miles into the Atlantic. This was made possible by the efforts of S/L N.E. Small, RCAF, of 162 Squadron, who arrived in

Newfoundland with a detachment of Cansos in late December. Small had 5 Squadron strip their Cansos of all non-essential equipent, like guns, stores, and ammunition. By doing so, they extended their operational range to about 700 miles, making them 'virtual'VLR aircraft. It was a remarkable feat of initiative, which shaved hundreds of miles off the western side of the air gap. According to the RCAF official history, it was the intervention of two Cansos from 5 Squadron RCAF that 'blunted the U-boat onslaught' on ONS 166 on the 24 February, damaging both U-604 and U-621. But the U-boats hung on for two more days as the battle spilled onto the Grand Banks, where two of Western Support Force's weather-beaten destroyers reinforced A.3. When all was said and done, fourteen ships were lost, against three known U-boat kills.

WAC staff found little basis for criticism, and ONS 166 provided Horton with even more ammunition for his plans to reorganise the mid-ocean battle. In early March he established support groups by drawing one large escort from each WAC group, while the Admiralty reassigned a half flotilla of destroyers from the Home Fleet. That much was good news. But the nine B groups left in MOEF following the departure of the Canadians in February were soon unable to sustain the pressure of the winter weather and the brutal convoy cycle. By late in the month, B groups, which should have had a five-day layover in Newfoundland, were heading back into the Atlantic after forty-eight hours. Realising that the problems of late 1942 were not uniquely Canadian, the Admiralty now wanted the C groups returned to the mid-ocean starting in mid-March.

In fact, by late February the first fruits of the decisions taken at Casablanca were beginning to appear, particularly in the form of increased air support and important changes in command and control. The RAF's 120 Squadron Liberators were able to intervene successfully in the eastern portion of the air gap, but the lack of VLR Liberators in Newfoundland was now evident. The Canadians had been pressing hard for Liberators since autumn 1942, against British doubts that the RCAF could employ them effectively. A review of the situation in Newfoundland by S/L Bulloch, 120 Squadron's young commander, revealed that the Canadians had the skill and experience to operate VLR aircraft. By early March the Canadian request was under 'urgent consideration' by the British. In the meantime, the strength of 120 Squadron was doubled.

The increase in British VLR aircraft in the mid-ocean was facilitated in part by the USAAF, which joined the anti-submarine war in October 1942 and vastly expanded its role. In late January two Liberator squadrons of the newly formed 25th Anti-Submarine Wing, USAAF, arrived in the UK to participate in the renewed Biscay offensive. These medium-range B-24s not only released Coastal Command VLR Liberators for the mid-ocean, but they came equipped with American 10cm radar sets. Coastal Command had been trying to secure the release of the British 10cm radar for its ASW operations since autumn 1942, only to be blocked by the RAF bomber commanders who did not want its secret revealed until they could use it over Germany. The crash of a pathfinder aircraft equipped with Bomber Command's H2S 10cm radar into Rotterdam on 2 February broke the impasse, and by March the first 10cm equipped Leigh Light Wellingtons appeared over the Biscay and a second squadron was forming. In the meantime, in February Coastal Command, relying heavily on the SC 517 sets of the USAAF Liberators – one of which sank U-519 – renewed the Biscay offensive. The air campaign intensified over the next three months as more and more aircraft joined the patrols in the North Atlantic and the sweeps in the Biscay, and new weapons were introduced.

Important changes in command and control were also in the air by February. The British had been trying to regain control of the mid-ocean since early December 1941. Meanwhile, the Canadians, growing in strength and importance in the north-west Atlantic, chaffed under American operational control. By late 1942 the Canadians made it plain that they wanted CTF-24 out and they began to consolidate their own commands, while restricting the ability of the Americans to control their forces. By early 1943 Admiral Murray, now in Halifax, assumed control of the RCN in both eastern Canada and Newfoundland, the RCAF had assumed control of air operations – including those of the USN and USAAF in Newfoundland – and naval headquarters in Ottawa had restricted CTF-24's ability to move Canadian escorts around. The need to resolve the outstanding command and control issues in the mid-ocean and the north-west Atlantic, and increasing Canadian obstructionism, forced Admiral King, the USN Commander-in-Chief, to convene a major conference in the first week of March.

The Washington Convoy Conference settled the structure of the Atlantic campaign for the balance of the war. The Americans agreed to withdraw from involvement in North Atlantic trade convoys, while retaining overall strategic control over their zone. CTF-24 was to be reduced to the local USN commander and A.3 was to be disbanded. WAC obtained operational control over convoys and escort operations westward to forty-seven degrees west, roughly the Grand Banks, which allowed the British to run the mid-ocean war on their own. In between WAC and the USN's own Eastern Sea Frontier a new 'Canadian north-west Atlantic' command was created, placing convoy and naval and air escort operations under Admiral Murray in Halifax. The new command arrangements were to come into effect on 30 April.

An increased convoy cycle was also agreed to at Washington, one that would double the volume of shipping moving across the Atlantic by the end of March. To escort the increased traffic it was agreed that the C groups would be repatriated as soon as possible from their exile in the eastern Atlantic. They were, by now, fully re-equipped, had integrated new destroyers and frigates, brought in new SOEs and continued to kill U-boats along the UK-Gibraltar route. Support Groups, which Horton was already forming, would be added to the mix, and the British agreed to help the RCN with the formation of its own Support Group for the mid-ocean.

While senior officers from the three major Allied naval powers sorted out their problems, the war at sea moved towards its climax. It was precipitated by a sharp decline in the ability of British code breakers to penetrate the U-boat's weather code, which in turn had provided a key to the daily settings of their operational signal traffic. During January and February the British had been able to break most German traffic within twenty-four hours, fast enough to be used operationally. That quickness began to falter in late February, and delays contributed directly to the interception of ONS 166. By early March, and especially during the period from 10-19 March, long delays were experienced breaking the daily settings of German coding machines. With now nearly seventy U-boats in the North Atlantic, ably directed by their own signals intelligence, the Germans achieved their highest interception and attack rates of the war. In fact, in early March all North Atlantic convoys were intercepted, over half were attacked and twenty-two per cent of all shipping that set out to cross the Atlantic in the first three weeks of March failed to arrive.

During the week of the Washington Conference MOEF group A.3 endured another horrific passage, this time with SC 121. It was beset by twenty-seven U-boats, which sank thirteen ships without sustaining any loss to themselves. It was the best battle of the year so far for Dönitz. For 'Heineman's Harriers' of A.3 the losses brought to twenty-seven the number of ships lost in two successive battles. It was a dubious distinction, and Heineman complained that the expected support from an auxiliary aircraft carrier had failed to materialise. In fact, the escort carrier (CVE) USS *Bogue,* still brand new, provided cover for HX 228, which was following close astern of SC 121 through the air gap, to the southern tip of Greenland. Moderating weather also allowed B.3 to use its radar to good effect in defence of HX 228 and only four ships and the destroyer *Harvester* were lost. During the battle the little French corvette *Aconit* achieved the remarkable feat of sinking two U-boats, U-444, the U-boat which had just been rammed by *Harvester*, and U-432, the U-boat which had torpedoed the crippled destroyer.

But the German high point was unquestionably the combined battle for HX 229 and SC 122 between 16 and 20 March. While British code breakers struggled to read German signal traffic, on

13 March *B-Dienst* intercepted and read HX 229's signalled position and course, doing the same with SC 122's report the next day. Forty U-boats were assigned to attack the two convoys in what British intelligence described – once they had broken the codes days later – as 'the largest pack of U-boats that has ever been collected into one area for the same operation'. Despite intense air support around the convoys throughout the daylight hours on 17 March in the depth of the air gap, the naval escort could not cope with the swarms of attackers. British authorities gradually brought the two convoys together to economise on escort strength and air support, but not until the arrival of overwhelming air coverage on 20 March were the U-boats driven off. By then they had sunk twenty-one ships for the loss of only one U-boat. By the end of the battle for HX 229 and SC 122, some senior British officers felt that the convoy routes were becoming untenable. During March 1943 U-boats sank a record seventy-one ships from convoys (including stragglers). Only 'a storm of such violence as to warrant classification as a hurricane,' in the words of Stephen Roskill, British official historian, saved the next series of convoys. By the time the storms cleared in late March so too did the way ahead for the Allies.

Since 1939, Allied fortunes in the North Atlantic war had always improved with the onset of better weather and longer days. Both of these brought a dramatic improvement in the efficacy of Allied sensors and weapons, and concurrent reduction in the darkness and rough seas needed by U-boats to operate around convoys. But spring 1943 also brought with it Allied Support Groups – five in the last week of March – two auxiliary aircraft carriers and swarms of new, well-equipped aircraft. Over the Biscay transit routes Coastal Command, now operating thirty-two Leigh Light and 10cm radar-equipped Wellingtons in two squadrons, launched Operation 'Enclose' from 20-28 March. During that period forty-one U-boats crossed the bay, twenty-six were intercepted and fifteen attacked. The fact that only one U-boat was sunk was attributed to teething problems with the newly deployed Leigh

Light Squadron, 407 (RCAF). Operation Enclose II produced similar results from 6-13 April, with 172 Squadron again accounting for the lone kill. By the time Operation 'Derange' was mounted late in April, No. 19 Group of Coastal Command could deploy no less than seventy-two 10cm radar-equipped Wellingtons, Liberators and Halifaxes over the Bay. On 27 March Dönitz once again ordered U-boats to transit submerged during the night and surface only briefly during the day to recharge batteries. He had suspected since March that the increase in night-time attacks was the result of new radar, but German scientists were taking an inordinately long period to produce a naval 10cm warning device.

Air power was pouring into the mid-ocean in late March as well. The strength of 120 Squadron doubled over the month, and a second VLR squadron, No. 86, joined them, bringing the total of VLR Liberators available by late March to thirty-eight. These were augmented at the same time by a dramatic increase in the number of USAAF Fortresses and medium-range Liberators based in Newfoundland. And on 23 March the RCAF was assigned sufficient VLRs from the British allocation to begin forming their own squadron, No. 10, which began to fly operational missions on 10 May.

Equally importantly, as the weather improved in late March, so too did British intelligence and – even more importantly – the way in which it was used. For at the end of March the British saw an opportunity to convert their increasing numbers of very well-equipped naval and air escorts, their problems with reading U-boat signals and the improving weather into a major offensive against the Wolf Packs. Since February, the British had observed a sharp increase in the number of U-boats destroyed, up to nineteen over the six sunk in January. At the same time British intelligence revealed increased timidity, fear of counter attack – especially from the air – and an increase in 'defects' reported by the new captains of the rapidly expanding U-boat fleet. Dönitz had noticed much the same thing. Although the number of U-boat kills went down in March to sixteen, battles around convoys were intense and prowling aircraft were ever more present. When forty U-boats were sent to attack HX 230 in late March, British intelligence thought they noticed a very sharp decline in German morale. The convoy was well protected by a CVE and a Support Group, and none of the U-boats pressed home its attack. Nor did they press home against SC 123 a few days later. When HX 231 was intercepted on 4 April Dönitz sent out an admonishment to deal the Allies a 'heavy blow', and then reprimanded the group when only six ships were sunk from the convoy. The appeals continued through April, calling on one occasion for the U-boat captains to display 'healthy warrior and hunter instincts'. By mid-April the British had detected an 'incipient decline in U-boat morale.'

Under these conditions, the ability to avoid U-boats – which had been the whole premise of convoy routing since 1939 – was less important than the opportunity to crush the U-boat fleet. Vastly increased and well-equipped naval and air forces, operating in much better weather, now provided the means to deal a crippling blow to Dönitz's submariners: this was 'the great moment' which the British had worked towards for nearly four years. Indeed, the ink was hardly dry on the minutes of the Washington Conference, which had agreed that defence of convoys was the primary objective of North Atlantic operations in 1943, when the British quietly shifted to the offensive. By late April they had reneged on their promised commitment of escort groups to the mid-ocean in order to divert them to an offensive campaign in the Bay of Biscay, and they were planning to bring the battle in the mid-ocean to a climax by abandoning evasive routing entirely. Now they wanted to drive heavily reinforced convoys into the heart of waiting packs, and were prepared to lose two merchant vessels for every U-boat killed.

During April the Allies played the mid-ocean war very carefully, not least because the British could not launch their offensive in the mid-ocean until they gained full operational control of it at the end of the month. Most convoys, especially those of the recently returned C groups, were routed well clear of danger. Those that were threatened were heavily reinforced the day before they entered a danger area, and provided with intense air support. It was not until late April that the U-boats, brow-beaten and prodded by appeals from BdU, managed to gather in strength again around a series of convoys when British code breakers suffered another brief lapse.

The climactic battle of the Atlantic war, and the one which finally broke the spell of the Wolf Packs, centred on ONS 5, a slow westbound convoy (which adopted their own series designation at the end of March following ON 171). The escort was provided by B.7 under the skilled leadership of Cdr Peter Gretton, RN, one of the best of the Atlantic war, in the destroyer *Duncan*. Gretton had under command the destroyer *Vidette*, the new frigate *Tay*, his stalwart corvettes *Sunflower*, *Loosestrife*, *Pink* and *Snowflake*, and the trawlers *Northern Gem* and *Northern Spray*. Their routing carried ONS 5 well into northern latitudes, skirting south of Iceland and down towards the southern tip of Greenland through atrocious weather. *B-Dienst* tracked them all the same, and Dönitz deployed sixteen U-boats to intercept. USN Catalinas flying from Iceland forced the first U-boat in contact, U-650, down several times on 28 April, but Leutenant von Witzendorff's signals brought up two others on the first day. All were attacked and one damaged by the ships of B.7 during the first night's action. The next day a surprise underwater attack by U-258 sank one ship, while a USN Catalina from VP 84 damaged U-528. WAC immediately reinforced ONS 5 with five destroyers, four from the 3rd Support Group, as the convoy steamed into extremely heavy weather and its pursuers lost contact. Round one had gone to Gretton and his escorts.

While Dönitz tried desperately to relocate ONS 5, most of his U-boats were redeployed into a pack of some twenty-eight submarines and were drawn off in a largely futile search for SC 128. ONS 5 skirted west of that concentration and by 4 May began to receive excellent air support from the Cansos of 5 Squadron RCAF, operating again more than 600 miles from their Newfoundland bases against Wolf Packs Fink and Amsel, which now lay in ONS 5's path. One of these aircraft sank U-630 thirty miles astern of the convoy, and three others were attacked. But owing to bad weather the larger ships of B.7 and the reinforcing destroyers were unable to refuel, and most departed on 3 May, leaving Lt Cdr R.E. Sherwood, RNR, of *Tay*, as SOE, with three corvettes and three other destroyers. Meanwhile, *Pink* and *Northern Spray* were well astern, collecting groups of stragglers driven from the convoy by the storm. So with the escort reduced and the convoy somewhat scattered, ONS 5 stumbled into group Fink late on 4 May. During that night U-boats sank six ships from the dispersed portions of the convoy, but much worse was in store. On 5 May the convoy once again encountered poor weather that restricted air support from Newfoundland. One 5 Squadron Canso crashed on take-off, killing the whole crew, while another failed to find the convoy in the patchy fog. Only a Liberator from Iceland – over a thousand miles from its base – found ONS 5 on 5 May, but could do little to help through the poor visibility. Daylight attacks by submerged U-boats sank a further four ships. By the end of that day some fifteen U-boats had established contact: it appeared that ONS 5 was facing disaster.

But two hours before dusk, as ONS 5 steamed on a glassy sea, a heavy fog descended upon the convoy. That night the U-boats made some twenty-six attempts to get at ONS 5; every attempt failed. As the U-boats groped through the fog, B.7's 10cm radar picked them up easily. *Sunflower* located four in quick succession and damaged one with gunfire. *Loosestrife* located two trying to attack the convoy and sank U-192 with depth charges. *Vidette* drove off three attackers, while *Snowflake* found three almost simultaneously on her radar and eventually blew one, U-531, to the surface with depth charges. The U-boat then escaped, only to be sunk later by *Vidette* using her hedgehog. Meanwhile *Oribi*, a fleet class destroyer of the 3rd Support Group, made a hash of ramming U-125 and the sub had to be finished off by *Snowflake's* gun. About the same time *Sunflower* rammed U-533, which escaped but was seriously damaged. In the frantic action around the convoy the destroyer *Offa*, another fleet class, just failed to ram a U-boat, while *Loosestrife* drove off three others.

Towards morning the 1st SG arrived to join in the fray, the sloops *Pelican* and *Sennen*, and the frigates *Jed*, *Wear* and *Spey*. They wasted no time getting into action, when *Pelican* and *Jed* located U-438 on radar and promptly sank it. In the murk Pelican had two brushes with icebergs, which she detected by radar and – based on the sound the bergs made as they rode through the sea – classified both as U-boats, an enduring peril of convoy battles on the Grand Banks. Meanwhile, *Sennen* nearly sank U-575 with gunfire, and drove off another. Dönitz called a halt to the battle the next morning. ONS 5 had lost twelve ships, but the naval and air escorts had sunk seven U-boats, while U-439 and U-659 were lost when they collided in the fog. In particular, the loss of so many U-boats in a single night's action was unprecedented, the greatest success ever achieved by the type 271 radar. In one action the mystique of the Wolf Pack had been broken.

In fact, the carnage around ONS 5 was simply the beginning. Starting in May convoys routed into northern waters followed a standard Great Circle route, which reduced transit times for westbound convoys by three days (a southern Great Circle 'tram line' was established in June). The British used the new rigid routing to punish U-boats bold enough to attack. Most of the serious fighting was done by British escorted convoys, well reinforced by naval and air forces, even though RN groups only made up sixty per cent of MOEF. According to the Washington Conference agreements, with the disbandment of A.3 (whose last transatlantic convoy was HX 233 in late April), British forces were supposed to make up the vast majority of MOEF, ten out of fourteen groups. But many of the British ships were syphoned off for other duties in April, among them the long anticipated reopening of the Mediterranean to shipping, which in a stroke dramatically eased the burden on British carrying capacity by eliminating the need to go all the way around Africa.

As a result, by May MOEF numbered only twelve groups, five of which were now Canadian. The Admiralty offered the loan of two newly commissioned River Class frigates to help get the 'Canadian

Support Group' into the mid-ocean, and all the RCN ships on loan to both the British and the USN were returned. But the increased convoy cycle inaugurated in March absorbed whatever slack the RCN hoped for into the expanded demand on what was now the Western Escort Force, based in Halifax. So the battles of May were almost exclusively British. With the U-boats on the run and the Americans out of the Atlantic war, the British now gripped the enemy with Nelsonic fervour and were intent on winning a decisive victory.

And so they did. U-boats rash enough to close with a North Atlantic trade convoy in May 1943 were simply inviting destruction. Air escorts were devastatingly effective, and with some fifty VLR aircraft now based on both sides of the Atlantic the air gaps were effectively eliminated. In May, Allied aircraft sank nine U-boats along the main convoy routes. British VLR Liberators and many US aircraft now carried the new 'Mark 24 Mine', actually an air-launched acoustic homing torpedo designed to be dropped into the wake of a diving U-boat. The power of both land-based and sea-based aircraft was ably demonstrated in mid-May during a series of battles around HX 237/SC 129. F/L J. Wright of 86 Squadron, RAF, hit U-456 with an acoustic torpedo on 12 May while flying in support of SC 129. The submarine surfaced in a damaged state and was sunk the next day by a warship. That same day a Swordfish biplane ASW aircraft operating off the CVE HMS *Biter* called up a destroyer and frigate to sink U-89. Air patrols on 14 May by both 86 Squadron Liberators and Catalinas of the USN's VP 84 sank U-boats using acoustic homing torpedoes, while Liberators sank another around SC 130 with a torpedo on 18 May. Attempts to attack ON 184 were disrupted by Avengers flying from USS *Bogue*, which achieved the first kill by CVE-based aircraft on 22 May when they sank U-569. Not to be outdone, the next day a Swordfish from HMS *Archer* found U-752 on the surface and punched a hole in her pressure hull with a well-placed armoured piercing rocket projectile, another first. During the two weeks from 10-24 May, ten convoys passed through the waiting packs in the mid-ocean. Only six of the 370 ships in those convoys were sunk, and three of those were stragglers. In contrast, the attackers lost thirteen U-boats: seven to aircraft, two shared between naval and air escort, and four to warships.

Meanwhile, the air assault on the transit routes in the Biscay increased in intensity and air patrols independent of convoy movements proved remarkably successful at sinking U-boats as well. As before, Dönitz ordered U-boats crossing the Bay to travel on the surface only in daylight hours to avoid radar-equipped aircraft at night, and once again that sharply increased the number of daylight interceptions and attacks by Coastal Command. In the first week of May no fewer than four U-boats were sunk by daylight patrols over the Bay, in part because Dönitz ordered them to fight back. Unfortunately, the quadruple anti-aircraft guns and armoured plating for the conning towers ordered in 1942 had not yet arrived, and the U-boat captains who chose to fight often paid dearly for their boldness. The Germans became more coy in the last three weeks of the month, choosing to dive rather than fight it out with the attacking aircraft. But still the Bay patrols sank three more U-boats before the end of May.

By any measure, May 1943 was a catastrophic month for the U-boat fleet. No fewer than forty-one submarines were sunk, the single highest loss rate of any month in the war. One of them carried Dönitz's only son to a watery grave. They were swarmed by aircraft and hounded by well-equipped warships at every turn, especially when the British drove convoy after convoy through their waiting packs in order to bring them to battle. The Germans suspected a new form of radar, probably the 10cm 'Rotterdam' set found on the downed aircraft in February. However, their preliminary attempts to augment the effectiveness of the *Metox* warning system had failed and for the moment there was no solution in sight.

On 24 May, Dönitz admitted tactical defeat and recalled the Wolf Packs from the mid-Atlantic. 'The situation in the North Atlantic now forces a temporary shifting of operations to areas less endangered by aircraft,' Dönitz wrote in his war diary. 'This is necessary in order not to allow the U-boats to be beaten at a time when their weapons are inferior...'. Max Horton and later historians were under no illusions about the significance of the victory of May 1943. Late in that month he signalled his forces: 'The last two months of the Battle of the Atlantic has undergone a decisive change in our favour.... The climax of the battle has been surmounted.' He was right, and historians of the Second World War usually abandon the story of the Atlantic at this stage. However, the struggle between the U-boat and anti-submarine forces was just beginning to enter its most interesting phase.

7
Driving the U-boat Down
June-December 1943

On the afternoon of 8 July 1943, Liberator 'R' of 224 Squadron RAF Coastal Command was on patrol off Cape Finisterre, Spain, when the waist gunner spotted a U-boat. The pilot put the Liberator into a sharp turn. Unknown to the officers and men of U-514, their assailant was no ordinary pilot and Liberator 'R' was no ordinary aircraft. S/L Terence Bulloch, refreshed from seven months' leave and now returned to war in command of a new squadron, had spent the last portion of his leave testing the new 'Leigh Light' Liberators and the unique A/S rocket system fitted to 'R' itself. In addition to the eight rockets, Bulloch's plane carried eight depth charges and a single Mark 24 Mine – code for the acoustic homing torpedo nicknamed 'Fido'.

U-514, caught completely unaware, remained on the surface, held its course and did not fire at the lumbering Liberator as Bulloch put it into a tight turn and began his attack. At 800 yards range,

Bulloch let loose the first two rockets, followed within seconds by another pair and then, finally, at 500 yards the last four in one salvo. As the aircraft swept over U-514, one of Bulloch's gunners saw a single rocket emerge from the water on the other side of the U-boat. This was assumed to be a hit, since the armoured piercing rockets were designed to plunge into the water well short of the target and then shoot up from beneath, puncturing the pressure hull. It appeared that at least one had passed right through U-514.

But while Bulloch's crew speculated on the accuracy of the rocket strikes, their pilot threw Liberator 'R' into a tight turn and roared in over U-514 once again. This time he placed a 'stick' of all eight depth charges across the U-boat, burying it in a spray of shattering explosions. Then, as U-514 slipped beneath the waves, Bulloch dropped his homing torpedo, which produced a satisfying underwater explosion. No one was sure which of the attacks was lethal: it's possible that they all were. U-514 was lost with all hands.

Bulloch's attack on U-514 was indicative of the lethality of Allied A/S weapon systems by the summer of 1943, particularly those of the aircraft. Until early 1943, aircraft had played a Cinderella role in anti-submarine warfare, although their contribution shaped the war at sea. Aircraft determined where U-boats could and could not operate on the surface with impunity, and therefore where pack operations were possible and when convoys were largely safe from attack. But until 1943 they had never been serious U-boat killers. Having made the mid-ocean untenable for pack operations and claimed nearly half of all the U-boats sent to the bottom from January to the end of May 1943, in the last seven months of 1943 aircraft drove submarines from the surface of the sea entirely. By December 1943, the Germans ordered their U-boats to remain submerged as much as possible and not to reveal their positions by routine radio traffic.

In fairness, aircraft did not achieve this victory on their own. During 1943 they were part of a massive Allied offensive designed to crush the U-boat fleet using naval and air forces, sophisticated and effective inter-Allied command and control methods, and intelligence of all types. It proved to be a highly successful onslaught, and it crippled the U-boat fleet until the very last days of the war.

On 24 May 1943 Dönitz recalled his U-boats from the North Atlantic – 'to lick their wounds and mourn their dead,' as Churchill put later in the summer to the British Parliament. In fact, Dönitz did not abandon operations. Instead, he deployed a concentration west and south of the Azores, into an area still difficult for aircraft to reach. U-boats also operated in the South Atlantic and in a broad arc stretching from West Africa to South America and into the Caribbean. By dispersing his U-boats to distant theatres and into the very heart of the central North Atlantic, Dönitz hoped to maintain a presence at sea until some new weapons and detectors were available.

His moves did not go unnoticed. Much of the Allied effort coming out of the Washington Conference of March 1943 was devoted to developing a well co-ordinated response to the U-boat in the North Atlantic. Although no supreme commander was established, an Allied Anti-Submarine Survey Board travelled througout the area to ensure that the three national theatres – Western Approaches Command along the main convoys routes to forty-seven degrees, the new Canadian north-west Atlantic, which ran operations from the Grand Banks to the Gulf of Maine, and the new USN Tenth Fleet, which was formed at the end of April to handle all ASW in the North Atlantic – worked well together. Most important was the proper sharing of information from the operational intelligence centres in London, Washington and Ottawa. By late spring this intelligence system was maturing quickly, with relevant information passed routinely and promptly between centres.

It was this excellent use of intelligence, especially DF and Ultra, combined with the flood of new aircraft, weapons, sensors and ships that allowed the Allies to launch their offensives in 1943 and to achieve such devastating results. Only in the Canadian zone were preparations for offensive action frustrated, largely by the inability of the Germans to move safely across the Atlantic. Once this was evident, Canadian ships were released to join in the British offensive along the Biscay transit routes.

In the summer of 1943, the growing power of the USN allowed the Americans to span the Atlantic, and strike hard with powerful hunting forces at the U-boats trolling south and west of the Azores. Dönitz had put them there in hopes that they would enjoy some success against the direct US-Mediterranean convoys that supported American operations in North Africa. This deployment was watched closely by the USN's intelligence centre, Op 20G, and the Tenth Fleet. Over the late spring and summer the burgeoning fleet of American 'jeep' carriers was assigned to the area to protect the convoys and kill U-boats. They did both superbly.

The first to go was the USS *Bogue,* which sailed from Argentia, Newfoundland, on 31 May with her four destroyers to support GUS 7A and UGS 9 in the mid-Atlantic, east of Bermuda. *Bogue,* the lead ship of her class, was a converted C-3 type merchant ship, displacing 13,000 tons fully loaded with a top speed of eighteen knots, a 443-foot flight deck and room for twenty-eight aircraft. By size, equipment and performance she and her sisters were ideally suited for convoy support and U-boat hunting. Guided by intelligence fed from Tenth Fleet, *Bogue*'s airmen soon sank their share of U-boats.

Their targets in early June were the seventeen U-boats of Group Trutz, refugees from the German defeat further north in May. Captain Giles E. Short, USN, brought *Bogue* and her escorts to the south end of Trutz to screen the passage of GUS-7A, and then moved eastward to clear a path through the U-boats for UGS-9. On 4 June *Bogue*'s airmen attacked three U-boats, damaging two of them with well-placed depth charges, but all three escaped. Late the next day Short turned *Bogue* south to close with UGS-9, when one of his patrols – at this stage typically a Wildcat fighter and Avenger A/S aircraft carrying depth charges and a homing torpedo – chanced upon U-217. Following proscribed doctrine, Lt Rogers swept in over the sub first in his Wildcat, spraying U-217 with .50 calibre machine fire from his six guns in hopes of clearing the decks. During his first pass Rogers saw six men fall into the sea, but the fire from U-217 did not slacken until his third strafing run. Then Lt McAusland brought his squat Avenger in out of the sun and placed four depth charges alongside U-217 from 100 feet. As the U-boat slipped into a final dive, Rogers emptied his guns into it and *Bogue* was credited with the kill.

Things did not go so well for *Bogue's* airmen two days later when they encountered U-758, which was en route to the Caribbean when it stumbled upon UGS 9. U-758 was the first to be fitted with the new quadruple 20mm anti-aircraft guns, and Kapitänleutnant Helmut Manseck intended to follow Dönitz's orders to use them. Fighters several times swept U-758's gun deck with withering machine gun fire. Manseck replaced the stalwart but doomed gunners after each pass, diving once to ease the pressure from the swarming aircraft, before returning to the surface to continue the battle. Eventually, even Manseck had had enough, and the ferocity of U-758's fire allowed the U-boat to dive safely and escape. A few hours later Manseck signalled triumphantly – and somewhat erroneously – to Dönitz, 'Eight carrier planes warded off: one shot down, four damaged'. For Dönitz, U-758's victory with the quad mounting 'confirmed' the tactic of staying on the surface to fight it out with Allied aircraft, a confirmation which would have dire consequences for the U-boat fleet over the next two months.

Of equal portend in the campaign against the U-boats in the mid-Atlantic was *Bogue's* sinking of U-118 on 12 June. Having seen UGS 9 clear of danger on 10 June, the carrier and her escorts steamed back into the U-boat area and happened upon U-118. In fact, the interception was no simple fortune of war. U-118 was a U-tanker standing by in her rendezvous area to meet four outward bound U-boats when in the late morning a patrol from *Bogue*, directed by Ultra intelligence, found her. The U-boat was swarmed by eight aircraft, which made repeated strafing and bombing runs dropping fourteen 325-lb depth charges and firing over 5,000 rounds of machine gun ammunition. All of U-118's officers died in

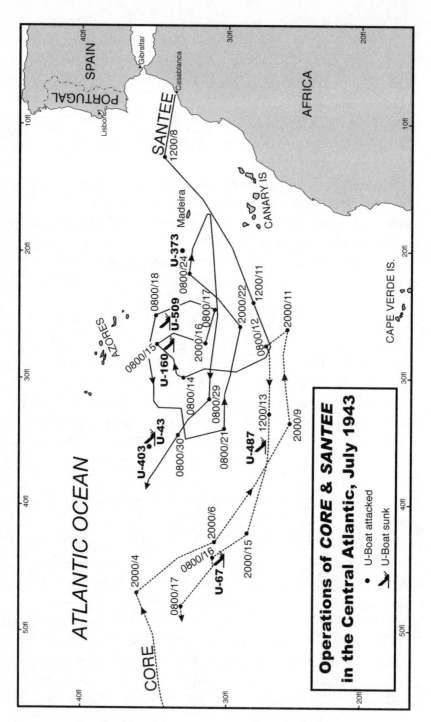

Operations of *Core* and *Santee* in the Central Atlantic, July 1943.

the conning tower directing the U-boat's defence. Seventeen German sailors were rescued from the stricken vessel; some of them were wounded men already transferred from Manseck's U-758.

The sinking of U-118 marked the tentative beginning of a trend in USN CVE operations over the rest of the summer. From late June to early September a relay of CVE's that included *Bogue, Card, Core,* and *Santee* operated in the central North Atlantic, as Tenth Fleet made a special effort to get the U-tankers which were supporting operations further afield. During July they sank five U-boats south of the Azores, four of them in the period lasting from 12-16 July. On 13 July aircraft from *Core,* operating on Ultra intelligence, surprised the tanker U-406 at its refuelling rendezvous and sank it with a swarm of aircraft. The British protested this use of Ultra. They were anxious that the hard won secret not be revealed by so deliberate a use. 'Too true to be good!' the British exclaimed of the American penchant for arriving at the rendezvous like they were supposed to refuel.

But Admiral King preferred to kill off the U-tanker fleet, and so the assault continued. On 14 July aircraft from *Santee* found and sank U-160 with a single acoustic homing torpedo, and then did the same to U-509 the next day. *Core* added to her score on 16 July by sending patrols out to an area determined by Ultra to find U-67 and sink her. The remaining U-boats in the area were finally dispersed when a report from a Spanish freighter that an aircraft carrier was in the area was passed on to BdU. Nonetheless, Tenth Fleet continued to find U-boats using Ultra because U-boats needed to top up their fuel. Thus, on 23 July aircraft from *Bogue* found U-527 refuelling from U-648 and an Avenger promptly sank U-527. A week later a patrol from *Santee* caught U-403 fuelling the minelayer U-43. Both U-boats were driven down and U-43 destroyed by a homing torpedo in a catastrophic explosion that detonated her mines.

The pace continued into August, by which time *Card* was leading the charge. After aircraft from *Card* damaged U-66 on 3 August, Tenth Fleet followed BdU's efforts by wireless to have the U-boat rendezvous with the nearest tanker, U-117. As a result, aircraft from *Card* found the two U-boats on the surface, refuelling and exchanging personnel and supplies, on 7 August. U-66 escaped again, but U-117 was mortally damaged by depth charges and destroyed by a homing torpedo. Now BdU desperately needed to find fuel for fourteen U-boats, and the buzz of signal traffic and planned rendezvous were all tracked by Allied intercept stations. So, too, were the orders given to U-262, which was damaged by *Card*'s aircraft later that same day, as was U-664 – although both U-boats had shot down their attackers. While BdU ordered U-262 to meet with U-664 and U-760 to pass supplies prior to returning to France, and Allied intelligence worked out the site of the rendezvous, the airmen of *Card* changed their tactics. They now added a third aircraft to their normal patrol, an Avenger armed with two 500-lb bombs fitted with instantaneous fuses. And so when the air patrol met U-664 at the rendezvous on 9 August the U-boat was met with a hail of fire and a swarm of aircraft, driven down and then, when U-664 surfaced again twenty minutes later, more aircraft were there. Strafed, bombed and depth charged, the crew of U-664 finally abandoned ship.

Card's fliers scored again on 11 August, when a patrol followed an HF/DF bearing to U-525. The sinking of this U-boat was unique only in that when the final coup de grace was administered, the attacking pilot Lt Charles Hewitt was able to watch the homing torpedo acquire the target and strike the U-boat halfway between the stern and the conning tower. *Card*'s captain summed things up nicely when he observed, 'the 500-lb bomb breaks the enemy's morale and at the same time improves ours... [but] It is believed that the Mk.24 Mine is far more effective than commonly given credit... when the mine functions as it is supposed to – the show is over...'. And so it was. *Core* sank two more U-boats and *Card* one more in this central Atlantic offensive before it ended in late August. By then the 'air gap' near the Azores had been all but eliminated by an Anglo-Portuguese agreement signed on 8 August which allowed Coastal Command to base aircraft at two airfields.

The first squadrons arrived in October, closing the final key gap in North Atlantic air cover. In those waters USN CVE hunter killer groups sank fifteen U-boats in June, July and August 1943, including much of Dönitz's U-tanker fleet, an average of about one U-boat a week in a campaign which crippled the Germans' ability to conduct long-range submarine operations.

Over those same months Allied land-based air power, again supported by warships, inflicted even heavier casualties on U-boats transiting the Bay of Biscay. By early June the Allies deployed twenty long-range and VLR anti-submarine squadrons onto the Bay transit routes. Most of these, a dozen, were RAF, four were American (including the USN's VP 63 Catalina's equipped with Magnetic Anomaly Detectors and retro-bombs), two Australian, and one each from Canada, Poland and Czechoslovakia. All the key aircraft types were represented: Sunderland and Catalina flying boats, Wellingtons, Liberators, Halifaxes and Flying Fortresses. Backing them up were Beaufighters of 248 Squadron RAF and the Mosquitos of No. 10 Group, RAF Fighter Command.

In fact, the Bay offensive, which really began in May, was a complex naval and air battle. F/L C.B. Walker of 461 Squadron Royal Australian Air Force found this out on 2 June when his lumbering four-engine Sunderland flying boat was set upon by eight Ju88 long-range fighters. During the hour-long engagement Walker's gunners shot three of the Ju88s down – which spoke volumes for the qualities of the German fighter – and eventually flew 350 miles home on three engines. The RAF quickly deployed Mosquito and Beaufighter two-engined fighters into the Bay, and the process of escalation began. When Captain Johnny Walker's sloops of EG 2 arrived in June to join in the Bay offensive they were supported by the light cruiser *Scylla*, lest the Germans send out some of their powerful destroyers. By the time B5 arrived from the mid-ocean for a turn at U-boat hunting, they were supported by a cruiser and three fleet class destroyers. They needed that weight, since on several occasions flotillas of German destroyers and torpedo boats sortied to rescue survivors from U-boats.

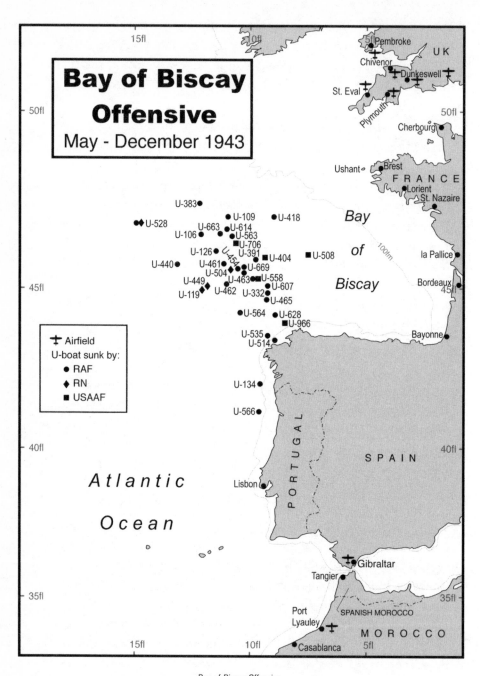

Bay of Biscay Offensive..

Through June, July and early August the escalation of forces in the Bay did little to slow the campaign against U-boats. In May Dönitz ordered U-boats to fight back, but the fire-power which a lone U-boat then possessed offered little deterrence even to a lumbering anti-submarine aircraft. And so in early June Dönitz made the fateful decision to order U-boats to travel across the Bay in groups, trusting in their combined fire-power. The first few transits under this new system were successful, and Dönitz was encouraged by the experience of U-758 with the new quad 20mm gun in its battle with *Bogue's* aircraft on 7 June. But Allied airmen soon learned to swarm the U-boat groups with aircraft. After a group of five U-boats were seriously beaten up by four Polish Mosquitos, Dönitz revised his orders yet again: U-boats were to travel together, but surface only to recharge batteries. Meanwhile, the battle against aircraft was to be carried on by U-441, specially converted into a flak trap by the addition of two quad mountings and one semi-automatic 37mm cannon.

During June the Bay offensive accounted for six U-boats, two of which were sunk by EG 2 on 24 June. Walker's sloops were clearly the class of naval U-boat hunters: powerful, well-equipped long-range warships manned by superbly trained personnel and led by a talented and determined hunter. They were only a short distance off on 24 June when a patrolling aircraft alerted them to the presence of two U-boats. EG 2 soon located the tanker U-119 by asdic. A few well-placed depth charges blew the U-boat to the surface, where Walker drove *Starling's* bow into the sub for the fatal blow. Meanwhile the rest of EG 2 started sniffing around for U-449, which they soon located by asdic as well. By then U-449 had gone deep and she proved a much tougher nut to crack. It took five hours of steady pounding with depth charges using 'barrages' controlled by another ship which stood off and maintained contact on the very deep target. The final barrages which destroyed U-449 were set to explode between 500 and 750 feet, well beyond the designed maximum diving depth for the U-boat and just about at the limit for Walker's weapons and sensors. The problem of deep diving U-boats only got worse as the war went on. On 24 June Walker was also lucky. Most of the time warships deployed to the Bay offensive were too far from the U-boats when they were diverted to them by aircraft, and subsequent searches proved futile.

In July the campaign in the Bay intensified and the airmen got into their stride, sinking fifteen U-boats. Four went down in the first week, including Bulloch's sinking of U-514. Between 7-9 July, aircraft from Gibraltar, called upon to help in the Bay offensive, accounted for three U-boats waiting off Portugal. When U-441 went to sea again to troll for Allied aircraft she got more than she could handle. On 12 July the flak U-boat was located by a trio of Beaufighters and, with one of her quad mountings momentarily defective, U-441 suffered heavy casualties. The Germans got some revenge when a flight of Ju88s arrived in time to shoot down two ASW aircraft orbiting the sub. But Dönitz now abandoned the absurd idea of an anti-aircraft submarine. Meanwhile, eight more U-boats attempting to cross the Bay were sunk before July ended. One of these, U-459, succumbed when the 172 Squadron Wellington was shot down and crashed on top of the U-boat – no one ever claimed that Allied airmen in their slow and vulnerable long-range aircraft lacked courage. When the wreckage was cut away the Germans found two depth charges logged in the U-boat's upper casing. They tried to dispose of them by going to full speed and pushing them off, but aerial depth charges now had very sensitive fuses and the charge exploded almost immediately. U-459 was so damaged the crew was forced to scuttle the sub. Seventeen were rescued, along with one survivor from the attacking aircraft.

The final telling act of the month was the swarming of a group of three U-boats, two of them U-tankers, that had set out from France in late July. The group was spotted on 30 July and soon drew a USN Catalina, an RAAF Sunderland, a RAF Liberator and an RAF Halifax to the scene, followed shortly by another Sunderland and another Halifax. Walker's EG 2, patrolling nearby, was also summoned. By the time Walker arrived the U-boats had been bombed – with some effect – by the Halifaxes using a new high-level depth charge, and depth charged at low level by the others, some of whom suffered serious damage from the anti-aircraft fire. Nonetheless, a Sunderland of 461 Squadron RAAF managed to sink – curiously enough – U-461, while the other despatched U-462. EG 2 arrived in time to find U-504 with asdic and sink it in turn, thus annihilating the U-boat group.

The peak of the air offensive was reached in the first two days of August, when Coastal Command squadrons sank four U-boats in the Bay. In a period of twelve days the Bay offensive had accounted for ten of the seventeen U-boats in transit. Dönitz reacted on 2 August by ordering U-boats to disperse and surface only at night to recharge batteries. Since the end of April the Biscay offensive had accounted for a U-boat about every four days. After 4 August 1943 the rate dropped to one every twenty-seven days for the next ten months.

Despite the declining results and increasing danger from German attack, the Bay offensive did not stop right away. U-boats still moved in and out of their French bases. Through much of August, however, Dönitz routed them south to cross the Biscay under the lee of the Spanish coast, where neutral waters and a sharply rising coastline sheltered U-boats from preying aircraft and their radar. As a result, the British shifted their patrols south, too, to the area off Finisterre, where by late August the Biscay offensive was a major operation. Several support groups of British and Canadian warships now trolled for U-boats, directed and supported by fighter and A/S air patrols, and covered by fleet class destroyers and cruisers. The danger from German forces based in France had not diminished, but no one was ready for the new threat unleashed on 26 August.

On that day the RN's EG 40 and the Canadian EG 5 were conducting an A/S sweep north-west of Finisterre, shadowed by three Condors of KG.40. At noon an American Liberator, 'going hell for leather for Gibraltar,' swept over EG 5 and warned that 'Twenty-one enemy planes are headed this way!', and then promptly dived into the nearest cloud. When the enemy finally arrived Allied sailors counted 17 Dornier 217 long-range bombers and seven Ju88 fighters. The tiny anti-submarine ships braced themselves for attack, but the Dorniers just circled. Eventually small black objects trailing jets of smoke were seen to fall from the wings of the bombers. These raced towards the ships and seemed to follow the evasive movements of the vessels. When the chief engineer of the Canadian corvette *Snowberry* was told that there were 'fifty German aircraft overhead' he found a reserve of speed in his little ship which even the designers did not anticipate. All the escorts of EG 5 and EG 40 were pushed to their maximum speed trying to avoid the miniature aircraft. One by one the little 'glider bombs' – actually remote-controlled and rocket-propelled 'smart bombs' – crashed into the sea, with only two British ships suffering near misses. As the captain of *Snowberry* wrote in his report, this being the Germans' first attempt, their homing technique was poor'.

The Do 217s did much better the next day, when they found EG 5 now joined by EG 1 and screened by the destroyers *Grenville* (RN) and *Athabaskan* (RCN). One of the jet-propelled 1,100-lb radio-controlled bombs struck *Egret*, the flagship of EG 1, destroying the sloop in a terrific explosion. Another bomb which struck *Athabaskan* had been set for a cruiser and the mistaken identity saved the ship: the bomb passed right through the destroyer's super-structure before exploding. This new danger, and the renewal of pack operations in the mid-ocean, brought the Bay of Biscay offensive to halt by mid-September. No fewer than seventeen A/S aircraft and seven long-range fighters were lost by Coastal Command over the Bay in August. In return, only two U-boats were sunk from mid-August to mid-September. The Bay offensive was, nonetheless, an overwhelming success for the Allies, costing the Germans about one U-boat every five days through May to mid-September. But changing German tactics, the introduction of the *Wanze* detector for 10cm radar in August, and the intensity of the naval and air battles plus the diminishing success all urged a reduction in Allied effort.

So, too, did a looming change in German intentions. Since the defeat of May, Dönitz had pursued major changes in the U-boat war on two fronts. The completion of Allied air defences, especially the domination of radar-equipped aircraft throughout the Atlantic, meant that the old submarine was no longer an effective weapon. Something radically new was required: a true submarine with a high submerged speed, capable of diving to great depths and armed with new weapons and sensors that would allow it to fight without ever having to surface or show a periscope. The ideal solution was an air-independent design, but the experimental Walter boat driven by hydrogen peroxide was more difficult to perfect than initially thought. In the interim in June Dönitz accepted a design for the 'electro boat'. This was a conventional diesel-electric air-breathing submarine with a fully streamlined hull, a massive increase in storage batteries and an underwater breathing device called 'schnorkel'. With these improvements Dönitz was promised an underwater speed of eighteen knots for one-and-a-half hours, and an economical submerged speed of twelve to fourteen knots for up to ten hours. Soon two basic designs were set, the type XXI for oceanic work and the smaller type XXIII for inshore. These were now given priority. Orders for 180 type VIIc/42 U-boats were allowed to lapse, leaving just enough of the old submarines to cover losses until the type XXI was ready in mid-1944.

Over the short term, however, Dönitz had to keep fighting, and to do that the existing fleet needed new equipment. During the summer of 1943 this came in three forms. The quad anti-aircraft mounting was seen – at least until August – as the solution to the lone large A/S aircraft, a situation which Dönitz hoped still prevailed in the mid-Atlantic. The final arrival of the *Wanze* warning device for 10cm radar in August promised to give ample warning of approaching aircraft and warships. And finally, the advent of an effective acoustic homing torpedo for U-boats in the late summer gave them a fighting chance against surface vessels. The T-5 *Zaunkonig* (Wren), known to the Allies as the German Naval Acoustic Torpedo (GNAT), was designed to home-in on the propeller noises of high-speed ships like escorts. An earlier version of the torpedo introduced in April was only contact fused. The T-5 was not scheduled for operational service until 1944, but Dönitz pushed for it because its new magnetic pistol greatly reduced the requirement for accuracy. By mid-September Dönitz had a group of twenty U-boats re-equipped and ready to restart the war in the mid-ocean. They would shoot their way through the naval and air escorts and once again devastate Allied convoys – at least, that was the plan.

A German return to the mid-ocean was anticipated over the summer of 1943; they had to use their two hundred operational U-boats somewhere. The Allies knew that the enemy was working on new weapons and tactics, and as Dönitz issued his orders and positioned U-boats in early September, their movements – and tasking signals – were followed closely by Allied intelligence. So the deployment of Group Luethen west of Ireland around 12 September was no surprise. By 16 September it was clear that convoys ONS 18 escorted by B3 and ON 202 escorted by C2 were heading into danger. The newly formed Canadian support group EG 9 was diverted to help the two convoys and VLR Liberators began to sweep a path ahead. On 19 September Dönitz's final admonition to his U-boats was intercepted by Allied intelligence, revealing with complete clarity the position, purpose and tactics of Group Leuthen. That same day a Canadian VLR Liberator opened the battle by sinking U-341.

The British had sailed ONS 18 and ON 202 so that the faster convoy would overtake the slow one as they reached the danger area. This allowed support to be concentrated. By 19 September they were re-routed north-west, to try to slip around Luethen, as the thirty-eight ships of ON 202 closed in on the twenty-seven ships of ONS 18. The combined escort of the two convoys included four destroyers (one a Canadian), two River Class frigates, eight corvettes (three RN, three French, and two Canadian), one trawler, and ONS 18 contained the merchant aircraft carrier *Empire MacAlpine*, a bulk carrier fitted

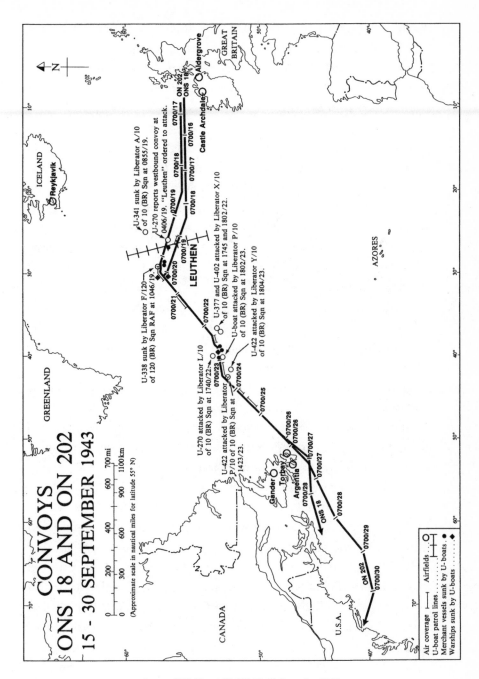

Convoys ONS 18 and ON 202 15-30 September 1943.

with a flight deck and equipped with three Swordfish aircraft. On 19 September the Canadian support group EG 9, led by Cdr C.E. Bridgeman, RNR, in the frigate *Itchen* (RN), with destroyer *St Croix* and the corvettes *Chambly*, *Morden* and *Sackville*, was ordered to assist ONS 18.

As things turned out, the first convoy seriously threatened was ON 202 coming up astern. On the night of 19 September an HF/DF contact drew C.2's British frigate *Lagan* out to investigate, supported by the destroyer HMCS *Gatineau*. The destroyer arrived just in time to watch *Lagan's* stern disintegrate in a towering explosion from a torpedo fired by U-270: the first hit by a GNAT. *Lagan* was taken in tow by a tug and eventually made port as a constructive total loss. Meanwhile U-238 slipped into ON 202 and sank two ships.

On 20 September the escort's senior officers agreed to combine their convoys, use the corvettes for the close screen and shift all the larger ships to the support role. The arrival of Liberators from Iceland helped drive off the shadowers and bring the convoys together, while U-boats and escorts engaged in a day of frantic action. Things were so hectic that at one stage the destroyer *Icarus* rammed the corvette *Drumheller*, which prompted the Canadian corvette's captain to signal the larger vessel, 'Having no Submarines?' Late that afternoon when in pursuit of U-305 the Canadian destroyer *St Croix* was struck by a GNAT and disabled. *Itchen* arrived to help just as a huge explosion from the second GNAT ripped the old destroyer in half, the first ship sunk by an acoustic torpedo. As *Itchen* closed to rescue survivors another GNAT exploded in her wake and Bridgeman left the area to find the corvette *Polyanthus*, thought to be nearby, in order to do the rescue work while the frigate provided a screen. But *Polyanthus* was never seen again. U-952 had completely shattered the little escort with a well-placed GNAT. All *Itchen* ever found was wreckage and three survivors. It was not until the morning of 21 September that *Itchen* returned to the scene of *St Croix's* loss and recovered eighty-one men from a company of 147.

Heavy fog shrouded the battle on 21 September, making the U-boats' task harder. But the air was filled with Liberators from Iceland and the Swordfish off *Empire McAlpine*. During a brief gap in the fog, everyone was astonished to find that ONS 18 and ON 202 were now nicely placed, side by side. Cdr M.B. Evans, RN, the SO of the combined escort, thought some one else had arranged the junction, and in the end reported that it apparently had been 'ordered by a higher authority' than any on earth. In the fog Evans' destroyer *Keppel* managed the only kill by the naval escort, when she ran down an HF/DF bearing, and surprised and rammed U-229.

When the fog finally lifted late in the afternoon ONS 18 and ON 202 were still in formation, spread over some thirty square miles of ocean, and the sky was 'filled with Liberators', now from 10 Squadron RCAF operating from Newfoundland. Nonetheless, ten U-boats remained in contact on the night of 21 September and the combined convoys lost four ships. Most escorts reported GNAT's exploding in their wakes. When *Itchen* and the Canadian corvette *Morden* raced ahead of the convoys to investigate a contact U-666 fired two GNATs in a confused night of action. *Morden* sheered away to avoid the torpedo and it exploded in the corvette's wake. *Itchen* was not so lucky. Her torpedo was a perfect shot, travelling down half the length of the ship before detonating. The explosion probably countermined the frigate's magazine since she disappeared in an enormous explosion. Only three men survived, two of *Itchen's* own crew and one from *St Croix*. The three survivors of *Polyanthus* rescued by the frigate all perished.

At dawn on 22 September the sky was once again filled with Canadian Liberators, as the air assault on Leuthen continued. Dönitz finally called off the battle on 23 September, content with his victory. The U-boats of Luethen claimed no fewer than twelve escort vessels and seven merchant ships sunk, and three escorts and three merchant ships damaged against only two U-boat losses. This, for Dönitz, vindicated his new weapons and tactics. Leuthen had blown its way through the escort screen and inflicted heavy damage on the two convoys. The reality, however, was much different; six merchant vessels and three escorts. At no time had the escort or the Allied authorities ashore panicked. The battle had been hard fought and the novelty of the new weapon and rough seas accounted for the failure of the naval escort in particular to repeat the success of ONS 5 of May, when a huge pack had stumbled around a convoy in fog and suffered terribly for its rashness.

The British assumed that the new weapon was a homing torpedo, but they remained uncertain through the balance of the autumn of that year. Indeed, as late as November when HMS *Chanticleer* was struck, they thought the Germans might be sowing acoustic mines ahead of convoys. Moreover, they were unable to decide – if the problem was a GNAT – how the mechanism worked and they feared that the torpedo was capable of fairly sophisticated guidance. For this reason the British solution to the GNAT, a towed pipe noise-maker dubbed Foxer, was a complex and heavy piece of equipment, requiring elaborate winches and paravanes to set it. And since they believed that the GNAT was capable of continuous and subtle changes in course, the British practice was to stream two Foxer gears to protect each quarter of the ship. The complex Foxer took many men a half-hour to launch, it could only be towed at fifteen knots and the noise-makers lasted for only a few hours.

In contrast, the Canadians had a solution to GNAT the very day they heard of *St Croix*'s loss. Scientists in Halifax, who had invented the original pipe noise-maker for sweeping acoustic mines in 1940, understood the problem. They assumed that the GNAT had a rudimentary rudder system with only three settings – left, right and centre – and would simply be drawn directly to the loudest noise. One noise-maker would therefore be enough. On 21 September, even before *Itchen* was sunk, they built a prototype in their shop and conducted trials in Halifax harbour the next day. Technical specifications were signalled to St John's and fifty sets were sitting on the wharf when C 2 and the remnants of EG 9 arrived from the battle. This Canadian Anti-acoustic Torpedo

(CAT) gear was elegantly simple: one five-foot pipe (soon reduced to thirty inches) bolted to a bracket with another loosely fitted above so the two rattled, and the whole thing attached to a light wire yoke. The pipes lasted for over fourteen hours and it could be towed at nearly eighteen knots. CAT was launched by one man heaving it over the stern; recovery was done by a small hand winch. CAT gear was adopted by the USN. The British stuck to their Foxer gear, and Canadian deference to British concerns kept the CAT coiled on deck until early December.

The other solution to the GNAT was to go slow, under eight knots, and 'side step' during the approach to an underwater contact. Some escort commanders preferred to maintain a listening watch on asdic for the sound of the torpedo, but this was hazardous and not encouraged. Caution and much-reduced speed were now the keys when attacking a submerged U-boat.

With battle rejoined in the mid-ocean, the British soon moved resources there to counter the threat. Over the autumn support groups poured in, including Walker's sloops in EG 2 assisted by the CVE *Tracker*, the four destroyers of EG 3, the new American-built Captain Class destroyer escorts of EG 4, sloops and frigates of EG 7 and five destroyers and the CVE *Fencer* of EG 8. The RCN's solitary support group EG 5, with two RN frigates and four corvettes, also joined in (EG 9 was disbanded after the loss of its larger ships in the battle for ONS 18/ON 202). They all provided essential close escort and striking forces, but again the lion's share of U-boat killing went to aircraft. In the battle for SC 145 in early October, the only other serious engagement of the autumn campaign, the convoy's escort and EG 3 fought a furious battle against U-boats without killing any. For their part, all the Germans' GNAT's missed. But the airmen did not: three U-boats were sunk by RAF Liberators and another by a Canadian Sunderland. More distressing for the Germans was the presence of night support around SC 145 by Leigh Light equipped Liberators. Now even in the middle of the broad Atlantic it was not safe to be on the surface at night. The pattern of SC 145 repeated itself a week later around ONS 20, now escorted by EG 4 with Cdr Peter Gretton's crack B.7 acting in support. The naval escort had no luck, but RAF Liberators flying in support sank three U-boats.

Excellent intelligence, oppressive air support and powerful naval escorts all made the German autumn 1943 campaign on the North Atlantic a complete failure. GNAT did not inflict the much needed tactical defeat on naval escorts, lumbering maritime patrol aircraft still pushed through the U-boats' anti-aircraft fire, and the anxiously awaited *Wanze* radar detector proved ineffective against 10cm radar. All of Dönitz's ambitions were unfulfilled. In October only four ships were sunk from Allied convoys, barely half of September's dismal toll of eight. In November of that year U-boats sank only nine ships worldwide, and none from convoys at all. The shipping situation that had so dominated the Atlantic campaign for the last few years was now over. Not only had losses plummeted, but in 1943 the Americans alone produced 14 million tons of new merchant vessels, and the opening the Mediterranean in the summer dramatically improved the efficiency of the British merc-hant fleet. The Atlantic war was now very much about keeping the U-boat down and mastering the riddle of increasingly complex anti-submarine warfare.

In contrast to the vastly improved Allied situation in the last four months of 1943, forty-six U-boats were lost in the mid-ocean, Biscay and Gibraltar areas; twenty-four to land-based aircraft, nine to USN CVE groups, and thirteen to naval vessels alone. Two of the latter went to Walker's EG 2 on 6 November when they crashed through a U-boat concentration east of Newfoundland, sinking U-226 and U-842. On 12 November Dönitz confided that the enemy 'has all our secrets and we have none of theirs.' Apart from the overwhelming superiority of Allied weaponry and sensors the key to this second and final victory, the one which drove the U-boats down and made them fugitives for much of the rest of the war, was superb intelligence. According to the RCAF official history, the British read German signal traffic with such facility during the autumn of 1943 that Allied information on U-boat locations was 'often as good as, or better, than BdU's own.' The Germans never figured that out.

Victory over the U-boats was so complete by autumn 1943 that in late October the British Admiralty announced the cancellation of virtually all their escort-building programmes. This included most of the programme of British Loch Class frigates, specially designed to take the latest in A/S weaponry, and the lion's share of the massive Captain Class destroyer escort programme in the United States. In the end only seventy-eight Captains entered RN service, 222 contracts were cancelled and the balance of the 520 ship programmes abandoned. American and Canadian escort-building programmes were scaled back sharply as well, a circumstance which left the RCN fleet, which had not yet acquired the latest types, largely frozen a generation behind the final wartime developments in ASW.

Dönitz responded to the disaster in the mid-ocean by introducing his own VLR aircraft in an attempt to find the illusive convoys and get his U-boats ahead of them. Blohm and Voss 222 long-range flying boats, He.177 and Ju290 aircraft, now joined the venerable Condors over the North Atlantic, but they could not bring the U-boats and convoys together in the mid-ocean.

Once again the fall back position was to redeploy west of Portugal, where aircraft and U-boats might work better under more favourable conditions and in a new spirit of co-operation. However, the results in that part of the Atlantic were no better. On 27 October Luftwaffe aircraft reported the sixty ships of the combined convoys SL138/MKS28 west of Portugal and eight U-boats were deployed to intercept. They were harried by air patrols from Gibraltar and the UK, and – for the first time – RAF patrols operating from the Azores. The first U-boat to make a sighting report, U-306, was promptly located by HF/DF and sunk by the escort. The next to arrive managed to hit one ship, but barely escaped the counter-attack. Dönitz soon abandoned the chase.

When a large battle eventually developed around SL139/MKS30 in mid-November, it proved to be the last battle of significance along that route. The combined convoy was reported by German air patrols on 15 November and twenty-six U-boats were deployed to intercept. Forewarned by intercepted wireless traffic, the British moved quickly to reinforce the air and naval escort. Air coverage from land bases, even at night, was almost continuous. EG 7 arrived to reinforce the screen shortly after the convoy passed through the first U-boat line on 18 November, while a Leigh Light Wellington flying from the Azores sank U-211 near the convoy early the next morning. Later that day the RCN's EG 5 joined, followed closely by two British destroyers. SL129/MKS30 was now surrounded by nineteen escorts in a double screen as it passed through the second U-boat line at dusk on 19 November. By then the convoy was west of Cape Finisterre and under threat from German air attack as it approached a third U-boat patrol line. As the pack closed with the convoy most were intercepted and driven off, with EG 5 sinking one sub on the morning of 20 November. That same day air patrols from England intercepted two long-range German patrol aircraft sent to shadow the convoy and shot them down off the north coast of Spain. The Germans got a little revenge that day when shadowing U-boats shot down a British Liberator and a Canadian Sunderland. But RAF Wellington patrols from the Azores helped keep the U-boats at bay overnight. On 21 November two British escorts sank U-538 astern of the convoy, and Dönitz finally called off the U-boats. However, the battle was not quite over. Later that day two dozen glider bomb-equipped German aircraft appeared over the convoy, just as it was joined by the Canadian anti-aircraft cruiser *Prince Robert*. The combined fire of the escort and cruiser forced most of the glider bombs to be released against two stragglers astern of the convoy; one was sunk and another damaged. Three of the new four-engined He.177's were shot down. With that the battle ended.

For the Germans, the results of the attack on SL139/MKS30 were deeply disappointing. Over twenty U-boats managed to damage one escort and shoot down two aircraft. None hit a ship from the convoy with a torpedo. In exchange, three U-boats were lost and one heavily damaged. For its part, the Luftwaffe sank one ship at a cost of five of its precious long-range aircraft. Dönitz, nonetheless, tried to push his U-boats through the increasingly oppressive Allied naval and air protection around the SL and MK convoys for several more weeks. The Allies responded by sending in British and American CVEs to hunt them, and the results were predictable; an unequal battle in which a few Allied warships were sunk along with a few U-boats, all with no impact on Allied merchant shipping at all. By mid-December Dönitz had given up the campaign on this route, too.

By mid-December 1944, Dönitz ordered his U-boats to remain submerged most of the time, to run on the surface only in bad weather or to recharge batteries, and to sharply reduce the volume of their wireless traffic. Swarms of radar-equipped aircraft had finally driven the submarine down for good; the problem now was how to find these fugitives in a vast ocean.

8

Troubled Waters
January-August 1944

The defeat of the U-boats in 1943 effectively ended German attempts to achieve a strategic result against Allied shipping. Only the convoys to Russia remained under serious threat, and even that was reduced in late December when *Scharnhorst* tried to attack a convoy in the Arctic night off North Cape, Norway. Here, too, darkness no longer provided cover. *Scharnhorst* was tracked down and beaten into a wreck by the radar directed guns of British battleships and cruisers. By the end of 1943, the best the Germans could hope for at sea was to use their remaining forces to tie down Allied resources and try to impede the development of Allied operations by temporary, local victories. The U-boat's adoption of new methods and equipment allowed them to survive and fight – barely. They also forced the Allies to adapt to a radically new, in fact modern, form of anti-submarine warfare.

It therefore fell to the U-boats to maintain a semblance of German presence at sea, and they did this for the balance of the war. But the objective now was primarily to survive, to hold on until the radically new type XXI and XXIII U-boats could arrive to restore the initiative. To help in the process Dönitz finally appointed a Naval Scientific Operations Staff at the end of 1943, under his personal direction, to oversee the development of new weapons and sensors. Such a staff, a hallmark of the Allied system for years, was long overdue. One of the first things these scientists did was to develop a directional antenna for the new *Naxos* 10cm radar warning set. Then, based on their own estimates of what the Allies would do next, Dönitz's scientists developed countermeasures for the next generation of centimetric radar – 3cm – which was ready by the spring of 1944, before Allied 3cm sets entered widespread service. This was the first time that the U-boat fleet had been ahead in the electronic war. Work had also started in earnest on the new U-boats, with orders for 290 placed in 1943. They were to be built using a new system of prefabrication, with parts for eight major sections drawn from sixty plants throughout Europe, and then the sections transported to assembly yards at Bremen, Hamburg and Danzig. This was intended to minimise the effects of Allied bombing and ease the pressure on limited space at the major shipyards. The first were scheduled for delivery in April 1944, and Dönitz hoped to be receiving thirty-three a month by September.

By the end of 1943, the Germans were also experimenting with the new 'schnorkel' breathing device. The idea was not new, since the Dutch had such a device in service prior to the war. But so long as U-boats had unfettered use of the surface for movement, there was little point in adopting it. The new conditions of total Allied air supremacy forced Dönitz to take a serious look at the schnorkel in 1943, and by early 1944 U-264 and U-575 were nearly ready for sea trials. Schnorkel consisted of an intake tube with a float valve at the top paired to an exhaust tube, which vented just below the surface, housed in a streamlined flaring. As fitted to the old U-boats, the schnorkel mast was hinged and laid along the forward deck when not in use. When raised, the snort allowed the U-boat to cruise at periscope depth at moderate speed (depending on sea-state) and recharge its batteries. In theory – and by 1945 in practice – it was no longer necessary for a submarine to surface at all.

In the meantime, pressure had to be maintained in the Atlantic and so by early 1944 Dönitz deployed a concentration of U-boats west of Ireland between fifteen and seventeen degrees west, where he hoped that the convoys would come to them. In addition, individual U-boats were still sent on distant operations, and into the Mediterranean. With an average of sixty-six U-boats at sea at any one time in early 1944, Dönitz had some hopes of modest success, and with nearly 200 operational ocean-going submarines, the U-boat fleet still constituted a major threat.

But the powerful impact of radar-equipped aircraft in 1943 had created an entirely new operational environment at sea, and it was difficult for Dönitz to use his U-boats in the old way. The requirement to spend a great deal of time submerged or watching anxiously for sudden air attack sharply reduced the operational radius and time on station for most submarines. Crossing the Atlantic, a task that had taken little more than a week in 1942, now took up to a month. Even getting on station west of Ireland could take a couple of weeks. U-boats were now very slow in all respects, strategically, operationally and tactically. And invariably they were now lone wolves. The dynamic of a pack attack, which upset the defence and forced escorts to concentrate on protection of the convoys, was long past. Naval and air ASW forces were now free to concentrate on sinking any U-boat they came in contact with.

This trend had been in evidence since the late spring of 1943, but the cowing of the U-boat fleet and the comparative immobility of submarines by early 1944 now made U-boat hunting a top priority for the Allies. In this they were greatly assisted by excellent intelligence, which was well collated and distributed. Starting in the spring of 1943 the British Operational Intelligence Centre began to issue daily U-boat threat estimates, code-named 'Stipple'. The reinforcement of convoys was based on these estimates. Coastal Command, and soon the other Allied air forces, quickly based their daily flight plans on the Stipple signal and in turn issued their own U-boat probability estimates and searches for U-boats in a daily signal code named 'Tubular'. Aircraft not committed to convoy cover were then diverted to patrols according to the quality of the intelligence estimates – an 'A' estimate being a confirmed recent sighting, and a 'C' being weak or old information. The idea of the Tubular-based sweeps was to try to relocate the U-boats and then commence a hunt to exhaustion, a 'Swamp' in RAF parlance. Since a submerged U-boat could only make about two knots, it could only be a maximum of 100 miles from its original location before all of its oxygen supply was depleted. Most likely, the U-boat would be forced to the surface before that. Four aircraft equipped with 10cm radar could therefore sweep the 'probability area' within which a confirmed U-boat was likely to resurface. And even if a second sighting did not result in an attack, it would result in an exhausted U-boat being driven down again. The search could then recommence, with every likelihood that the submarine would surface again soon.

The concept of hunting to exhaustion became the mainstay of anti-submarine air operations for the balance of the war, guiding patrols in transit areas in the eastern Atlantic, in the approaches to North America and in the Straits of Gibraltar. In early 1944 USN Catalinas of VP 63 equipped with Magnetic Anomaly Detectors also began a standing patrol of the Straits of Gibraltar, maintaining two aircraft in continuous sweeps at 100 feet over the centre of the passage. U-761 was detected on 12 February and sunk in a combined naval and air search; U-392 followed on 16 March. RAF Swamps in the Mediterranean were particularly successful in early 1944; conditions were good and distances short.

But where conditions were poor and distances great it was still tough to run a U-boat to exhaustion. Eastern Air Command of the RCAF based in Atlantic Canada and Newfoundland, which by then was well integrated into the British system, adopted these methods in 1943, and their search for U-845 in early 1944 illustrates the new approach well – even if the execution was faulty. Based on Ultra intelligence, an 'Otter' – the RCAF equivalent of a

Tubular signal – area was promulgated for U-845 on 22 January, and a series of Liberators from 10 Squadron RCAF began to fly out to the mid-ocean to search. As many as five aircraft a day flew U-845's estimated track until early February, when the search was finally abandoned. However, a DF fix on a signal from U-845 put aircraft back on track on 9 February, or so it was thought. U-845 actually came to Newfoundland about fifty miles north of the Allied estimates of its track, and its precise location was not determined until it torpdoed the steamer *Kelmscott* ten miles off St John's. A three-day hunt to exhaustion, code named 'Salmon' by the Canadians, followed without result. While the RCAF flew air searches, the newly reformed RCN support group EG 9 searched as well. In dreadful winter weather, and amid poor co-ordination between navy and air force, U-845 slipped away. EG 9 was sent overseas to help the RN and the RCAF began to fly 'Otter' patrols in search of the next inbound U-boat, U-539, south of Flemish Cap when an RCAF Liberator actually found and attacked U-845 on 14 February. By then the U-boat was too far out to sea and no 'Salmon' operation was possible. Ironically, EG 9 sank U-845 on 10 March, west of Ireland.

Hunts to exhaustion in the Canadian zone were never success-ful, in part because of bad weather and poor co-ordination between ad hoc naval forces and widely scattered air forces. But the Canadians did push U-boats into the waiting grips of USN CVE's, patrolling on the edge of their zone. The search for U-856, for example, off Nova Scotia in late March absorbed over 300 flights and more than 3,000 hours of flying time, plus naval searches, without producing even one contact. When U-856 reached the comparatively uniform water conditions south of Sable Island USS *Croatan* and her escorts were waiting, as were two additional groups of USN destroyer escorts. Radar-equipped Avengers found the U-boat at night and tracked it using sonobuoys, until the destroyers arrived to pound the U-boat with depth charges and eventually sink it. As the RCAF official history observed, the sinking of U-856 by the USN was evidence of what 'experienced surface and air escorts working in close harmony' could achieve.

The sinking of U-856 also demonstrated that by 1944 the burden of killing submarines – now immobilised and driven down by air power – had fallen once again to warships. The Allied navies went at this problem with renewed energy in early 1944. At the end of January the RN began an offensive against the U-boat concentration to the west of Ireland using its own CVE's, *Activity* and *Nairana* sailing with EG 2 and *Fencer* and *Striker* with EG 16. But flying operations were plagued by severe winter weather. This was nothing like the sunny climes of the Azores where USN CVEs had scored so successfully the previous summer. Only *Fencer* recorded a kill, and the carriers were soon withdrawn.

For the warships, however, the offensive west of Ireland was much more successful. Over a two-week period – a single patrol – the sloops of Johnny Walker's EG 2, well directed by Ultra, sank six U-boats in what the Admiralty's *Monthly Anti-Submarine Report* described as, 'The most outstanding success of the Anti-U-boat war.' EG 2's cruise began on 31 January while screening the carriers. Quick action on an asdic contact by *Wild Goose* probably saved *Nairana*. Three of Walker's sloops prosecuted the contact for an hour before evidence of the destruction of U-592 rose to the surface. On 8 February *Wild Goose*'s alert lookout spotted U-762 lurking around SL147/MKS38. The U-boat promptly dived and three sloops closed the contact. *Woodpecker* delivered one 22-charge barrage, which killed the sub. Hours later, on the morning of 9 January, *Wild Goose* again detected another U-boat and once again called Walker's *Starling* up to help. Barrage attacks soon produced evidence of the destruction of U-734. Meanwhile *Kite* and *Magpie* had managed to get their teeth into U-238, and were still attacking when Walker joined following the sinking of U-734. This new contact went very deep and required nearly six hours of barrage attacks and 266 depth charges to end the job. EG 2 finished their patrol on 19 January by tracking down and sinking U-264, the first U-boat to go to sea with a trial schnorkel. U-264 had engineers aboard and – unfortunately for the crew – was required to signal reports on how things were going. EG 2's destruction of U-264 was therefore no accidental encounter. Nor, it seems, was the sinking of U-575, the second schnorkel-equipped U-boat to go to sea, by USS *Bogue*'s group, a Canadian frigate, and RAF aircraft on 13 March.

Most of the submarines killed by EG 2 in early February went deep, and their destruction represented the perfection of anti-submarine warfare based on depth charges and fixed asdic transducers. The typical asdic transmission was shaped like a searchlight beam, and was pointed about ten degrees from the horizontal to sweep the water near to surface immediately around the ship. It was assumed that most submarines would be relatively shallow divers, and at the start of the war British depth charges had a maximum setting of 150 feet. By 1942 settings of 350 feet were possible, and by 1943 depth charges could be set to fire at 550 feet. So long as U-boats attacked primarily on the surface, depth charge attacks tended to be both hasty and limited to a thin veneer on the surface of the sea; the technology, tactics and doctrine of both sides aligned to make it so. The designed maximum diving depth of the type VIIC U-boat, the workhorse of the Atlantic war, was 100 metres, roughly 350 feet, although in an emergency they were capable of 500 feet or better. For most of the war few U-boats had time to go that deep and if the escort's first charges missed, there was little time for it to develop a deliberate hunt before being called back to the convoy. Prolonged anti-submarine hunts prior to mid-1943 were rare and few escorts had the opportunity to track a U-boat at depths (in 1942 up to 600 feet) beyond the limits of existing A/S equipment.

The Germans too understood how increased depth complicated the A/S problem, and some U-boat captains risked crushing depths to escape their hunters. The type VIIC U-boats ordered in 1941 had a standard diving depth of 400 feet, a test depth of 600 feet and a destruction depth of as much as 1,000 feet. The type VIIC/42, abandoned by the decision to build the type XXI, pushed these limits even further, to 666, 1,000 and 1,666 feet respectively. By August 1943 the first of the type VIIC/41 U-boats began to appear, and even the older types were pushing the limits of their pressure hulls as a way of escaping hunters on the surface.

The ability of U-boats to dive very deep did not surprise the Allies, but by the autumn of 1943 escort commanders complained that their depth charges could not be set deep enough to reach them. Western Approaches Command often reprimanded its officers, like Lt Cdr E.H. Chavasse, RNR, senior officer of EG 4, for excessive expenditure of depth charges: 'I pointed out to my superiors that U-boats, when attacked, had recently developed the habit (and ability) of diving to the previously unheard of depth of 800 feet...,'Chavasse wrote after the war, 'and were jolly nearly safe as houses.' That was not strictly true. New pistols for depth charges were just coming into service. The Mk IXx had settings to 700 feet and the MK IXxxx could get down to 875 feet. In addition, depth charges fitted with the new, seventy per cent more powerful, explosive 'minol' were available by early 1944.

But new pistols with deeper settings were not a solution to the problem. The fixed beam asdic required the escort to stand well off in order to maintain contact, while depth charges had to be laid behind the attacking vessel. The result was a very long 'blind time' between the point at which asdic contact was lost and the depth charges were fired. Moreover, depth charges took a long time to sink, some ten feet per second and over half a minute to get to 600 feet. Since submariners could easily anticipate a depth charge attack by the increase in the attacking vessel's speed, the long blind time of a depth charge attack – up to ninety seconds on a U-boat at 600 feet – gave a deep submarine lots of time to take evasive action.

Allied sailors long knew that the best way to overcome this problem was to employ two or more ships. One held the U-boat in asdic contact while the others were directed over the target at a slow speed (hence the term creeping attack) as a form of 'ahead throwing weapon'. HMC Ships *Skeena* and *Wetaskiwin* used this method to sink U-558 in July 1942, and Walker's EG 2 used it in the autumn of 1943 to sink U–226 and U–842 on the Grand Banks. EG 2 often used two or more attacking ships at a time in what Walker dubbed 'barrage attacks'. The Admiralty promulgated the tactic in August 1943, but the success of early February 1944 brought the creeping and barrage attacks to prominence.

However, even as EG 2 boiled the ocean with its depth charges the wave of the future was upon them. A new support group, EG 10, operating in the vicinity of EG 2 and supporting the same convoys, sank two U-boats on 18 and 19 February 1944 using the new type 147B asdic and the 'Q' attachment on the standard type 144 set. The 'Q' attachment on the main asdic set produced a narrow, fan-shaped beam in the vertical plane. It was slaved to the main set but aligned at a sharper angle in order to maintain contact on a U-boat until the last possible moment of the run-in to fire

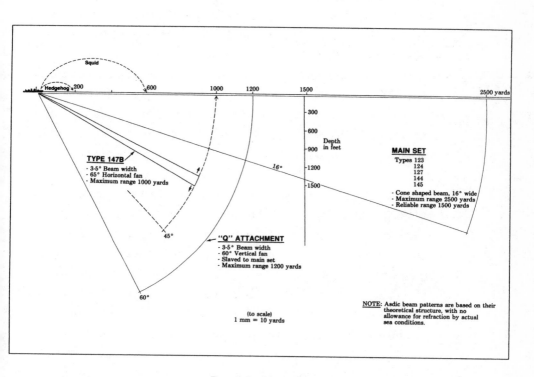

Theoretical asdic patterns.

depth charges. In the main asdic 'Q' system the depth of the contact had to be estimated from the range at which the fixed beam lost the target, a simple question of geometry. As the main set swept over the target during the approach, the asdic operator maintained contact by switching to his 'Q' attachment, which kept the attack on line. This combination of skill, experience and educated guesswork was not necessary with the type 147B set. The type 147B produced a thin fan-shaped beam in the horizontal plane and the transducer was articulated so that it could be pointed sharply down, maintaining contact until the ship was virtually right on top of the U-boat. The angle of the setting coupled with the very thin beam could be translated into an accurate depth reading, providing accurate measurements of depth of the target right up to the last moment.

The frigate *Spey* of EG 10 had all of this asdic equipment when she encountered U-406 and U-386 in mid-February. U-406 was found on asdic at 1,700 yards, and using 'Q' and the main set was held as close as 300 yards, indication of a shallow target. No creeping or barrage attacks were necessary. One ten-charge pattern was dropped, which inflicted mortal damage on the U-boat. *Spey* obtained her second U-boat contact on asdic less than a day later at a range of 1800 yards. The frigate began her attack at 750 yards with depth charges set shallow, to fifty and 140 feet. At 500 yards *Spey*'s type 147B revealed that the U-boat was actually 350 feet deep. Depth charges were reset immediately to 250 and 385 feet just before the first left the ship. As *Spey* turned to renew contact, U-386 broke surface 800 yards away and tried to escape. The U-boat was riddled with gunfire, but *Spey*'s captain resisted the temptation to ram, contenting himself with shattering the U-boat's final resolve with a shallow pattern of depth charges. Sixteen submariners were recovered.

The difference between the methods of EG 2 and EG 10 were apparent. Walker's methods required lots of time and plenty of depth charges, an average of four hours and 106 depth charges each. 'The danger of the creeping attack', the *Monthly Anti-Submarine Report* for February 1944 observed, 'lies in the fact that it tends to develop into a long, drawn-out struggle during which asdic conditions or weather may deteriorate, thereby causing the hunting vessels to lose contact and giving the U-boat then opportunity to escape.' Creeping attacks also required 'exceedingly close co-operation between ships and almost unlimited time and depth charges', and it was necessary to force the enemy to go deep. In contrast, *Spey* destroyed her two U-boats in minutes, blowing them to the surface with single ten-charge patterns and then riddling them with gunfire. 'It is obviously tactically advantageous,' the *Report* went on, 'to kill the quarry as quickly as possible and the latest developments in asdic and anti-submarine weapons are designed to assist in the accomplishment of this object.'

In 1943 the preferred solution to this problem was to use the new A/S mortar, hedgehog, which threw a pattern of 32lb contact-fused bombs ahead of the ship. Hedgehog bombs descended at twenty-two feet per second. Allowing for 7.5 seconds in the air, that meant about thirty-five seconds blind time on a target at 600 feet. However, only about thirty per cent of attack situations favoured the use of hedgehog and its theoretical lethality of sixty per cent on targets at 300 feet was never realised. In fact, hedgehog had obtained only thirteen per cent lethality by the end of 1943. The limited range of the weapon, only some 200 yards ahead of the ship, and the fixed beam of the type 144 asdic, meant that hedgehog was only accurate down to about 350 feet. Hedgehog attacks on deep U-boats in early 1944 were made using a stopwatch and firing the weapon manually – which accounts for their universal failure. The accuracy and usefulness of hedgehog against deep targets could be improved by using the 'Q' device or a type 147B asdic. Even so, the bombs were contact-fused and a miss was as good as a mile. Moreover, the 32lb torpex warhead was not powerful enough against the reinforced pressure hulls of the type VIIC/41 U-boats, and could not be counted on to breach the hull should they strike other parts of the U-boat (such as fuel tanks or deck plates).

The real solution to the problem was the new, much more powerful, ahead-throwing weapon called 'squid.' In crude terms, squid was a small depth charge – 200 lbs. of lethal Minol II – fired forward of the ship, which produced a large and powerful explosion. More importantly, squid was slaved to the new asdic type 147B and featured fully automated control. Once contact had been made, the 147B set the fuses on the squid bombs and fired the weapon. According to Cdr L.P. Denny, RCNR, who sank U-877 with a single bomb in late 1944, 'With Squid it was like Duck Soup... Difficult to miss if you were careful.' A fast descent time of about forty feet per second – roughly twenty-five seconds on a target at 600 feet – helped give squid a lethality rate of nearly sixty per cent on deep targets. Unfortunately for the Allies, only the latest British-built escort classes – the Loch and Bay class frigates and Castle Class corvettes – carried the complex squid and type 147B suite, and retrofitting existing ships to take the equipment was very complex and time consuming.

The new equipment also worked best under ideal conditions in deep water. The sea is not a uniform medium, and changes in temperature and salinity, as well as bottom and tide conditions, affected the operation of asdic. Submariners, in particular, were aware of the 'afternoon effect' produced by the warming of the surface layer of the sea during the day in warm areas like the Mediterranean and the Caribbean. German submariners operating the St Lawrence River, off Canada, in 1942 knew that if they punched through the top layer of water down into the more saline sea water below that no escort could find them. As one submariner observed, once below the layer they were 'safe as in the bosom of Abraham', and they could drift on the current without having to operate a single piece of machinery.

By 1942 the USN was already wrestling seriously with this problem, using the new science of bathythermography (BT), the changing temperature of water according to depth, to produce charts of likely asdic ranges for the North Atlantic. By 1943 USN groups were taking BT readings every watch, which revealed where the 'thermocline' (the key sharp change in temperature between the top and lower layers) lay. This may account for their

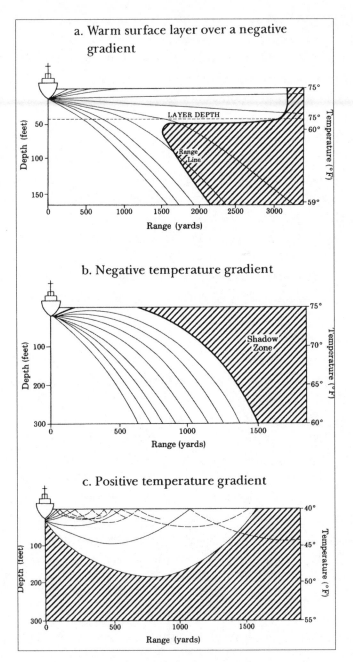

Asdic sound propagation under different conditions

success just outside the Canadian zone in 1944, where waters were generally 'isothermal' (i.e., had no temperature layer). In contrast, waters inside the Canadian zone were the worst in the North Atlantic – comparable only to those experienced by the Arctic convoys. In the winter, water temperature increased with depth, which bent asdic beams back up to the surface making even shallow diving U–boats safe. In the hunt for U–845 in February it was believed that no asdic sweeps got deeper than 200 feet. In the summer a sharp warm layer on the surface trapped sound in the top fifty feet and gave long ranges on very shallow U–boats, while making it equally impossible to locate those which had gone deeper.

This much was known by early 1944, and scientists were busy trying to understand how ocean conditions affected anti–submarine warfare. The problem did not prevent the loss of twenty-nine U–boats in the deep waters of the North Atlantic during the first quarter of 1944, eighteen of them to warships. In exchange, Dönitz's submariners accounted for only three of the 3,360 ships that passed through the U–boat concentration west of Ireland over that period. The monthly average toll was barely twelve ships, most of these independents sunk in distant theatres. By this stage the Allies had more shipping available than they knew what to do with: 14 million tons of new construction arrived in 1943 alone. The submarine problem, at least as far as the war on shipping was concerned, had ceased to exist. Some senior Allied officers advocated sharply scaling back maritime air power in particular, simply accepting a monthly shipping loss rate of 300,000 tons to U–boat attacks. In short, the U–boat had become a tactical problem for ASW forces, and in early 1944 the U–boat fleet therefore paid a heavy price for their holding action during this difficult phase of the war.

As things turned out, what Allied navies in particular needed in the next phase of the Atlantic war was not expertise and equipment for deep water, but skill and the right kit for ASW in wreck strewn shallow water. In the spring of 1944 the Allied invasion of France was an open secret, the only thing really unknown was the precise location and the actual time. The Allies knew that Dönitz had over 400 U-boats in service, and intelligence officers anticipated that he would commit them en masse to crush the landing in a final Wagernian Gotterdammerung in the English Channel. Even assuming that the Germans committed only the 170 operational U-boats available, it was projected that as many as 240 Allied ships per week might be lost. Defending the Allied invasion of France from this onslaught was the primary concern of Atlantic ASW forces in the spring and summer of 1944.

The key to securing the invasion route from the U-boats was massive use of air power. No. 19 Group, RAF, which was charged with closing off the western entrance to the English Channel, was increased in size to twenty-five squadrons of 350 aircraft – enough to keep thirty aircraft on patrol at any one time. Their task, code-named Operation Cork, was to fly a huge Swamp Operation covering 20,000 square miles between the Loire River estuary in western France to the south of Ireland, and into the Channel as far as the Cherbourg peninsula. Patrol routes were laid out to ensure that the surface of the sea was swept by radar at least once every thirty minutes. Air patrols over the Northern Transit routes, between Britain and Iceland, were also intensified to keep U-boats based in Norway from reaching the Channel.

Operating below the air umbrella were 286 of what Roskill called, 'the best and most experienced' A/S vessels the Allies could muster. Many were assigned to close escort of the invasion and follow-on convoys, but ten designed hunting groups closed the western end of the Channel to U-boats. Six Escort Groups, the RN's 1, 2, 5 and 15, and the RCN's 6 and 9, supported by two CVE's carrying fighter aircraft, patrolled between Land's End and Brest in an outer barrier, while four veteran anti-submarine destroyer groups – the RN's 3 and 14 and the RCN's 11 and 12 – established an inner barrier west of the Cherbourg peninsula. Many of the groups were issued wreck charts of the Channel and were also fitted with new radio aids to help them do precise navigation. The British Admiralty expected U-boats operating inshore to be timid, and to prefer to keep moving, even in shallow water. Setting the U-boat on the bottom was seen as an act of desperation, and it is fair to say that Allied ASW specialists and veterans were highly confident that their equipment and experience would be transferable to in-shore conditions.

The Allied anti-submarine measures to defend the invasion of France were overwhelmingly successful. In the event Dönitz assigned only forty-nine U-boats to the English Channel, and only nine of these were equipped with schnorkel. Therefore, the great bulk of the U-boats had to try to make their way through oppressive air and naval surface surveillance and it simply could not be done. Within three days of the Allied landing on 6 June, six U-boats had been sunk by aircraft and a further six driven back to port with damage. Of the eight non-schnorkel U-boats which set off from Brest on 6 June, two were damaged by air attacks on the first day and had to return. On the night of 7–8 June a Liberator of 224 Squadron, RAF, flown by F/O Kenneth Moore, RCAF, was credited with sinking U-629 and U-373 with depth charges in less than a half hour flying in bright moon light: a unique achievement. Of the four remaining Brest U-boats, U-413 was damaged by a Halifax of 502 Squadron, U-740 was sunk by a Liberator of 120 Squadron and U-821 was beaten-up by Mosquitos of 248 Squadron and then sunk by a Liberator from 206 Squadron. By 9 June only U-441 was still edging her way into the Channel. On 12 June Dönitz recalled all non-schnorkel boats. On 18 June U-441, still struggling to get home, was caught by a Wellington of 304 (Polish) Squadron and sunk. It was not until 15 June that the first schnorkel equipped U-boat reached the main assault area.

That same day the first of the Norwegian-based schnorkel-equipped U-boats announced her presence, when U-767 sank the frigate *Mourne* off Land's End. Air patrols over the northern transit routes were supposed to stop the arrival of these U-boats. But with fewer aircraft, worse weather and much greater distance they could only hope to impede movement and sink as many as fortune allowed. During June these patrols nonetheless accounted for eight U-boats, four of them claimed by 162 Squadron RCAF. The squadron was made up of the best Canadian aircrew in the western Atlantic and had been sent overseas in early 1944 to participate in the offensive against the U-boats. The General Officer Commanding No. 18 Group attributed their success to a 'magnificent system of training' within the squadron. If No. 18 Group got 'really good operational intelligence' the GOC recalled, 'we said, "Go on, we'll put 162 right in the middle."'

But it was dangerous work. In June 1944, 162 RCAF Squadron lost three Cansos, suffered thirteen dead aircrew and one POW. F/L David Hornell won a posthumous Victoria Cross for diving through withering fire from U-1222, sinking the U-boat and crashing into the sea on 24 June. F/O John Cruikshank, flying a Catalina of 210 Squadron, RAF, also won a VC flying the northern patrols in the summer of 1944. On 17 July he attacked U-347 well above the Arctic circle. When his depth charges refused to fall during his first pass, Cruickshank came back for a second run. This time U-347's fire was more accurate. One shell from the 37mm burst inside the Catalina, killing the navigator and wounding most of the rest of the crew, some seriously, and starting a fire. Cruikshank was later found to have seventy-two separate shrapnel wounds, two serious ones to the lungs and ten in his lower limbs. But he pressed on with the attack, placed the depth charges alongside U-347 and sank the U-boat without survivors. After the attack, Cruickshank collapsed at the controls and was laid on a bunk for the five hour return flight to Sullom Voe in the Shetlands. Refusing morphine lest it dull his senses, Cruickshank took the controls once again to set the battered Catalina down, and then the co-pilot taxied hard and drove the sinking aircraft ashore. Cruickshank survived; his was the only non-posthumous VC awarded for sinking a U-boat.

While airmen sank U-boats during June and July 1944 – the last occasion when air power was able to catch non-schnorkel-equipped submarines on the surface under normal operational conditions – the best of the Atlantic's naval A/S forces found the inshore an unforgiving place to hunt U-boats. Non-sub contacts abounded. There were an estimated 700 wrecks in the Channel, and the difficulty of classification of bottomed contacts led A/S specialists to hope that the Germans would stay in motion, since getting the submarine moving in the water mass greatly simplified the problem. The Germans knew this too, and their adoption of bottoming and schnorkel inshore created a whole new tactical problem. By operating in known shipping lanes, and using the ocean environment for cover, U-boats now simply allowed targets to come to them. For their part, the Allies also did not have to worry about diverting convoys, since the lurking submarines became a known and accepted risk, and support groups were used increasingly to reinforce escorts as shipping passed around or through choke points.

With U-boats now operating almost exclusively submerged, the hardest job which Allied hunters faced was localising them so they could be attacked. Schnorkel was virtually impossible to locate with existing radar, and it was estimated that snorts reduced the effectiveness of air searches by as much as ninety per cent. Naval escorts were then reduced to classifying every asdic contact, a task made even more laborious by the German practice of bottoming when being hunted – contrary to Admiralty estimates. The Canadian frigate *Grou*, operating without wreck charts, classified seventy bottom contacts during her first thirty-eight days in the Channel, about one every twelve hours. And this represented only one in every twenty bottom contacts she was likely to encounter in a twelve-hour period. HF/DF was never a success in the Channel because since the receiving stations were too far away, the accuracy of the fixes was seldom better than thirty miles, and few U-boats signalled anyway. Once a U-boat was located, all the problems of classification of the contacts and dealing with a cagey opponent remained. Difficult asdic conditions, a tide to move silently on and schnorkel allowed a skilled submariner a great deal of latitude in the last year of the war. The extent of this problem was yet to be fully demonstrated by the end of June 1944, but the trends were already apparent.

In the end, most hunting groups 'classified' suspicious contacts with high explosives. On 27 June off Cherbourg the RCN's EG 11 classified a contact by towing a depth charge on a length of cable fitted with a grappling hook. Once the grappling hook snagged the target, the charge was fired electronically. On the first occasion the towed charge produced evidence of a merchant ship. There were better ways. The officially sanctioned method was to lay depth charges alongside the contact with the aid of an echo sounder, creeping slowly along, placing the charges set to their maximum depth and then going full speed ahead while they 'cooked off' on the bottom. It was, as one Canadian recalled, an effective 'but damned dangerous' procedure. More than one ship was seriously damaged by her own charges in shallow water.

These methods were being developed through June, while the hunting groups dodged fleet class destroyers, GNATs, minefields, coast artillery and glider bombs. Only three U-boats were sunk in the Channel or its approaches by warships in that month. One of these went to fleet class destroyers of the 10th Flotilla. It was not until 25 June that the British Captain class frigates *Affleck* and *Balfour* sank U-1191 and HMS *Bickerton* sank U-269 that the A/S specialists began to sink submarines. Even Walker's illustrious EG 2 was shut out in June, and his sudden death on 9 July meant this most famous of submarine hunters – with more than twenty kills to his credit – made no contribution to this new kind of ASW.

Over the same month, the U-boat failed completely to interfere with or disrupt the Allied landings and the follow-on support. The great Wagnerian Gotterdammerung in the Channel, with the last of the U-boat fleet being thrown into a massive assault in the crucial area between Portsmouth and the invasion beaches, simply did not happen. Nor, indeed, was there a concurrent assault on the main transatlantic routes, which had been pulled tight in order to release escorts for the D-Day landings. To a considerable extent, the U-boat fleet, most of which was not yet equipped with schnorkels, was cowed by the quantity and quality of Allied anti-submarine operations. But the passivity of the still huge German submarine fleet in June 1944, while the Wehrmacht fought ferociously to expel the invasion from France, is one of the unexplained – indeed unexplored – issues of the war.

The U-boat fared no better in July, when the burden of anti-submarine work inshore shifted to warships. Of the nine U-boats destroyed off the French coast and in the Channel in the second month of the campaign, six fell to surface vessels. The only air successes, two U-boats destroyed, occurred in the Bay of Biscay. One U-boat was sunk by a mine in the approaches to Brest. The six sunk by surface vessels were all credited to different ships or groups: one each to EG 1, EG 2, EG 3, EG 11, 10th DF, and the escorts HMS *Wanderer* and HMS *Tavy*. The sinking of U-333 on the very last day of July by *Loch Killin* and *Starling* of EG 2 well to the west of Land's End was the first kill by squid during the campaign. If there was pattern to the July U-boat kills, it was geographical. Whereas action in June was concentrated either around Ushant or between Cap de la Hague and Start Point, in July activity was in the middle of the Channel, close to the main convoy routes to the Allied beach head. The assault area was the principal operational zone for U-boats, and the schnorkel-equipped U-boats revealed their presence by attempting – without much success – to attack shipping.

August brought yet another shift in pattern, one occasioned by the Allied breakout from Normandy and the rapid collapse of German armies in the west. This spelled the end for the U-boat bases in France. Hasty preparations were made to get every submarine to sea as quickly as possible, while those still on patrol were ordered to Norway. The evacuation of bases from Bordeaux to Brest presented the Allies with an excellent opportunity to destroy what remained of the German navy in France – especially the U-boat fleet. By early August patrols by striking and A/S forces were extended into the Bay of Biscay. It was there, on 6 August, that *Loch Killin* of EG 2 began the new Bay of Biscay campaign by sinking U-736 with her squid. EG 2, even without Walker, killed two more U-boats over the next week, getting a little help from aircraft. Their record was matched by the RCN's EG 11, a group of ageing destroyers taken off the North Atlantic convoys for the D-Day operations. They were manned by anti-submarine veterans and led by Cdr J.D. Prentice, RCNR, who was driven by the same zeal to kill U-boats as Walker. By the end of August Prentice's EG 11 had sunk three U-boats all on their own, including one 'classified' by using the new Mk X depth charge, a ton of high explosive fired from the old destroyers' torpedo tubes. During August much of this work was done within range of German coastal batteries while skirting mine fields, GNAT's, fast attack craft and more glider bombs. Reports and memories of the period indicate the men of the A/S groups were tired and edgy by August.

In many ways the new face of inshore ASW was characterised by the final U-boat kill of the summer campaign off France and England. On 31 August the Canadian frigate group EG 9 was patrolling off Land's End when they made contact with U-247. Surging tides and falling darkness made the contact hard to hold, and it was soon lost after a number of attacks by depth charges and hedgehog that produced a trace of oil. An organised search down the set of the tide resulted in a new contact early on 1 September, sitting on the bottom in forty-two fathoms. The frigate *Saint John* ran over the contact and made a trace with her echo sounder that produced a tell-tale spike in the middle indicating a conning tower. The frigate then laid two depth charge patterns over the U-boat, which resulted in a tearing explosion and more oil. CinC, Plymouth ordered EG 9 to remain on the contact, which it did throughout the night. Morning light revealed a long oil slick trailing off from the point of contact. *Saint John* was left to monitor the contact. Early in the afternoon she laid five depth charges alongside the contact using echo sounder, and then stood off to see what happened. The explosions finally brought a surge of debris to the surface, including an engine room log, charts, clothing, fittings, and other equipment, proof of U-247's catastrophic destruction.

The destruction of U-247 on 1 September 1944 marks the end of the summer inshore campaign that began with the invasion of France on 6 June. Only thirty schnorkel-equipped U-boats operated in the Channel, making forty-five individual sorties, a far cry from the numbers the Allies anticipated. On the whole, they found it difficult to get into the central Channel, although once there they found operational conditions good. Conditions in the U-boats were, nonetheless, appalling. U-218, which laid mines off Land's End on 20 June, suffered damage to her diesels that resulted in the venting of some exhaust gases into the submarine. Her log on 20 June reported,

> Several men suddenly taken ill during the forenoon. By noon two thirds of the crew are suffering from severe headaches and stomach ache, nausea and retching and are no longer fit for duty. The remainder... keep things going. There are several cases of fainting due to over exertion and carbon monoxide poisoning.

Navigation, too, was difficult from a submarine that spent all its time submerged. Charts were inaccurate, the coast hard to discern precisely through a periscope, and echo sounders difficult to use without giving away positions. U-boats struck bottom with some regularity. The navigation of U-763 was so far off that she eventually found herself – unwittingly – in Spithead, the very entrance to Portsmouth harbour.

In the end, the Allies took a heavy toll: twenty-two U-boats and a thousand crewmen lost between Ushant and Dover in the summer of 1944. In exchange for this sacrifice, twelve Allied ships (of all types) were sunk and five damaged. Over June, July and August the Allies sank thirty-six U-boats in the English Channel and the Bay of Biscay. Ten of these fell exclusively to aircraft and two to mines. Seven were accounted for by convoy escorts and fleet destroyers, and seventeen wholly or partly claimed by the A/S support groups.

Nothing the Germans did at sea in the summer of 1944 – the midget submarines, one-man torpedoes, glider bombs, aerial torpedo attacks, mines, coast artillery, small craft – affected the campaign in France or the movement of shipping in the Atlantic. In that sense, the Allied effort was entirely successful. But given the ultimate objective of preserving the integrity and morale of the U-boat fleet, and learning how to fight inshore and with the aid of schnorkels, the same might be said of the German campaign. As the British *Monthly Anti-Submarine Report* for December 1944 noted, 'We had been disappointed of a holocaust when U-boats failed to storm up the English Channel in the first week of June...', and '...we were again disappointed when they were flushed out of their French bases' in August. Moreover, as the bulk of the U-boat fleet escaped from France in August, the first serious attacks on cross-Channel shipping occurred in which four ships were sunk and two damaged. The attackers got clean away. One of them, U-480, which sank the Canadian corvette *Alberni*, the British minesweeper *Loyalty* and one freighter south of the Isle of Wight, was completely covered in a special rubber coating designed to absorb sound waves from asdics. Whether that new 'Alberich' skin saved her, or, like U-989, survival was primarily due to the skill of her captain is open to speculation. The fact remained that U-boats had struck and escaped retribution. The summer campaign of 1944 made it evident that there was much to learn about A/S operations against an enemy who was now never seen. The ocean environment and schnorkel gave submariners new life by late 1944. If that could be matched by high submerged speeds – and a way to keep Germany in the fight long enough – a successful renewal of the U-boat campaign in the Atlantic was likely.

9

Defeating the Old U-boats... Again! September 1944-May 1945

On 16 August 1944 U-482, an early type VIIC commanded by Count von Matushka, sailed from Bergen for the North Channel. The U-boat carried some of the latest improvements including schnorkel, the new 10cm radar detector *Tunis*, the first successful U-boat radar, the usual mix of acoustic and pattern-steering torpedoes, as well as 'submarine bubble-target' (SBT) asdic decoys. Matushka intended to operate in less than thirty fathoms and to use the inshore environment to his advantage.

Three aircraft and three anti-submarine vessels were sighted during the transit, but U-482 remained undetected and located two ships on its own radar. By 28 August Matushka was in the approaches to the North Channel, where he remained for the next two weeks. Navigation, often difficult from a schnorkelling U-boat, was easy because radio beacons and lighthouses were 'still operating as in peacetime'. During his whole cruise, the Count

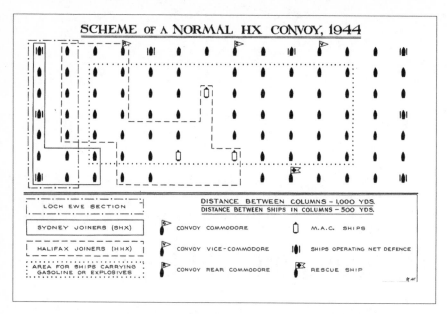

Scheme of a normal HX Convoy, 1944.

Convoy HXS 300 from a contemporary illustration.

surfaced only once to fix his position. Naval forces were all around, their Foxers and CATs creating a regular din, but Matushka was not intimidated. He kept his battery charged by schnorkelling briefly at night and resting on the bottom during the day, and then allowed targets to come to him.

The first to do so was the ten thousand ton tanker *Jacksonville* of convoy CU 36, on 31 August. The sinking prompted an intense search. Undeterred, Matushka destroyed the British corvette *Hurst Castle*, part of the force sent to hunt him. On 3 September U-482 was overrun by ONS 251, from which Matushka sank the Norwegian steamer *Fjordheim*. Finally, on 8 August, the tanker *Empire Heritage* and the small steamer *Pinto* were sunk from HX(F) 305 just fifteen miles from shore. With that U-482's cruise effectively ended. She arrived in Bergen on 26 September having travelled 2,729 miles – all but 256 of them fully submerged. Matushka claimed that he was never located by aircraft and never firmly fixed by asdic, a claim the British official historian accepted as 'well-founded'. As Roskill observed, the loss of these ships 'almost on our front doorstep and at our most sensitive spot [where the main transatlantic convoys funnelled into the Irish Sea]...was an unpleasant shock, the more so because all the victims were sailing in convoy.' The sinkings by U-482 suggested that the U-boat fleet retained significant combat power by the late summer of 1944. Admiral Horton, Commander in Chief, Western Approaches, was particularly anxious that this old U-boat fleet be decisively beaten and its morale crushed before the radically new type XXI and XXIII U-boats entered service.

However, in August and September there seemed little likelihood that this would happen before the Allies crossed the Rhine and ended the war. The British made plans to transfer the bulk of their fleet to the Pacific, leaving what was left of the Atlantic war for the Canadians to finish. The main transatlantic convoys were now entirely under RCN escort, and new Canadian support groups were forming almost weekly. Allied shipping moved safely in a complex web of well-escorted convoys, and the main routes

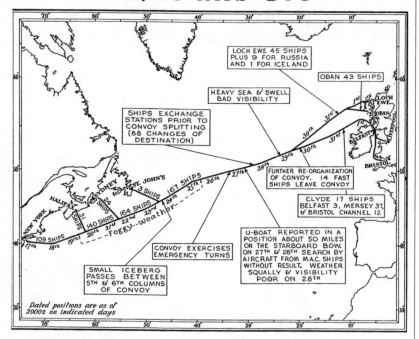

CONVOY HXS-300

LARGEST NORTH ATLANTIC TRADE CONVOY OF SECOND WORLD WAR

Sailed New York July 17, 1944 . Arrived Mersey August 3, 1944
Escort: one frigate and six corvettes of the R.C.N.

TOTAL MERCHANT SHIPS 167 (INCLUDING 4 M.A.C. SHIPS—1 NON-OPERATIONAL)

BRITISH	50		FOR U.K.	157
U.S.	75		FOR RUSSIA	9
OTHER ALLIES	39		FOR ICELAND	1
NEUTRAL	3			

Convoy in 19 columns covered area of about 30 square miles

CARGO CARRIED TO U.K.

	TONS		TONS
GRAIN	84,561	MOLASSES	37,500
SUGAR	84,948	IRON AND STEEL	36,705
OTHER FOODSTUFFS	47,167	OTHER GENERAL CARGO	80,699
LUMBER	35,588	VEHICLES AND TANKS	53,490
OIL	307,874	OTHER MILITARY EQUIPMENT	251,297

TOTAL 1,019,829 TONS

COMMODORE SIR A.T. TILLARD, K.B.E., D.S.O.
CASUALTIES-------------NONE
SHIPS RETURNING-----NONE
STRAGGLERS-----1 (ARRIVED AUGUST 5)

Convoy HXS 300.

were little more than tramlines. HX(S) 300, the largest convoy of the war, arrived in Britain in early August without loss, 167 ships under a modest close escort routed without diversion.

But the western Allies stalled at the Rhine in late September and it was soon clear that the war would not end before the spring of 1945. Sabotage, shortages of skilled workers and material, and Allied bombing delayed completion of the new U-boats, while their training areas in the Baltic were under continuous pressure from the Russians in the east and Allied aerial mining operations. The clock was winding down on the U-boat war, but new U-boats poured from yards and crews were found. Only the very low rate of U-boat losses through the last half of 1944 helped preserve the U-boat fleet's expanding expertise in inshore operations. Few submarines were now sunk by A/S aircraft and kills by warships over the autumn proved disappointingly low for the Allies. The hard-won expertise in inshore and fully submerged operations developing within the existing U-boat fleet was passed on to the crews of the new U-boats.

Reliance on schnorkelling coupled with dependence on bases in Norway nonetheless severely limited the operational range of the existing U-boat fleet. As the BdU war diary noted on the 15 September, 'the US coast, the Newfoundland area and also the St Lawrence' were the only overseas stations where type IX U-boats could operate with any hope of success. The smaller type VII U-boats were now considered so limited in range (in part because of habitability problems) that even the English Channel was thought beyond reach from Norwegian bases. The British expected the Germans to concentrate their efforts west of Ireland again, in the open ocean, in a repeat of the winter 1943-44 campaign. However, the Germans adapted quickly to inshore conditions and preferred to patrol where the Allies had difficulty finding them. For that reason, U-boat operations in September and October 1944 concentrated in the waters off northern Britain and eastern Canada.

The preferred Allied solution to this new problem was to establish barriers in deep water and kill U-boats before they got inshore. The burden of mid-ocean barrier operations in late 1944 fell to the USN. In mid-August two U-boats were en route to the Gulf of St Lawrence, U-802 and U-541, while U-1229 was on its way to land spies in Maine. All were boldly making time on the surface as they approached the Canadian coast. USS *Bogue*'s group operated against them, while RCAF aircraft flew sweeps along their estimated tracks, and RCN support groups patrolled the outer edges of the Canadian zone. Only U-1229 was sunk, by aircraft from *Bogue*. The other two operated with limited success inside the Canadian zone.

Thus, there were at least two U-boats loose in Canadian waters when the Admiralty appealed to the RCN in early September for additional support groups in British waters. To find them, the close escort groups in the mid-ocean were reduced to five ships, all fast escorts were withdrawn from 'B' groups, escorts for the Sierra Leone and Mediterranean convoys reduced to three corvettes (with the French coast now clear, these convoys were well away from any major threat), and the new Canadian support groups went overseas almost as fast as they were ready. The British also occasionally now used close escort groups for searches in the approaches to the North Channel, which accounted for two U-boats in early September. These, and the frigate *Saint John*'s U-boat in the early hours of 1 September, represented the only kills by Allied warships in the main North Atlantic theatres during a month when some twenty U-boats operated in northern British waters.

Hunting forces from the Channel and Biscay began to redeploy northwards at the end of August. Here patrol areas were much larger than the Channel and it took time to become familiar with all the non-subs and local conditions. One saving grace for the Channel veterans was that the northern areas contained far fewer wrecks, only two-and-a-half per ten square mile area. But the lower incidence of non-sub features in northern waters was offset by the absence of the radio navigation aids and shore-based radars. Wrecks and non-sub contacts were reported and buoyed, but not with the same accuracy as further south. A crash programme of extending radio navigation in the north was begun, so 'that escort vessels should not waste their time hunting and attacking charted wrecks in a mistake for bottomed U-boats.'

To reduce the problem posed by U-boats on the bottom, the Admiralty also began a large-scale inshore deep mine laying scheme that continued to the end of the war. Mining St George's Channel was part of the plan to change the main entrance to Britain for ocean convoys from the North Channel – now clearly within reach of Norwegian-based U-boats – to the Southern Approaches. The first ocean convoy to use St George's Channel since June 1940, HX 306, passed through in mid-September.

Meanwhile, much of the action concentrated north of Britain, where an attempt was made to establish a surface and air barrier to stop the movement of U-boats. This effort was almost entirely futile. Bomber Command sank more U-boats (four) in a single raid on Bergen on 4 October than A/S forces achieved in two months of patrols. The best chances came in September, when the traffic was highest, and two U-boats in transit were sunk by Coastal Command aircraft. But October was a dismal month for the A/S specialists and the northern barrier forces. Most of the U-boat fleet was regrouping for a major offensive and there were few U-boats at sea. Of the six sunk in the North Atlantic during that month, the Germans themselves accounted for four: two were lost in collisions with other German ships, one by a German mine off Norway, and one was believed lost due to a schnorkelling accident. Of the two sunk by Allied forces, one went to the Fleet Air Arm and the other – the only kill of October by a Support Group in the North Atlantic – was by the Canadian frigates *Annan* and *Loch Achanalt* of EG 6. The few U-boats at sea were suppressed, but this was put down to a generally passive nature on their part.

There was no gainsaying that something had to be done to increase the chances of killing submarines, but Horton was also anxious to keep the Germans from sinking ships, too. These were not mutually exclusive tasks. He instructed support groups in September that, 'During the present inshore threat to our shipping in the Western Approaches,' their duty was to concentrate on 'the safe passage of the convoy through the local area'. That signal was reinforced a month later when a new set of patrol instructions for support groups in British waters was issued. The best place to find U-boats was around the targets they sought. One major post-war British study attributed this shift in emphasis back to close support of convoy movements with a noticeable increase in the number of U-boat kills by early 1945. There were, however, other mitigating factors by then, not least of which was increased U-boat activity and improving skills on the part of the Allies.

Concentration of hunting around convoys was also a much better way to use very limited resources. With some 300 destroyers and escort vessels slated for departure to the Far East, the RN was hard pressed in the autumn of 1944. Canada eased the RN's problems somewhat by providing about forty per cent of the hunting groups in UK waters in this last phase of the war. This was done by stripping virtually all of the available ships from the Canadian north-west Atlantic – just about the only foreign theatre that schnorkelling U-boats could reach – and relying on a deep-sea barrier of USN hunter killer CVE groups patrolling in deep water just outside the Canadian zone.

By the autumn of 1944 the mastery of schnorkel by Germany's submariners had all but eliminated the possibility of locating U-boats on the surface or even with 10cm radar. Airborne 10cm radar could detect a schnorkel only under good conditions, and at barely one tenth of the range possible on fully surfaced U-boats. It helped if the radar operator had some inkling of what to look for in the clutter of his screen. The situation was better, but only just, for 10cm sets fitted to warships. Trials on a mock-up schnorkel under 'good sea conditions' revealed that it could be detected, but only at comparatively short ranges. A practical maximum range under moderate conditions for the 271Q set was about 4,000 yards. Ships equipped with type 272 and type 277, like some of the Lochs and Castle class ships, stood a much better chance. By early October it was clear that the best solution to the schnorkel was 3cm radar, and some sets were already at sea. The best was the USN's SL radar, which was also fitted to the RN's American-built Captain and Colony (a version of the River) class frigates. Historian Peter Elliott claimed that the SL was so good that, 'even planks with nails in them, floating in the water, were easily detected at a mile or two'. As the last winter of the war wore on, the Allies came to rely more and more on their new 3cm sets, including those carried by aircraft.

But it would take more than good radar to solve the riddle of inshore ASW, especially the problem of finding the U-boat in the first place. The localisation problem could be solved by expanding the use of harbour defence asdics, a series of asdic transducers laid on the seabed and operated from ashore. A variation on this theme, a line of moored sonobuoys, was eventually tried off Ireland by the RN in 1945, but with little success. The concept evolved after the war into an extensive system of seabed sensors known as SOSUS. Blimps equipped with magnetic anomaly detectors were considered, but nothing came of the effort. Perhaps the most ingenious idea was sowing the Cabot Strait, between Canada and Newfoundland, with acoustic homing torpedoes which would respond to the distinctive sound of U-boat engines, an idea that had to wait for the invention of the microchip to permit the necessary discrimination between friend and foe. For the most part, the Allies had to rely on a 'flaming datum' – a vessel hit by a torpedo – to be sure that a U-boat was present. It was not the best way to proceed.

However, localising the U-boat was only the start of the problem. It then had to be precisely located and attacked, and that meant a good understanding of the ocean environment itself. The Americans were already using bathythermography (BT) readings in deep water to obtain an 'assured range' for their asdic searches. There was no question that these USN operations were highly effective. But in the autumn of 1944 no one was sure that BT would work well inshore. In August 1944 the RCN's scientists reported that, 'Assured ranges are zero during the winter months', off Halifax, 'and deep submarines could approach to close quarters without detection.' Things were little better in summer months when, because of the warming of the surface layer, 'assured ranges are very short.' The best conditions, as sailors already knew, were in the spring and autumn months. Nonetheless, the report concluded that BT readings would be 'of great importance in the operations of A/S flotillas.' The impact of bottom conditions was another matter entirely. Scientists suggested that it was often better to listen for U-boats than to fill the water with noise. But naval officers preferred to harass U-boat commanders with active searches in hopes that it would get them moving and eventually into the asdic's search beam. Nonetheless, by autumn 1944 the RCN was using BT under all conditions for its 'tactical value.'

The British, too, were no strangers to the problem of layers and their impact on sound propagation. They had noticed the effect of daily surface warming on asdic ranges in the Mediterranean before the war (the same phenomenon noticed by the USN in the Caribbean which led to the development of the BT), and had published a confidential book on the subject (CB 1835[2]) in 1931. However, the initial British request for BT equipment from the US in late 1943 was destined for use by submariners. By mid-September 1944 the Admiralty reported that 'all the bathythermographs in the United Kingdom have been fitted or allocated to submarines.'

What seems to have prompted RN interest in BT use in 1944 was not the problem in UK waters, but those on the arctic route. Asdic conditions for the Russian convoys were so poor that Captain Walker believed that only aircraft could kill U-boats effectively in that area. The problem was better defined by BT readings done by HMS *Saumarez* during a Russian convoy in September 1944. These revealed frequent sharp negative drops in temperature at roughly 150-200 feet – the deep, arctic current, which lay under the vestiges of the Gulf Stream. As *Saumarez*'s captain, Cdr P.G.L. Cazalet, RN, reported, this 'confirmed, in the main, what many of us suspected, i.e., that the submarine at 200 feet or more was almost impossible to detect.' In other areas BT readings revealed uniform temperature with depth, which produced good asdic conditions. Cazalet wanted to use BT to determine when conditions were good for asdic to ensure that time would not be wasted hunting for a U-boat that could never be found.

While the Allies brought the new science of oceanography to bear in the ASW, the war at sea continued unabated. In late 1944 the U-boat fleet remained a serious threat, and the only military arm of the Reich that showed real growth in fighting potential. Its crews were now experienced and confident in inshore operations, new equipment and a more efficient schnorkel design introduced in October greatly improved operational performance and survival rates. By the autumn of 1944 the loss rate among U-boats was down to its 1942 average, a factor which not only sustained operations well but had a positive influence on morale. Moreover, despite the virtual collapse of the German air defences and the presence of Allied armies on the border, U-boat construction reached its wartime peak in December 1944 with thirty-one submarines launched; twenty-one were type XXI.

As early as 9 October British Naval Intelligence warned that Germany 'planned to renew her U-boat offensive with new types of U-boats at the end of the year.' Further intercepts confirmed this warning. German agents in Madrid were instructed that information on sailings from North America was 'most urgently desired from December', and plans for U-boat co-operation with long-range aircraft were deciphered. At the end of October a special appreciation issued by the RN Operational Intelligence Centre concluded that an 'all out U-boat campaign' would commence in the near future: probably sometime between mid-November and mid-December.

The drift towards such a renewed campaign was evident by November, as the Germans also discovered that they could get more range out of their schnorkel-equipped U-boats than previously thought. *Annan*'s U-boat, U-1006, was one of four type VIIc despatched in October to the English Channel. Eight more followed from Norway in late November. The movement of U-boats back into the Channel eventually drew most UK-based support groups south again by December. The deployment was timed to meet the arrival of the U-boats from Norway. Not all of them made it. Two were sunk in transit by British support groups in mid-December, and U-1209, harassed by the RCN's EG 26, ran aground on Wolfe Rock and was a total loss. However, the remaining five arrived on station for the commencement of the new offensive. Meanwhile, others were deployed into the mid-ocean to provide the weather information crucial to the launching of the last great German offensive in the west.

The German army struck through the Ardennes forest on 16 December, taking the Allies completely unaware, and threatened to drive a wedge between the Anglo-Canadian and American armies. Western Approaches' forces were stretched and barely up to the task of handling the surge of U-boat attacks which followed. The RAF complained that its U-boat sightings were not quickly pursued by naval vessels, the Russian convoys were under attack again, the RN was five support groups short of the twenty-three estimated minimum required and the number of U-boats in UK waters was rising. More support groups were also needed for the mid-ocean, where Dönitz was likely to strike first with his new U-boats, and for the Canadian zone. Sinkings of Allied shipping had not increased, but the aim of British anti-submarine policy was to ensure that they did not, for fear it would enable U-boat commanders 'to regain confidence and get their tails up again'.

In fact, the first blows of the final offensive had already fallen. One ship was sunk in St George's Channel on 10 December and the steamer *Silverlaurel* off Cornwall on 18 December, despite the presence of eight support groups in the area. On 23 December U-772 sank two ships off the Cherbourg peninsula and then late in the afternoon of Christmas Eve U-486 found and sank the 11,000-ton American troopship *Leopoldville* off Cherbourg, with the loss of about 800 men. U-boat activity also increased 3,000 miles away. On 21 December an explosion rocked the freighter *Samtucky* in the approaches to Halifax harbour, and on Christmas Eve a GNAT from U-806 destroyed the minesweeper *Clayoquot*. The war that would not end was heating up. The attacks caused a wave of anxiety in senior British circles, with the First Sea Lord's presentation to Cabinet on 27 December 'rather a sorry tale of losses'. Three ships had been sunk and two escorts damaged off Cherbourg since 19 December. Three ships went down in the Channel on 28-29 December. The RN delayed the despatch of ships to the Pacific and two escort groups were moved from Gibraltar to the Channel.

In exchange, only four U-boats were sunk by anti-submarine forces during that month, a slight increase from November. For the Allies the only good news at the end of December was the stalling of the Ardennes offensive, the intelligence report of a delay of at least two months in the expected arrival of the new German type XXI and XXIII U-boats and the fact that Bomber Command was being brought onside to stem the rising tide of new high-speed submarines. Nonetheless, there was a sense that a final confrontation with the U-boat fleet was looming. With the new types available for service, the British warned in early January, the Germans would have at sea by March 1945 more submarines than they did during the crisis of March 1943. This time, however, there would be a 'two front' war – major campaigns inshore and in the mid-ocean. This was, in fact, just what Dönitz hoped to achieve.

The Allies now scrambled to assemble as many A/S vessels and ships in the North Atlantic as they possibly could, even if it meant delaying the British build-up in the Pacific. 'We are,' the First Sea Lord wrote to the Commander of the British Pacific Fleet on 19 January 1945, '...having a difficult time with the U-boats.'

There is no doubt this schnorkel has given them a greater advantage than we first reckoned on. I believe some of them have done as much as six weeks at sea without surfacing. The scientists have not yet caught up and the air are about ninety per cent out of business. The asdic is also failing us. The U-boat has found out that, if he conducts his patrol close inshore or in confined waters where there is a good tidal stream the tide rips will to a great extent defeat the asdic – so it is about fifty per cent, I imagine, out of business. As you probably know, they have been active and caused us losses in the last few weeks in the Channel, off Holyhead and one especially bold one penetrated into the Firth of Clyde. Science having failed us for the moment we are entering on an extensive deep mining programme, starting by mining them out of the Irish Sea and the English Channel and then extending the minefields to the seaward to try and keep them in deep water again. This, of course, will take time but we hope to finish in the early summer.

Adm Sir Andrew Cunningham's gloomy estimation reflected his own ignorance, badgering by Churchill and the need to explain to Adm Bruce Fraser why his ships would not be coming. The air was indeed largely out of the business of killing U-boats. But it was air power that kept the submarines down. As for the asdic, it would work well enough once the U-boat was localised and increased German attacks on shipping would provide that information for waiting hunters.

The USN, accustomed to operations in deeper waters with better asdic conditions, watched the Anglo-Canadian struggle with inshore waters with interest in 1944. Since September their highly successful carrier-based hunter killer groups had been without targets in the mid-Atlantic. In the autumn of 1944 the USN kept one Task Unit of four destroyer escorts at Argentia in readiness to forestall westward U-boat movements. The USN also sent help into the Canadian zone in early 1945, where they could gain some experience in inshore ASW and to 'familiarise themselves with every phase of Canadian anti-submarine warfare technique'.

Strapped for resources because most of the RCN's hunting forces were in UK waters, the Canadians welcomed the American offer. By late December, Task Units 27.1.2 and 27.1.3, each composed of four destroyer escorts, were searching the comparatively deep and favourable waters south of Sable Island under Canadian operational control. The USN gained a much better appreciation of the inshore problem in January 1944, when Americans helped hunt in the approaches to Halifax. The first instance occurred on

4 January, when U-1232 attacked several convoys which, according to the enterprising Kapitänzursee Kurt Dobratz, had 'to maintain a tight and rigid route between shoals and banks and cannot escape.'

Such was the case with the Boston to Halifax convoy BX 141 on 14 January, nineteen ships strung-out in single file along the swept channel approaches to the harbour. Dobratz hit three ships in quick succession as the convoy, in Michael Hadley's words, began 'to pile up like a traffic jam.' The escort was ordered to 'adopt scare tactics', by dropping random depth charges in likely firing positions, which saved two other ships and nearly sank U-1232 when the frigate *Ettrick* ran right over it. The frigate's magazine crew heard a dull boom, which sounded like a glancing blow on a submerged rock. In fact, U-1232 missed certain destruction by a matter of inches, and was lucky to limp home with a crushed conning tower.

That was as close as the RCN's hunters would get. Asdic conditions were so poor that contact could not be made on the stern of *British Freedom*, which lay on the bottom as her bows pointed skyward in the crisp winter air. On 17 January the USN's Task Group 22.9 joined the hunt for a U-boat now long gone. The next convoy to leave Halifax was heavily escorted, and covered by a smoke screen maintained by minesweepers.

The inability of the searching forces to obtain any firm contact on U-1232 also highlighted the problem of asdic conditions inshore. The RCN followed current Western Approaches procedures: active searches during the day, and alternating 'transmitting listening watches' at night in hopes that the sound of a schnorkelling U-boat might be heard. Trials conducted later in the spring revealed that under good conditions ships travelling at four knots could obtain passive contact with schnorkelling U-boats at 2,500 yards, and 1,500 at speeds up to eight. Halifax-based groups also used bathythermographs to modify this British practice by indicating when a passive search might be better during daylight hours as well.

A further perspective on the intractability of the inshore problem was gained when USN Task Group 22.9 commander, Cdr V.A.

Issacs, USN, reported candidly to the CinC, US Atlantic Fleet on 21 January that USN procedures and doctrine, designed primarily for deep ocean operations, were inappropriate and would have to be substantially altered. A more detailed American assessment of the difference between inshore and offshore ASW was produced by the commander of TG 22.10, who arrived with his group in Halifax at the end of January. Hunting inshore, the report noted, was affected by 'the proximity of land and shoals, the positions of two swept channels, numerous aids to navigation, including two lightships, the presence of several small A/S vessels assigned continuous patrol in the same area, the presence of a similar task group (EG) in an adjacent area, and the constant flow of merchant shipping...'. 'One regular encounter,' the report noted with some pique, 'was with a minesweeping group which maintained the right of way whether we had a good contact or not.' This was a new experience. After spending February off the Canadian coast, Cdr E.H. Headland, the senior officer of TG 22.10, went to Block Island Sound to conduct trials on locating a bottomed submarine.

The drama off Halifax in January had its counterpart overseas, when U-boats penetrated the Irish Sea for the first time since 1939. Six merchant ships were sunk, two others and two escorts damaged in an area long considered safe. Three new Task Forces were promulgated under Operation CE: TF 37 covering the North Channel and area north of the Isle of Man, TF 36 from the Isle of Man to the northern edge of Cardigan Bay and TF 38 covering St George's Channel. These were tasked first and foremost with destruction of the enemy. A major redeployment of forces took place during January, with up to six support groups assigned to these new duties. The increase in U-boat activity in the eastern Atlantic brought only a slight rise in the number of kills by naval A/S forces during January; there were four, one up from December. All of these fell to RN warships.

At the end of January 1945, then, the Allies experienced a marked increase in shipping losses with little improvement in the rate of U-boat kills. This was, however, a transitory phase.

According to the RN's official historian, by early February there were fifty-one U-boats on patrol off, or on passage to and from, the British Isles. Eight Allied merchant ships were lost in those waters during February 1945, three in the Irish Sea and five in the Channel, and two warships. However, A/S forces destroyed nine submarines, a marked improvement over January and one usually ascribed to increased support for convoy movements. That was only true in part.

The laurels in the A/S war in February 1945 went to the frigates of the RN's EG 10, and their senior officer, Cdr P.W. Burnett, RN, a qualified anti-submarine specialist who had led the Canadian group C.2 through 1943 and early 1944. In February Burnett's group – a nice combination of Captain Class carrying the latest 3cm radar and Loch Class with the latest in asdic sensors and weaponry – was on patrol north of the Shetlands when they sank three U-boats during an epic two-week offensive patrol. In all instances the U-boats were discovered on asdic by the same operator in the same ship, HMS *Bayntun*. The first, U-1279, was located on 3 February in deep water (600 fathoms, so no chance of bottoming) and was destroyed by the squid of *Loch Eck*. On 14 February, *Bayntun*'s asdic operator got a second firm contact on U-989. The U-boat was fatally damaged by squid bombs from *Loch Dunvegan*. EG 10's final success came three days later when *Bayntun* located U-1278 and sank her with the first hedgehog attack. Burnett knew and trusted his asdic operator, and never doubted the rating's faith in his ability. For the staff at Western Approaches Command, EG 10's kills demonstrated 'the very great hitting power of the Squid...'.

Four other U-boats were sunk in the Channel during February, where the action was concentrated. One was by an RAF aircraft, one was shared by various forces and one each was claimed by EG's 2 and 3. In the Channel many of the large and important oceanic convoys were heavily supported, with advanced screens to push them through any wayward attacker. But much of the action off Cornwall centred around the small coastal BTC-TBC convoys.

These were 'supported' by taking station three to four miles behind and waiting to pounce on any U-boat rash enough to attack. Such 'trolling' for U-boats suggests a relationship between higher shipping and higher U-boat losses.

U-boat hunting off Cornwall in February 1945 demonstrated clearly to the senior officer of the RN's EG 3 that it was 'difficult in inshore anti-submarine operations for an assorted force to co-ordinate in close harmony as a team.' This, he went on to point out, was not due to unwillingness on the part of the escorts sent to help, but because the job required 'experience, training and the best equipment'. Ships not equipped or trained to recognise non-sub contacts simply wasted ammunition and time, and confused the search 'by unreliable reports.' In its next contact with a U-boat on 24 February EG 3 restricted its help to EG 15, when they found and sank U-480 after another attack on a BTC convoy. The other kill in February was recorded by the Canadian frigate *Saint John* of EG 9 in Moray Firth.

The destruction of U-309 on 16 February also marked the end of EG 9 as an operational group due to the stress of inshore operations based on depth charges. 'In recent months the 9th EG has been [on] operation almost entirely in shallow coastal waters,' the group's SOE wrote, 'making daily and sometimes hourly attacks on bottomed contacts, and the average monthly expenditure of D/C's and H/H has been equivalent to the normal annual expenditure by ships operating in deep water.' All of these attacks, he noted, were made at the proper speed (fifteen knots), but the cumulative effect on the ships of such regular pounding in shallow water effectively eliminated EG 9 from the war. By 18 February, only HMCS *Loch Alvie* was fit for operations. *Saint John* was shipping thirty tons of water a day and could only keep compartments clear by continuous pumping. *Port Colborne* had leaks in her distiller machinery attributed to the pounding of explosives and was declared unfit for operations, as was *Nene*. *Monnow* leaked badly enough to require immediate docking 'before any serious damage was done'. The men, too, were exhausted by the constant vigil. Some Canadian groups adopted the habit of steaming into deep mine-fields and lying dormant for several hours while key personnel slept.

EG 9's modest contribution to sinking U-boats was part of a brightening picture overall for the Allies during February. U-boat kills were up, and the type XXI submarine was further delayed by bomber strikes and the mining of training areas. By mid-February British operational intelligence estimated that the sixty-four already in commission were plagued by problems. According to deciphered signals, the Germans did not expect the type XXIs to become operational in numbers before June. Only one, U-2511, was well advanced and the intelligence people watched her progress with great interest.

The delay in the arrival of the type XXI also meant that the Allies could concentrate efforts on defeating the old U-boats and thereby avoid the spectre of a 'two front' war. Everything was now to be sacrificed to holding, or defeating the existing U-boat threat for the next six months and, if possible, driving them out into deep water. Destroyers were recalled from the Mediterranean as Cunningham collected all 'the escort vessels I could lay my hands upon...', even to the point of battling Churchill over the release of trawlers to the fishing fleet, and ordering that 'all refits were to be postponed, and that even ships with only one propeller working were to continue to run'.

That victory was achieved over the next month. During March fifteen U-boats were sunk in British waters, for the loss of ten merchant ships and three warships. The result was the best score of U-boat kills by A/S forces for over a year. Six U-boats were sunk in the English Channel, two on mines, one by grounding and three by British support groups. By the end of March the Channel was largely abandoned by the Germans. The RN also accounted for all three U-boats patrolling the channel between the mainland and the Outer Hebrides, all of them succumbing to the hedgehog and depth charges of EG 21's Captain Class frigates. One U-boat operating off Scotland was sunk by the South African frigate *Natal*. Canadian support groups claimed two of the three U-boats sunk in the Irish Sea and the North Channel during March. One of them, U-1003, was awarded after the U-boat, travelling on its schnorkel at night, rammed the frigate HMCS *New Glasgow* of EG 26. To the war-weary staff at the Admiralty the incident was an occasion for some mirth. 'Does *New Glasgow* get an 'A'?!!' an Admiralty staff officer wrote with a delightful double entendre – an 'A' assessment was given to a U-boat 'Known Sunk'. As one staff officer noted rather puckishly, if *New Glasgow* was awarded credit for U-1003, 'won't this lead to a claim by [the] Wolf Rock light-house keeper?' – where U-1208 grounded in December while being pursued by the same Canadian group (EG 26 had tried to claim that one, too!). The solution in the case of U-1003 was to award the 'kill' to *New Glasgow* and say no more – but the frigate's captain was not awarded the usual DSC!

The total for March of fifteen brought the number of U-boats sunk by A/S forces in UK waters since the start of 1945 to thirty-five. This, at last, was U-boat sinking on a significant scale. The trend was not lost on the Germans either. Although their command and control system was collapsing, and few U-boats used radios at sea (only thirty of the 114 U-boats which sailed on operations from February to the end of the war reported their arrival in the Atlantic) BdU was generally aware of the increased level of losses in British inshore waters. These could not be sustained, and so at the end of March large-scale deployments to inshore UK waters ceased. This was the victory Horton had sought since the previous summer.

By mid-April U-boats had largely abandoned British coastal waters, and were concentrated 200-300 miles out to sea. Eighteen U-boats operated in the South Western Approaches during April and the first week of May, and the Admiralty deployed support groups of Captain Class frigates to deal with them. They accounted for three and aircraft sank three more. The total of U-boat kills by A/S forces in the eastern Atlantic in April 1945 was fifteen. The bulk of killing in the last days of the war, roughly twenty-three U-boats sunk at sea from 1-10 May, was the work of

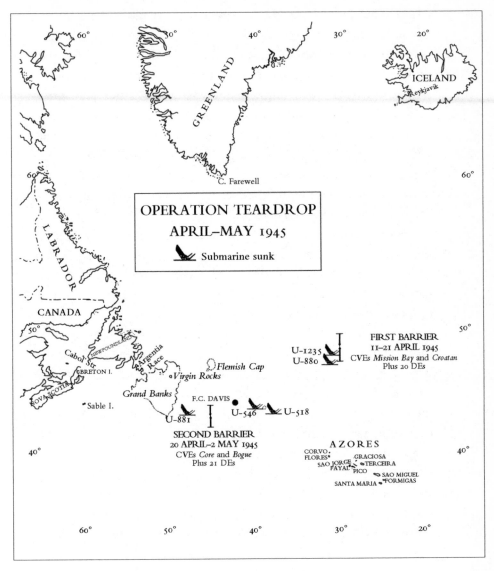

Operation Teardrop.

Allied tactical air power, as Germany collapsed and U-boats made one final desperate attempt to save themselves by fleeing to Norway.

The qualified victory in the eastern Atlantic was mirrored in the mid-ocean and off eastern North America, where U-boat operations also continued uninterrupted until the bitter end. USS *Lowe* sank U-866 a few miles south-west of Sable Island at 10:19 Z on 18 March. When the group's senior officer was not satisfied with oil and a bit of debris, *Lowe* and *Menges* pounded the wreck with the new Mk 8 depth charge. This weapon had a dual-action detonator and could be fired either by water pressure, like a standard depth charge, or magnetically in response to a target's magnetic signature. U-866 was plastered with nearly a hundred of these over the next two days. When they were done there was little doubt that U-866 lay shattered on the bottom. The USN repeated the feat a month later when U-369 was sunk just a few miles south of the wreck of U-866.

In the meantime the burden of the action shifted seaward, to the mid-ocean, where intelligence plotted a pack of seven U-boats sweeping westward along the convoy routes towards North America. Dönitz was staging his last pack operation of the war. But the Americans had been fearful since the end of 1944 of a submarine-launched missile attack against American cities, and had prepared for a massive barrier operation to forestall it. As a result, when group Seewolf deployed in early April, four escort carriers and over forty destroyer escorts in two successive barriers were ready. Code-named Operation Teardrop, the first barrier deployed north of the Azores on 11 April destroyed two U-boats on 15 April, and then a third on 21 April as the barrier moved westward following the movements of the pack. By then a second barrier force of two CVE's and over twenty destroyer escorts was deployed south of Flemish Cap. It destroyed a fourth U-boat of group Seewolf on 24 April following an exhausting ten-hour hunt. By then Dönitz had ordered three other U-boats westward to hunt off the American seaboard. All of this was followed by Allied intelligence, and as the Germans moved further westwards the Americans put every ship to sea, three carriers and over thirty DEs. On 5 May they located U-881 south of the Grand Banks and sank it. That accounted for five of the seven U-boats assigned to Seewolf. The other two surrendered at sea following the German capitulation.

The only U-boat to make it into American waters in the spring of 1945, U-853 revealed herself by torpedoing a ship off Block Island on 6 May. These were the same waters where TG 22.14 had conducted trials on a bottomed submarine two months before. Not surprisingly, the USN made short work of the U-boat. The success of American forces in the mid-ocean and western Atlantic in April 1945 was just a sample of the power latent in the US Atlantic Fleet. 'The USN had such enormous forces available,' the RCAF official history concluded, 'that in April and May 1945, without denuding American waters, it could and did maintain nearly as many ships and aircraft in the Canadian zone as the entire naval and air strength normally available to the commander-in-chief Canadian north-west Atlantic.'

Allied A/S forces inflicted a major defeat on German's old U-boat fleet in the dying days of the war, but there was little cause for celebration. Just a few weeks following the end of hostilities, Captain C.D. Howard-Johnston, Director of the Anti-U-boat Division of the Admiralty, observed, 'the new U-Boat with new propulsion, the new torpedoes, the new W/T gear, has enabled the U-boat arm to complete this war to all intents and purposes undefeated at sea'. His sentiment was widely shared. Captain Stephen Roskill, the RN's official historian, concluded in the penultimate draft of his history that, 'We never gained a firm and final mastery over the U-boats.' The British government objected to that conclusion, and forced him to change it to, 'we did not gain so high a degree of mastery as would have forced them to withdraw from our coastal waters – as the heavy losses inflicted in the Atlantic in May 1943 forced them to withdraw from that ocean'. The basis of Roskill's position was simply that, on 5 May 1945, there were twenty-five U-boats either inshore or on passage to or from inshore UK waters and that these in turn were tying down 400 A/S vessels and 800 aircraft.

It was, perhaps, a rather large price to pay to keep the U-boats in check, but the U-boat fleet and its personnel in particular paid an enormous price for their persistence. Of the 830 U-boats that participated in operations during the war (a total of 1,162 were built), no fewer than 696 were destroyed by the Allies, an operational loss rate of 83.9 per cent. Personnel losses were equally staggering. Of the 40,900 men who served in U-boats between 1939 and 1945, 25,870 died with their submarines, giving the U-boat service a fatal casualty rate of sixty-three per cent – the highest of any service during the war. When the 5,000 prisoners of war are added to this tally, the total casualty rate for the U-boat service jumps to seventy-six per cent. Despite all this, the U-boat service remained bowed but not broken when the war ended in early May 1945.

In contrast, Allied defence of shipping was so overpowering that at no point between the end of May 1943 and May 1945 were Allied plans or operations threatened by the German campaign in the Atlantic. Indeed, Atlantic shipping moved steadily and routinely throughout the war despite German efforts to disrupt it. Although some 2,452 ships were sunk in the Atlantic theatre (including the Russian routes) – almost half of all those lost to enemy action worldwide – nearly half of that figure, over 1,000 ships, went down in 1942 and most of these in the western hemisphere where the sensible precautions that formed the bedrock of Allied victory in the Atlantic were not taken. The German attack on shipping was dramatic and dangerous, and it had a profound impact on Britain's long-term economic viability. But it was also ultimately futile.

10
The Crisis That
Never Was

By the spring of 1945 Dönitz had struggled for nearly two years to introduce a radically new type of submarine, one which would turn the tide in the Atlantic war in Germany's favour. It was a monumental project, fraught with delays of all kinds, from technical problems and haste, to sabotage and aerial assault. In the last months of the war, in particular, as Germany's transportation crumbled under relentless attack from Allied bombers, the dispersed nature of the programme became one of its great handicaps. It simply became impossible to move the large sub-assemblies of the new U-boats to their final assembly yards – and those yards themselves were bombed ceaselessly as the war drew to a close.

The delay in the arrival of these new subs was, however, only partially due to the general impact of Allied strategic bombing. Dönitz's decision to go straight into series production before the problems evidenced in the early models were fixed meant that first type XXI's failed to reach their designed capabilities. So the first wave of this new generation of submarine was relegated to training. It was not until 31 April 1945 – nearly two full years since the programme had been given top priority – that the first type XXI U-boat, U-2511, left Norway on an operational cruise. Five more were scheduled to follow in early May; nearly 100 in total were in commission, working-up, undergoing trials or en route to their operational bases. It was little wonder, therefore, that senior British officials were deeply concerned about ending the war as soon as possible.

Allied intelligence in the autumn of 1944 had a very good picture of what to expect from the type XXI U-boat. Displacement was estimated at 1,200 tons (actually 1,600 tons), a surface speed of perhaps twenty knots (actually fifteen), and a maximum submerged speed of roughly fifteen to eighteen knots (actually a little over seventeen knots). By October the British believed that perhaps as many as sixty were completed, with fifteen ready for operations. By early November the estimates had grown to twenty-four ready for operations, with a further seventy-one under construction or fitting out, just about spot on. Estimates of the number of the smaller, inshore type XXIII U-boat, were good too, sixteen for operations and twenty-six building.

Dönitz's excitement – and Allied anxiety – about the type XXI was not misplaced. Schnorkel, improved acoustics and weapons made the type XXI a more potent weapon than the Allies realised. Improved design in the hull shape, in the schnorkel itself and in batteries meant that the type XXI had to schnorkel for only three hours a day to keep its batteries fully charged. Running on batteries alone it could cover 300 miles at five knots, three times farther and twice as fast as old U-boats on batteries, before needing to raise the schnorkel. This was enough to clear most barrier operations, and it more than doubled the area to be searched in hunts to exhaustion. Increased submerged efficiency gave the new type XXI enough range to go as far as Cape Town and back without refuelling, and to do so comfortably. It was also equipped with a sophisticated passive sonar array capable of tracking fifty individual ships up to 7,000 metres away, and sending targeting data to the torpedoes. Most of the latter were new pattern-running torpedoes that could be fired into a convoy with a theoretical hit probability of ninety-five to ninety-nine per cent – a result actually achieved on trials. Moreover, with the new passive sensor, the U-boat did not need to surface to fire. A type XXI could tuck itself under a convoy and engage targets until it ran out of torpedoes. And to tackle escorts, a new GNAT, the 'T 11', was developed with an improved homing head impervious to Foxer and CAT.

In the autumn of 1944 the British were less concerned with the offensive capabilities of the type XXI than with how they were going to find and destroy it. Operational scientists estimated that it would be five times harder to find than U-boats presently in service, and once found extremely hard to attack because of its high submerged speed. The problems of target movement at great depth had already complicated A/S tactics in the winter of 1943-44, when the old U-boats went down to 700 feet or more. But they were slow by comparison, and no weapon system yet in service – or even contemplated – could handle a target changing its position in three dimensions faster than the surface escort could move. Even Allied A/S ships were built to handle a slow target. Apart from destroyers, only the Captain Class frigates could outrun a submerged type XXI with certainty.

But simply keeping up was not enough. All existing asdic domes were also designed for comparatively slow speeds. Escorts travelling faster than twelve to fifteen knots quickly drown-out their asdics in the rush of water passing the dome. High-speed asdic domes with more power would be needed to track these 'beasts', as Admiral Murray described them. In short, high-speed submarines threatened to render the existing ASW system – ships, sensors and weapons – obsolete in a flash.

In fairness this problem did not develop overnight. Much work was done on high submerged submarine speeds in early 1944 in anticipation of the Walter Boats attacking the invasion forces off

France. That never happened. However, in June 1944 the British began modifying the submarine *Seraph* for high submerged speed trials by streamlining the hull and increasing the battery storage. Exercises conducted in October concentrated on the counter-attack problems of the escorts. At four knots or slower, *Seraph* represented a normal asdic target, although the streamlined hull made it a noticeably poor target at sharp inclinations. Active contact could be maintained at over nine knots. At high speed the submarine made enough noise itself that it could be followed by simply listening – using the asdic as a passive device (known as hydrophone effect, HE) – at ranges from 4,000–5,000 yards. Such ranges could be maintained by HE on *Seraph* at her best speed provided Foxer's were not used. These had a serious impact on active searches and 'almost completely destroys that of HE detection'. Contact could be kept quite easily by two ships working together, although it was easily lost by a single hunter.

Based on the *Seraph* trials, RN Operational Scientists placed heavy emphasis on developing passive means for tracking the type XXI. Using more VLR aircraft with extensive use of sonobuoys, flooding the U-boat's line of advance with ships and aircraft, and maintaining a listening contact with warships, it would be possible to conduct a much larger and more complex hunt to exhaustion. With its batteries exhausted, the type XXI might become simply a very large, and with luck, quite stationary target. It might have worked. But the high level of noise generated by *Seraph* in the nine to twelve knot range was not characteristic of the type XXI. American trials after the war with U-2513 concluded that, 'at twelve knots submerged speed she is quieter than our best fleet submarines at six'. Speeds above ten knots caused some noise by cavitation, 'but up to ten knots she is extremely quiet'. The USN found that it required at least seven ships to conduct an effective search. 'The prospects for successful search and detection by aircraft,' however, the report concluded, 'present a pessimistic picture. The prospects for successful attack are not much better'. In anticipation, Allied anti-submarine forces underwent an intensive retraining period over the winter of 1944-45, with each British-based group getting time with *Seraph*.

The final results of the *Seraph* trials were signalled to senior commanders in mid-December. The advice was that current equipment could handle the problem, but warned that, 'A high-speed submarine does not allow time to correct small errors in ship-handling and operating...', and therefore the very highest of training standards would be needed to cope with the type XXI.

In the end, the Allies never got to grips with the latest in submarine technology before the war ended. Forbidden to attack until she reached her war station, U-2511 conducted only a mock attack on an unsuspecting British cruiser before receiving the recall signal. The inshore type XXIIIs fared better. Several were on patrol off the British east coast in April and early May, sinking a number of ships. One, U-2326, which failed to hear the recall, sank two ships (one for each of its two torpedoes) off Newcastle on 7 May before returning safely. Others operated with impunity in the Thames estuary right to the end of the war. By all accounts, none of the type XXIII or type XXI U-boats to make operational cruises at the end of the war were ever detected by Allied forces. Probably for that reason many Allied A/S specialists wished the war had lasted a few months longer. And it was probably knowledge of the potential of the new U-boats to upset the whole Allied A/S system that prompted the RN's official historian to conclude that 'we never achieved a full and final mastery over the U-boat'.

The Germans, for their part, agreed. The U-boat fleet ended the war bowed but unbroken, the only arm of the Third Reich still in the fight as Dönitz, who took over from Hitler as head of state on 30 April, authorised unconditional surrender on 7 May 1945. We will never know if the type XXI and XXIII could have tipped the balance in the Atlantic war. There would have been much drama, and probably serious Allied losses, but any hope of influencing the outcome of the war was long past.

It seems, in the end, the Atlantic war was not within Germany's power to win – unless the Allies committed such colossal errors as to defeat themselves. But they did not. The British got the basic defensive system right in the early stages of the war, and had the time they needed to build up resources. The Allies even survived the carnage of early 1942, thanks in large measure to the power of American industry: something the Germans vastly underestimated.

And so, despite all the inter-service and international rivalries, the Allies won the war in the Atlantic and did it in convincing style. They proved superior on all fronts, from sheer industrial production to intelligence, equipment, operational research, and command and control. The bottlenecks which shaped Allied strategy – what forces to raise, what equipment to produce, what strategy to follow next, where to land, when and how to bomb – were all primarily problems of Allied planning, production and manpower. The German attack on shipping complicated effective management of the Allied war effort, but for all its drama it had no appreciable influence on the outcome of the war.

Afterword and Acknowledgements

The Battle of the Atlantic was a long, complex campaign fought over a vast area by several major and many minor players. In that sense there have been many 'battles' of the Atlantic, not the least of which the larger administrative struggle on the Allies' part to master the daunting task of simply moving men, material and ships across the ocean under wartime conditions. The battle this book focuses on, however, is the shooting war between the main protagonists in the main theatre of the broad North Atlantic. The Russian convoys and the South Atlantic I leave to others to describe.

If there is a central guiding theme here it is the effort of contending forces at what might be called the critical points, and the strategy, operations, tactics, equipment and doctrines employed by both sides to achieve their desired results. In that sense the book follows the usual, somewhat peripatetic, ramble through the years and theatres. That said, those familiar with existing Battle of the Atlantic accounts will find much that is new here. Not least is the attempt to write an overview from a mid-Atlantic rather than traditional Anglocentric perspective. That the British (and the Germans) maintained a proprietary interest in the Atlantic war goes without saying, and I hope that comes through. However, both the United States and Canada played salient roles in the Atlantic, and in time their efforts came to match and in some ways surpass, those of Britain. If, in the process, I have said more about the Canadian role – the subject of my own particular research – than has been the case in previous accounts, that is why. Moreover, the Atlantic war has been the subject of a large body of professional scholarship by Canadians over the last twenty years, which has probed most aspects of the campaign. In no small way, this is an attempt to integrate that exciting new scholarship into the wider story and create a modern paradigm for the Atlantic war.

Work on this volume also reveals just how much remains to be done in researching the subject. American and British literature on the Atlantic in general has been largely moribund for decades. No monographs or modern scholarships seem to exist on the Sierra Leone-Gibraltar convoys and the cruise of German raiders in the North Atlantic in early 1941. The American response to the carnage off their own coast has generated a small body of particular studies, but curiously the only extensive modern research and writing on the subject is a narrative prepared by the Canadian Forces Directorate of History and Heritage for the new official history of the Canadian navy, published in 2003. The development of tactics and doctrines within Western Approaches Command has never been looked at by modern scholars, and modern histories of RAF Coastal Command and US air operations are needed. The Canadian air force – which played a major role in the campaign – has a modern history but no one outside Canada seems to know that. The extent that this book reflects the strengths and weaknesses of the existing literature, therefore, I make no apology. There is much to be done.

The preparation of this book drew on the talents, kindness and goodwill of a great many people. I would especially like to thank Mr Mike Whitby, Head of the Naval History Team at the DHH, and Dr Roger Sarty, now Deputy Director of the Canadian War Museum – and both principle authors of the forthcoming official history of the Canadian navy in the Second World War – for their encouragement and for reading the manuscript. Glen Leonard, one of my graduate students, also read the manuscript and offered sound advice. They kept me from many egregious errors; any that remain are mine alone.

Many have helped with the photograph and map research and preparation. Thanks for the use of photographs goes to Marilyn Guerney at the Maritime Command Museum in Halifax, Bill Willson and his volunteers of the Naval Museum of Alberta in Calgary, Christine Dunphy of the Shearwater Aviation Museum in Halifax, Seb Cox of the Air Historical Branch, MOD UK, and Jurgen Rohwer and Thomas Weis of the Bibliothek fur Zeitgeschichte in Stuttgart. My graduate student Patricia Heckbert did the legwork in the UK looking for photographs. Jim Wood, another graduate student, braved the

Washington sniper's rampage – literally – to find photographs at the US National Archives. Dirk Lenentine, Bill Hamilton and Jorge Sayat of UNB technical Services provided invaluable help in scanning the photographs. I am grateful to Mike Bechtholdt for drawing some of the maps and diagrams, to Dr Serge Bernier, Director of the DHH in Ottawa, for permission to reprint maps and diagrams from Canadian official histories, and to the Militargeschichtliches Forsungsampt in Potsdam for permission to reprint one of theirs.

The secretaries of the UNB History Department, Carole Hines and Elizabeth Arnold were their usual stalwart best, and I thank them for their efforts. The financial support needed to complete this manuscript was graciously provided by the Security and Defence Forum of the Canadian Department of National Defence through the Military and Strategic Studies Programme at UNB. Special thanks goes to my wife Bobbi for putting up with the distraction and grumpiness of another book project.

The final vote of thanks and appreciation I reserve for the man who started it all many years ago, Dominick 'Toby' Graham. It was in Toby's undergraduate seminar in the late 1970s that my interest in the Battle of the Atlantic found root in serious scholarship, and it was under his guidance that I developed that interest into a professional career. Although better known for his army history, Toby was himself a student of that great British imperial and maritime historian Gerald Graham, and a firm believer in the importance of sea power in the study of modern war. To him I owe the two main features of my own approach to the study of the Atlantic war, a strong suspicion that the shooting war was only the most dramatic part of a more complex story, and – the subject of this book in many ways – an interest in how war is fought, how men learned from battle to battle and the important role that doctrine and national culture play in their responses to that challenge. When this process all began in the 1970s, with its revelations about special intelligence and the release of wartime documents, the mantra of the time was the need to revise our understanding of the Second World War. We have come a long way since then, and we still have a long way to go. But this particular turn of the wheel owes an enormous debt of gratitude to Toby Graham, and it is fitting that the book be dedicated to him. Thanks Toby.

Marc Milner
University of New Brunswick

List of Abbreviations

ACIs	*Atlantic Convoy Intsructions*
Adm	Admiral
AMC	Armed Merchant Cruiser
A/S	Anti-submarine
Asdic	British term for SONAR
ASW	Anti-submarine warfare
B group	British escort group of MOEF
BdU	Befelshaber der U–Boots (U-boat High Command)
BT	Bathythermography
C group	Canadian escort group of MOEF
CAM ship	Catapult Armed Merchant Ship
Capt.	Captain
CAT	Canadian anti-acoustic torpedo gear
Cdr.	Commander
CinC	Commander in Chief
CNA	Canadian North-west Atlantic
CTF–24	Commander, Task Force 24 (USN)
CVE	escort or auxiliary aircraft carrier
DF	Direction Finding (of radio transmitters)

EAC	Eastern Air Command, RCAF
EG	Escort Group
F/L	Flight Lieutenant
F/O	Flying Officer
Foxer	British and American anti-acoustic torpedo gear
FSL	First Sea Lord
GNAT	German Navy Acoustic Torpedo
HE	Hydrophone Effect (listening on asdic)
HF/DF	High Frequency Direction Finding
HG	Gibralter-UK convoy
HMCS	His Majesty's Ship
HX	Fast North America to UK convoy
Kplt	Kapitänleutnant
Kpzursee	Kapitän zur See
Lt	Lieutenant
Lt Cdr	Lieutenant Commander
MAC ship	Merchant Aircraft Carrier
MF/DF	Medium-Frequency Direction Finding
MKS	Mediterranean-UK convoy
MOEF	Mid-Ocean Escort Force
NCS	Naval Control of Shipping
NEF	Newfoundland Escort Force
NHB	Naval Historical Branch
NSHQ	Naval Service Headquarters, Ottowa
OB	UK-westward convoy
OG	UK-Gibraltar convoy
ONS	Slow UK to North America convoy
RAF	Royal Air Force
RCAF	Royal Canadian Air Force
RCN	Royal Canadian Navy
RCNR	Royal Canadian Navy (Reserve)
RN	Royal Navy
RNR	Royal Navy Reserve
SC	Slow North America to UK convoy
SL	Sierra-Leone-UK convoy
S/L	Squadron Leader
SG	Support Group
sqn	squadron
USN	United States Navy
VLR	Very Long-Range Aircraft
WAC	Western Approaches Command
WACIs	*Western Approaches Command Instructions*

Bibliography

Douglas, W.A.B., *The Creation of a National Air Force: The Official History of the Royal Canadian Air Force, volume II* (Toronto: University of Toronto Press, 1986)

Douglas, W.A.B., Roger Sarty and Michael Whitby, *No Higher Purpose: The Official Operational History of the Royal Canadian Navy in the Second World War: Vol II, pt I* (Vanwell: St Catherine's, Ontario, 2003)

Grove, Eric J. (ed.), *Defeat of the Enemy Attack on Shipping 1939–1945* (Aldershot: Ashgate Publishing for The Naval Records Society, 1997)

Hague, Arnold, *The Allied Convoy System 1939-1945* (Vanwell: St Catharine's, Ontario, 2000)

Hinsley, F. H., *British Intelligence in the Second World War* (abridged edition. Cambridge: Cambridge University Press, 1993)

Kahn, David, *Seizing the Enigma: The Race to Break the German U-boat Codes, 1939-1943* (Boston: Houghton, Mifflin, 1991)

Meigs, Montgomery C., *Slide Rules and Submarines: American Scientists and Subsurface Warfare in World War II* (Washington: National Defence University, 1990)

Milner, Marc, *North Atlantic Run: The Royal Canadian Navy and the Battle for the Convoys* (Toronto: University of Toronto Press, 1985)

Milner, Marc, *The U-Boat Hunters: The Royal Canadian Navy and the Offensive Against Germany's Submarines* (Toronto: University of Toronto Press, 1994)

Ministry of Defence (Navy), *The U-Boat War in the Atlantic 1939–1945* (London: HMSO, 1989)

Morison, Samuel Eliot, *History of United States Naval Operations in World War II: volume I: The Battle of the Atlantic, September 1939-May 1943* (Boston: Little, Brown, 1954)

Price, Alfred, *Aircraft versus Submarine: The evolution of the anti-submarine aircraft 1912–1972* (London: William Kimber, 1973)

Richards, D. and H. Saunders, *The Royal Air Force, 1939-1945*, 3 Vols (London: HMSO 1974)

Rohwer, J. and G. Hummelchen, *Chronology of the War at Sea 1939-1945* (Annapolis, Md. USNI Press, 1992)

Roskill, Captain S.W., *The War at Sea* (3 vols. London: HMSO, 1954-61)

Tarrant, V.E., *The U-boat Offensive 1914-1945* (Annapolis, Md. USNI Press, 1989)

Van der Vat, Dan, *The Atlantic Campaign: World War II's Great Struggle at Sea* (New York: Harper and Row, 1988)

Y'Blood, William T., *Hunter-Killer: U.S. Escort Carriers in the Battle of the Atlantic* (Annapolis, Md.: USNI Press, 1983)

List of Illustrations

List of Plates

15 MacPherson Collection, Naval Museum of Alberta

16 US National Archives

17 MacPherson Collection, Naval Museum of Alberta

18 Shearwater Aviation Museum

19 Air Historical Branch, MOD

20 Maritime Command Museum

21 Bibliothek fur Zeitgeschichte

22 Bibliothek fur Zeitgeschichte

23 Author Collection

24 National Archives of Canada, PA-135968

25 MacPherson Collection, Naval Museum of Alberta

26 National Archives of Canada, PA-135970

27 Maritime Command Museum

28 MacPherson Collection, Naval Museum of Alberta

29 MacPherson Collection, Naval Museum of Alberta

30 MacPherson Collection, Naval Museum of Alberta

31 Author Collection

32 Bibliothek fur Zeitgeschichte

33 US National Archives

34 MacPherson Collection, Naval Museum of Alberta

35 Author Collection

36 US National Archives

37 MacPherson Collection, Naval Museum of Alberta

38 MacPherson Collection, Naval Museum of Alberta

39 MacPherson Collection, Naval Museum of Alberta

40 National Archives of Canada, PA-34538

41 Author Collection

42 Air Historical Branch, MOD

43 US National Archives

44 MacPherson Collection, Naval Museum of Alberta

45 National Archives of Canada, PA-206625

46 Bibliothek fur Zeitgeschichte

47 Author Collection

48 Author Collection

49 US National Archives

50 MacPherson Collection, Naval Museum of Alberta

51 US National Archives

52 US National Archives

53 US National Archives

54 US National Archives

List of Maps

100 Reprinted from Gilbert Tucker, *The Naval Service of Canada, II: Activities on Shore During the Second World War*, Ottawa: King's Printer, 1952

105 Drawn by the author

112 Reprinted from M. Milner, *North Atlantic Run: The Royal Canadian Navy and the Battle for the Convoys*, Toronto: University of Toronto Press, 1985

114 Drawn by the author

121 Drawn by the author

127 Drawn by the author

130 Drawn by Mike Bechthold

132 Reprinted from M. Milner, *North Atlantic Run: The Royal Canadian Navy and the Battle for the Convoys*, Toronto: University of Toronto Press, 1985

141 Reprinted from W.A.B. Douglas, *The Creation of a National Air Force Vol. 2, The Official History of the Royal Canadian Air Force*, Toronto: University of Toronto Press 1986

162 Drawn by Mike Bechthold

166 Drawn by Mike Bechthold

173 Reprinted from W.A.B. Douglas, *The Creation of a National Air Force: Vol. 2, The Official History of the Royal Canadian Air Force*, Toronto: University of Toronto Press 1986

191 Reprinted from M. Milner, *The U-boat Hunters: The Royal Canadian Navy and the Offensive Against Germany's U-boats*, Toronto: University of Toronto Press, 1994

195 Reprinted from M. Milner, *The U-boat Hunters: The Royal Canadian Navy and the Offensive Against Germany's U-boats*, Toronto: University of Toronto Press, 1994

208 Reprinted from Gilbert Tucker, *The Naval Service of Canada, II: Activities on Shore During the Second World War*, Ottawa: King's Printer, 1952.

208 Courtesy of the Maritime Command Museum, Halifax

210 Reprinted from Gilbert Tucker, *The Naval Service of Canada, II: Activities on Shore During the Second World War*, Ottawa: King's Printer, 1952

227 Drawn by the author

Index

Battles & Campaigns

A series of illustrated battlefield accounts covering the classical period through to the end of the twentieth century, drawing on the latest research and integrating the experience of combat with intelligence, logistics and strategy.

Series Editor

Hew Strachan, Chichele Professor of the History of War
at the University of Oxford

Published

Ross Anderson, *The Battle of Tanga 1914*
William Buckingham, *Arnhem 1944*
David M. Glantz, *Before Stalingrad*
Michael K. Jones, *Bosworth 1485*
Martin Kitchen, *The German Offensives of 1918*
M.K. Lawson, *The Battle of Hastings 1066*
Marc Milner, *Battle of the Atlantic*
A.J. Smithers, *The Tangier Campaign*
Tim Travers, *Gallipoli 1915*

Commissioned

Ross Anderson, *The Forgotten Front: The East African Campaign 1914–1918*
Stephen Conway, *The Battle of Bunker Hill 1775*
Brian Farrell, *The Defence & Fall of Singapore 1941–1942*
Martin Kitchen, *El Alamein 1942–1943*
John Andreas Olsen, *Operation Desert Storm*
Michael Penman, *Bannockburn 1314*
Matthew C. Ward, *Quebec 1759*